Praise for the third edition
(*The Law Enforcement Guide to Wicca*)

"This book is a good resource to give to local police or social service agencies."
—*Circle Magazine*

"The single best book for non-practitioners seeking an understanding of our path ... And it's an excellent refresher ..."
—Christopher Penczak, author of *The Inner Temple of Witchcraft*

"An excellent resource ..."—Amber K, *Covencraft*, 336

"An invaluable resource to help identify and differentiate between vandalism, gang activity and ritualistic crime. A handbook that explains the tenets of some of the most misunderstood religious practices, and provides clarity for those unfamiliar with its associated history, symbology, and iconage. This book should be mandatory reading for all law enforcement personnel. It is a 'must have' for crime scene investigation. Every Chief of Police should have this book on their office shelf!"
—Rev. Angie Buchanan, Gaia's Womb – Earth Traditions

"An outstanding resource, and one I am glad to be able to recommend whenever I do training with law enforcement training classes, criminal justice college classes, victim advocates and others."
—Holli S. Emore, CFRE, Executive Director, Cherry Hill Seminary

"It is an excellent guide for those within the law enforcement field to better assist them in understanding alternative religions within all aspects of their jobs; whether it be crime scenes or the prison departments."
—Darla Kaye Wynne, Wiccan Expert Advisor to North Carolina Department of Corrections (NCDOC)

"I find the simplicity of the explanations makes this book a great teaching manual. I have it permanently placed on my workplace bookshelf and use it help colleagues understand what a client may be talking about in terms of their pagan beliefs and practices."
—Giovanna Zammit, Seasuns Counseling (www.seasuns.ca)

"When we are contacted by counselors, parents' organizations, law enforcement or schools wanting information on pagan religions and their practices, we are confident that *The Law Enforcement Guide to Wicca* (*LEGW*) will provide the practical overview they need."
—Warren Stott, Boulder Pagan Alliance, Boulder, CO

"It's good to know that a police officer has written a guide to tell other police officers just what Wicca is and is not."
—High Priest Daven, owner of Davensjournal.com

"Precise, clear information on Wicca and Neo-Paganism. One of the best overviews around."
—M. Woodling, Chesapeake Pagan Community, Maryland

"It offers a clear definitive and concise definition of what witchcraft is and is not."
—Covenant of Unitarian Universalists Pagans (CUUPS) Recommended Reading, http://www.cuups.org/resources/books/wicca.html

"Cuhulain's original work was created for the world of law enforcement. Because of that, the information it contains is very tight, concise and sharply focused. This powerhouse of information is a standard text I use to educate average people and seekers alike about the Pagan world. I always keep an extra copy on hand to give away!"
—Prometheus P.O., Minos, Temenos Catharmos, The Minoan Brotherhood

"How could someone write a 'law enforcement guide' to anything, even Wicca, and manage to make it interesting—even fascinating—to someone not in law enforcement? The next time I see Kerr Cuhulain, I must ask him, because that's exactly what he's done!"
—Mike Nichols, author of *The Witches' Sabbats*

"Having read Kerr's previous works, I am convinced he will do justice to this subject. In his work as a law enforcement officer, Kerr has a good deal of experience with diversity. It is most commendable that he works to create understanding and connectedness between the many paths of Pagan approaches to worship and reverence, and it is admirable and to be emulated by all Pagans and non-Pagans."
—Zanoni Silverknife, a cofounder of the Georgian and StarBornSothis traditions

"As a High Priest of the Wica, I have used this book when working with local law enforcement as a volunteer of the federal prison system, to educate those who need to know in the system. I highly recommend this book to anyone who works with law enforcement."
—Rev. Edward Livingston, Fire Dance Church of Wicca, Milton, FL

"I bought the *LEGW* over a decade ago, and have used it in my public relations work, with law enforcement, the media, and in my capacity as a volunteer Wiccan chaplain in the prison system across the nation. It speaks to truth, with fair minded, simple language. The information given dispels myths, combats superstition, and teaches that our common ground is more pervasive than we are taught.
—Rev. Velvet Rieth, APS, Covenant of the Pentacle Wiccan Church, New Orleans, LA (www.swampwitch.net)

PAGAN
RELIGIONS

Also by Kerr Cuhulain

The Law Enforcement Guide To Wicca
Wiccan Warrior: Walking a Spiritual Path in a Sometimes Hostile World
Full Contact Magick: A Book of Shadows for the Wiccan Warrior
Magickal Self Defense: A Quantum Approach to Warding

PAGAN
RELIGIONS

A Handbook for
Diversity Training

Kerr Cuhulain

Acorn Guild Press
Portland, Oregon

Published by Acorn Guild Press
4207 SE Woodstock Blvd # 168
Portland, OR 97206-6267
USA
http://www.acornguild.com/

Orders and desk copies: (800) 888-4741

Printed in the United States of America

ISBN 978-0-9710050-6-8

Part of this book was originally published as *The Law Enforcement Guide to Wicca* (1989, 1992, 1997).

Ásatrú Holiday Calendar used by permission of The Ásatrú Alliance.

Sonoran Sunrise Grove, ADF (Arizona), http://www.adf.org/about/photos/sacred-space/sonoran-sunrise.

Bilé of Red Oak Grove (New Jersey), http://www.adf.org/about/photos/sacred-space/red-oak.

Bilé of Sassafras Grove (Pittsburgh, PA), http://www.adf.org/about/photos/sacred-space/sassafras.

Manannan Mac Lir Grove Beltaine, http://web.archive.org/web/20080724173350/http://www.druidry-sf.org/ritual.html.

Photo "Author (in hat) carrying the Maypole at a Wiccan Beltaine ritual" courtesy of Phoenix McFarland.

Photo "Maypole dance at a Wiccan Beltaine celebration" courtesy of Kerr Cuhulain.

Library of Congress Cataloging-in-Publication Data

Cuhulain, Kerr, 1954-
    Pagan religions : a manual for diversity training / Kerr Cuhulain. — [4th ed.].
        p. cm.
    Includes bibliographical references (p. 155).
    ISBN 978-0-9710050-6-8 (pbk.)
    1. Neopaganism. I. Title.
    BP605.N46C84 2011
    299'.94--dc22
                                                        2011015237

Acknowledgments

I'd like to thank many people for assisting me with their expertise in various religious paths:

Dan Miller of the Heathen Freehold Society and Gary Penzler of Althing Canada for their assistance in writing the section on Ásatrú.

Tony Taylor, editor of the *Keltria* journal and *Henge Happenings* for information on Keltrian Druid practices.

Brendan Cathbad Myers, PhD, for information on Druidic practices.

David Foster, Administrator of the Ár nDraíocht Féin (ADF) and Senior Druid of the Sonoran Sunrise Grove, ADF; and Kirk Thomas, ADF Vice Druid, for ADF practices.

Daven, editor of Davensjournal.com, for information on OUD/Irish Druidry practices.

Druid author Kristen Madden, Tony Kornasiewicz, and Colleen Kelly for proofreading my Druid material.

CONTENTS

PHOTOS

ILLUSTRATIONS

Introduction
to the Fourth Edition

Fear of serious injury cannot alone justify suppression of free speech and assembly. Men feared witches and burned women. It is the function of speech to free men from the bondage of irrational fears.
—Louis Dembitz Brandeis (1856–1941), *Olmstead v. United States*, 277 U.S. 438, 478 (1928)

My first book, *The Law Enforcement Guide to Wicca* (*LEGW*), was published in 1989. In the introduction to the 1997 third edition I state, "It is most disturbing to me that there is a widespread misconception that Witchcraft and Satanism are synonymous." It was to combat such misconceptions that I wrote the *LEGW*. In the years since I wrote that sentence, the amount of accurate information on neo-Pagan faiths available in books and on the Internet has increased dramatically. Unfortunately, the misinformation has proliferated as well.

The surprising thing is how many people still actively promote misinformation in order to demonize minority religions. Intolerance is alive and well in the modern world; ignorance and fear still drive people to engage in hateful acts. I wouldn't be concerned if people, particularly some extremist Christians, were giving an accurate picture of us neo-Pagans. I don't mind people telling the world that I don't believe in Jehovah, or Jesus, or the Bible. I don't. Yet all too often others say things about us that aren't true, and I won't stand for that.

There is a lot of nonsense in circulation concerning what is popularly referred to as "the occult" and neo-Pagan religions. Much of it has been written by people who have never seen a Pagan religious ceremony (and probably never will). The word "occult," derived from the Latin *occultus*, translates as "concealed." When applied to a system of beliefs, it implies that one must be initiated into this system in order to have certain information revealed or to participate in activities that are not freely accessible to the public. The truth of the matter, however, is that most of the neo-Pagan spiritual paths listed under the title "occult" by "experts" aren't closed to the public. All of their practices are in print and available in libraries; they are entirely open to public scrutiny. In this book, I'm going to save you the legwork of research and summarize many of the Western world's major neo-Pagan beliefs and practices.

Many of the books on "the occult" or "occultism" that I've collected over the years were not written to inform. They contain misinformation calculated to create the illusion that the author's religion is the only valid one. Such books usually list every religion other than that of the author as "cults" or "occult" and often state that any belief not the author's own is demonically inspired. Such books typically are based on obsolete research, stereotypes, guesswork, unverified beliefs, and just plain nonsense. Hollywood shows for television and the theatre also perpetuate inaccurate and stereotypical images of Witches and the occult.

In recent years, many followers and scholars of earth-based tribal religions such as Wicca and Druidism have come to refer to their beliefs as "Pagan" or "neo-Pagan" (meaning "new Pagan"). This isn't how some people use the term, however. In Westhoelter's *General Information Manual With Respect to Satanism and the Occult,* a Pagan is described as "a person who is not a Christian or has no religion."[1] The *Colorado Bureau of Investigations Questioned Documents Examiner's Occult Guide* lists the same definition,[2] but then contradicts itself in its terms list by defining "Pagan" as "Non Christian believer in old Gods."[3] Lou Sloat's *Texas Ritualistic Crime Information Network Occult Crime Manual* includes "pagan" in its list of "occult terms."[4] These are misuses of the term "pagan" and are at odds with how the word is used in reputable schools of theology.

Many followers of neo-Pagan religions would like to tell their family, friends, coworkers, or partners about their spirituality. Due to the vast amount of misinformation about the occult in circulation, however, many are fearful of attempting this. Many are solitary practitioners who have no support network or Pagan friends that they can rely on if they were to become the targets of discrimination or harassment. Many police officers, particularly those dealing with youth, are encountering teens and parents involved in neo-Pagan religions. These police officers are trying to make informed judgements, but are hampered by the confusing array of misinformation on the subject directed at them by zealots with agendas. Because neo-Paganism is the most rapidly growing religious community in North America, this misinformation problem is growing more serious.

When I went public about my Wiccan beliefs in 1977, I quickly discovered that I was the first Wiccan cop to do so. There was little support for people like me in the 1970s. Back then, very few books were available, and many of those were inaccurate. I learned many lessons about antidefamation the hard way. Fellow Pagans were being wrongly accused, their lives ruined, living in fear. I experienced bigotry and harassment of minority religions firsthand, which led me to trace the development and use of various urban legends in modern Witch hunts. Over the next two decades, I researched and debunked the collection of urban legends that, gathered together, form what I call the Satanic Conspiracy Myth. These urban legends created an atmosphere of hysteria and rumour, fanaticism, and fraud. The misinformation contained in these urban legends resulted in countless hours of fruitless investigation by law enforcement officers. Copious tax dollars have been spent financing unproductive and unnecessary investigations, as well as the training courses offered by self-proclaimed experts who hoped to keep these investigations and the resulting discrimination active. I documented the power of information being deliberately misused. Of necessity, I found myself becoming a hate crimes investigator.

Compared to when I first started down the Wiccan path in 1969, there is now an enormous amount of accurate information on neo-Pagan spiritual paths available to the public. People can no longer excuse their discrimination or harassment with the statement, "I wasn't aware." Despite this, a misconception that Witchcraft and Satanism are synonymous persists. Thanks to centuries of religious propaganda, sensational Hollywood horror movies, and authors of sensationalistic do-it-yourself occult books, this myth is firmly entrenched in some parts of our society. For many, the word "witch" conjures up images of frightful crones with pointy hats and familiar cats, not everyday citizens, while the term "Odinist" may bring images of Nazi extremists. Ask your typical citizen what they think a Heathen is and they likely won't give you an answer involving Norse mythology.

I am a retired police officer currently working as a police dispatcher. When people saw me at work as a police officer, the last thing they would have thought was that I am also a Witch. Yet this is what I am. (The average citizen in Western society seems to be able to grasp the idea that a person could be one or the other, but not both.) A lot of baggage comes along with the *w* word. Centuries of myth and propaganda make it impossible for many people in today's world to see how "Witch" and "cop" can be combined in one person. Yet I have many colleagues in the emergency services (cops, firefighters, and paramedics) who are Vodou mambos, Ásatrú *gothar*, Native American shamans, or brethren of the Ordo Templi Orientis. Unless someone told you, though, you'd never know this to look at them.

Our assumptions color our perceptions. We are all looking at the same world, but because we all come from differing educational, social, and cultural backgrounds, we see different things. This is one of the reasons that there are so many religions to choose from. If ten different people standing in a field share a religious experience, one may see Gaia, one may see Jehovah, one may see Jesus, one may see the Virgin Mary, one may see the goddess Erzulie, one may see a UFO, and at least one will be standing there saying, "Hey! What are you all looking at?" People being what they are, however, will often assume that the person standing next to them sees the world the way that they do.

This book is not an attempt on my part to proselytize. I believe that all religions are paths leading to the same place, and I strongly support an individual's freedom to choose his or her own religious path, as guaranteed by the Canadian Bill of Rights and the Constitution of the United States. This book is an attempt to present an accurate picture of modern Paganism to the uninitiated. I've focused on Wicca, Druidism, and Ásatrú, all Pagan religions of Northern Europe.

If you are a Pagan, this book will give you the information you need to educate your friends, family, and coworkers. If you are not a Pagan, this book will tell you what neo-Pagan religions are and what they are not. I leave you to draw your own conclusions.

NOTES

1. Shane Westhoelter, *General Information Manual With Respect to Satanism and the Occult* (National Information Network, 1989), 67.
2. *Colorado Bureau of Investigations Questioned Documents Examiner's Occult Guide*, 4.
3. Ibid., 35.
4. Lou Sloat, *Texas Ritualistic Crime Information Network Occult Crime Manual*, 14.

Chapter One

Paganism and the Occult

Everyone would like to behave like a pagan, with everyone else behaving like a Christian.
—Albert Camus, French existentialist author and philosopher (1913–1960)

The word "pagan" first appeared in its modern spelling in 1425 in Higden's *Polychronicon*. In Mallory's *Morte D'Arthur* (circa 1400), it is spelled "paygan." The term can be traced back to the Latin root *pagus*, which originally meant "something stuck in the ground as a landmark"—in other words, a "peg." *Pagus* was derived from the root *pag*, meaning "fix." A whole family of English words can be traced back to this same root, including "page" and "pole." The noun *paganus*, meaning "country dweller," was ultimately derived from *pagus*.[1]

Etymologist John Ayto theorizes that because early Christians considered themselves "soldiers" of Christ and because *paganus* later came to refer to civilians, Christians adopted the word to refer to non-Christians.[2] Others have speculated that *paganus* was used by the predominantly city-dwelling early Christians in much the same way as we would call someone a "hick" or "country bumpkin" today. We may never know for sure which of these theories is correct, but the fact remains that "pagan" ultimately became a term used by Christians to refer to non-Christians. In recent years, however, theologians and folklorists have begun using "Pagan" and "neo-Pagan" to specifically refer to followers of certain earth-based religions.

Pagans can be organized according to ethnicity, pantheons, or structure. Druid scholar Isaac Bonewits proposed several overlapping categories, including:

- Paleo-Pagans: literally "old pagans." The original polytheists. Only a handful of remote tribes can lay claim to this category.

- Meso-Pagans: "Middle Pagans." These people mix one or more kinds of Paganism and one or more kinds of monotheism. Examples: Sikhism (combining Hinduism and Islam), Theosophy, Rosicruscianism, Freemasonry, Vodou, and many modern Druid orders.
- Buddheo-Pagans. Pagans who worship various Buddhas or Bodhisattvas.
- Neo-Pagans. "New Pagans." These are revivals of older paleo-Paganism, modified meso-Paganism, or new creations such as the Church of All Worlds or Discordianism.
- Recon-Pagans. "Recon" is short for "reconstructionist." Bonewits described these Pagans as scholars and conservatives leaning towards Luther's principle of "every man his own minister."[3]

This book, however, is organized by the traditions' ethnicities of origin and pantheons, as I believe that will be the easiest model for the reader who is new to this material to understand.

In the Diversiton census of religion and belief, based on the 2001 census in the United Kingdom, 30,569 people indicated their religion as "Pagan."[4] Other religious categories listed by respondents in this census include Wicca (7,227), Druidism (1,657), Celtic Pagan (508), Vodun (123), Ásatrú (93), and Santeria (21). Estimates vary widely as to how many Wiccans and other neo-Pagans there are in North America, the UK, and Australia. Author Phyllis Curott offers the highest estimate for Wiccans in the United States at between five and ten million.[5] The Covenant of the Goddess survey of October 2000 estimated that there were 768,400 Wiccans in the United States, of which 37 percent were under the age of twenty-five and 11 percent were under the age of seventeen. Of these, 80 percent were solitary practitioners. The 2001 Canadian Census data indicates that there are 21,080 Wiccans and other neo-Pagans in Canada, an increase of 281 percent over the 1991 statistics, which is the greatest percentage growth of any religion. The average age of these respondents was thirty.[6] The 2001 City University of New York's Religious Identification Study used a phone poll to estimate 134,000 Wiccans, 33,000 Druids, and 140,000 Pagans.[*] Nineteen percent (119,500) of the 629,000 Unitarian Universalists identified themselves in a 1999 study as "earth religionists." Bonewits estimates that 75 percent of the neo-Pagan community in North America is Wiccan, with 7–10 percent being Druid, 5–8 percent Ásatrúar, and the rest belonging to other Pagan categories.[7] One thing is certain: Wicca and other neo-Pagan faiths are rapidly growing in size and popularity.

---

[*]   http://www.gc.cuny.edu/studies/key_findings.htm. Eleven million people declined to respond to the CUNY study.

General Pagan Characteristics

I have often found it difficult to explain neo-Pagan beliefs to the uninitiated due to the nature of Western society. The predominant religion in Western society today is Judeo-Christianity. This faith has affected the nature of our society's laws, morals, and perceptions. Most people raised in Western society are thoroughly indoctrinated in Christian forms of thought, even though they may not attend church and do not consider themselves devout.

Many of those who have seen me take an affirmation rather than an oath on the Bible in court have asked me, "Aren't you religious?" or "Are you an agnostic?" when they really meant to ask, "Aren't you Christian?" They have been brought up to equate Christianity with religion. Some people find it difficult to believe that anything other than Christianity is a religion at all. Consequently, they have difficulty grasping what neo-Pagan religions are about, as Pagan religions have a different structure from Christianity. What I am attempting here is difficult, then, since the reader has likely not experienced a Pagan religion like mine before.

Since Christianity is well-known to Westerners, let's use it in comparison with neo-Pagan religions to illustrate some of the similarities and differences. This strategy is not meant to suggest that one is better than the other; it is simply provided for the convenience of the reader who is more familiar with Christianity than any other religion. It should also not be construed as implying that neo-Pagan religions and Christianity are opposites or opposed to one another. Naturally, both religions are diverse, and not all of these generalizations will apply to all Christian denominations or all neo-Pagan groups,but the table below provides a quick reference guide showing how a neo-Pagan's perception of the world is quite different from the Christian worldview.

Christianity	Neo-Pagan Spirituality
Monotheistic: One God.	Polytheistic: Many aspects of Divinity, including gods, goddesses, nature spirits, spirit guides, totems, elementals, ancestors, etc. All are worthy of respect.
Dualistic: Divinity is entirely separate from mundane world.	Monistic: Divinity is inseparable from everyday world. Divinity can be transcendent (surrounding and containing the world) or immanent (within all things).

Christianity	Neo-Pagan Spirituality
Original sin: Children are born tainted by sin.	Original blessing: Children are born holy.
Patriarchal/Paternalistic.	Men and women are spiritual equals.
Evangelism: Tendency towards exclusivism: "Only one true faith."	Pluralism: All spiritual paths are recognized.
Satan/the devil: Demonic or semi-divine personification of evil. Universe is often seen as a struggle between forces of light and forces of darkness.	No equivalent: No divine or semi-divine figure of ultimate evil. Neo-Pagans do not see the universe as a battle between forces of light and forces of darkness.
Rulers of nature.	Stewards of nature.
Redemption/Atonement/Confession: Conduct dictated by Commandments (Thou shalt not) and guilt for wrongdoing.	Karma/Wiccan Rede/Threefold Law/Nine Noble Virtues/Ardanes/Ordains. Ethics and morality are based on personal responsibility and respect rather than guilt. "Thou shalt not" is replaced with "I shall not."
Tendency to view spirituality as a serious, sober affair.	Spirituality is a joyful, pleasurable experience filled with love and humor.
Sex is viewed primarily as a means of procreation. Celibacy and sexual abstinence outside of marriage are expected of the priests of some denominations.	Sexual ecstasy is a divine blessing and a source of spiritual inspiration.
Psychic/magickal phenomena are generally discouraged if not actively opposed, except for certain "miracles" and transubstantiation/consubstantiation.	Magick* and divination are the birthright of everyone.

---

*See "Magick" in Chapter Three.

Christianity	Neo-Pagan Spirituality
Resurrection/Heaven: Chosen believers are restored to life in heaven after death. Only believers go to heaven.	Reincarnation: Belief in an afterlife (e.g., Summerland, Valhalla or Asaheimr, or Gwynvyd), often involving rest and recuperation before reincarnation. Neo-Pagans don't dwell on this, as they focus on the here-and-now.
Holy days based upon biblical and Christian historical events.	Celebration of the solar, lunar, seasonal, and life cycles (e.g., Sabbats, Esbats), including rites of passage.
Baptism.	Initiation.

For the purposes of this book, I will divide Pagan religions into several categories:

- Celtic neo-Pagans: this includes Wicca and Druidism.
- Norse neo-Pagans: this includes Ásatrú and Odinists.
- Ethnic neo-Pagans: Egyptian, Roman, Greek.*

Now that we are familiar with some general categories and characteristics of neo-Pagan beliefs, let's look at specific spiritual paths.

NOTES

1. Robert K. Barnhart, ed., *Barnhart Dictionary of Etymology* (New York: H.W. Wilson), 746; and John Ayto, *Dictionary of Word Origins* (Arcade Publishing; Ltr. Prtg ed., 1990), 379.
2. Ibid.
3. Isaac Bonewits, *Real Magic*, Berkeley, CA: Creative Arts Book Company (1970).
4. Diversiton Census of Religion and Belief, http://www.diversiton.com/religion/census/categories.asp.
5. Phyllis Curott, *Book of Shadows: A Modern Woman's Journey Into the Wisdom of Witchcraft and the Magic of the Goddess* (Broadway, 1999).
6. "Information about religion in Canada," http://www.religioustolerance.org/can_rel.htm.
7. Bonewits.

---

* I've made no attempt to include the African diasporan religions such as Vodou or Santería, as they are a vast, complicated subject and deserve a book of their own. Nor have I included more than a passing mention of occidental (Western) ceremonial magick groups, such as the Order of the Golden Dawn or the Ordo Templi Orientis. Their story deserves a separate book as well, and due to their Christian roots, I don't consider them to be neo-Pagan. I also haven't included the Greek, Roman, or Egyptian (Kemetic) revivals; they're out there, but they're rather small. Perhaps I will be able to include them in a later edition.

PART ONE
CELTIC
NEO-PAGANISM

The Celts

Anything that is evil to us, or that may witness against us, where we shall longest be, illumine it to us, obscure it to us, banish it from us, root it out of our hearts, ever, evermore, everlastingly ...
—Invocation from the *Carmina Gadelica*

The Celts were a collection of tribes spread over Western and Central Europe who shared common language and cultural patterns. They had a system of social castes, one of which served as teachers, adjudicators, and clergy. This caste of people was known as the Druids. The Romans conquered the Celts first on the continent and then in much of the British Isles in 43 CE under Emperor Claudius. The Romans then absorbed the polytheistic pantheon of the Celts into their polytheistic pantheon in many of the conquered areas. Later, Christian missionaries tried to stamp out remnants of Celtic beliefs. Fortunately, monks in Wales and Ireland wrote down some of the oral history and mythology of the Celts, thus preserving some of what was lost. An interesting collection of such surviving material can be found in Alexander Carmichael's *Carmina Gadelica.*

These Celtic traditions and beliefs found their way into two neo-Pagan religious streams in the modern world: Wicca and Druidism.

Chapter Two

Wicca

One can imagine the government's problem. This is all pretty magical stuff to them. If I were trying to terminate the operations of a witch coven, I'd probably seize everything in sight. How would I tell the ordinary household brooms from the getaway vehicles?
—John Perry Barlow

A Brief History

All religions were started by people, for it is people that they serve. The Wiccan religion is no exception. In the 1930s, a retired civil servant named Gerald Gardner attempted to reconstruct and revive Witchcraft, which he believed to be the indigenous shamanism of Northern Europe. Gardner was the first person to write publicly about Wicca, starting in 1949. Since then many others have followed his lead. There is no doubt that Gardner was instrumental in bringing Wicca out into the open. He founded a particular tradition of Wicca, which his followers call the Gardnerian Tradition, and in the process incorporated many of his own ideas into that tradition. Gardner presented a picture of a rediscovered ancient religion that had been preserved by isolated underground groups for years and had now surfaced more or less intact.[*]

Whether the historical records presented by a religious group are accurate has little to do with how the religion functions or how the religion meets people's needs, however. Wicca, like every other religion on earth, is based partially on mythology. Mythology isn't meant to be taken as literally true, though it often stems from a kernel of historical truth. Mythology is metaphor and allegory, a powerful set of archetypes and symbols, and religion is mythology in action. As my wife and fellow Wiccan author, Phoenix McFarland, says, "Myth is the address of magick."

---

[*] As Aidan Kelly, author of *Crafting the Art of Magic, Book 1: A History of Modern Witchcraft 1939–1964* has observed, this presentation of a religion as historically based is a typical characteristic of many religions, including Judaism and Christianity. An excellent history of how Wicca and related spiritual paths came to be can be found in the book *Triumph of the Moon* by Ronald Hutton.

Some Wiccans believe that Wicca can be traced back to a historical "Golden Age." They get upset when some people attempt to discredit Wicca by arguing that Gerald Gardner, considered by most to be the father of modern Wicca, "invented" the religion in the 1930s. Though it is true that Gardner created what we now call Wicca, he incorporated many ancient elements into it. Every religion in history had a starting point; every religion was invented by someone, somewhere. McFarland views it this way: "Religions are invented from shards of older practices. In an archaeology dig, we find that one building is built upon the ruins of an older one. Our mythologies, like the phoenix, rise from the ashes of dying faiths." As is well-known and documented by biblical historians, the Christian Church incorporated many old Pagan customs into its worship in its early years. Isn't this "inventing" religion? The "older is better" argument is a logical fallacy. Truth is truth, whether it was discovered five minutes ago or a thousand years ago. Age has nothing to do with it.

Whatever you choose to believe about Gardner and his religion, Wicca, it has become the fastest growing religion in North America today.

Gardner's original Wicca inspired many others to imitate it or improve upon it. It triggered the creation of a host of "Brit Trads," all originating in the British Isles. Examples of Brit Trads include the Alexandrian, Kingstone, and 1734 traditions. The appearance of Wicca in North America sparked the creation of still more Wiccan "denominations," such as the Georgian Tradition and the New Reformed Orthodox Order of the Golden Dawn (NROOGD). Each of these traditions differs slightly in their use of ritual and myth. Yet all have common threads of practice and unifying themes that identify them as Wiccan.

Wicca is now a legal religion recognized by all levels of government in the United States, Canada, and the United Kingdom. Every state in the United States and most provinces in Canada have legal Wiccan clergy, many of whom are involved in local interfaith councils. For example, Pete "Pathfinder" Davis, founder of the Aquarian Tabernacle Church, a Wiccan organization, went on to head the Washington State Interfaith Council. The U.S. Military has also recognized Wicca within its chaplain's manual since 1974.[1] "Wicca" is a religious choice that has been an option for the dog tags of U.S. service men and women since 1991. Most U.S. and Canadian prison systems now have Wiccan chaplains, as do many universities.

Etymology

The origin of the Old English (or Anglo-Saxon) word *wicca*, from which the word "witch" is derived, has been the subject of much debate. At one time, many believed that it shared a common root with the English words *wit* or "wise" and therefore meant "wise person" or "Craft of the wise." Another popular misconception is that it came from a root word meaning "to bend," and is related to the word "wicker."

Recent studies indicate that *wicca* derives from the eight thousand-year-old proto-Indo-European root word* *weik* (pronounced "way-ick"), meaning "pertaining to magic and religion." This became the word *wigila* in Old Frisian (which translates as "sorcery"), *wicken*, *weihen*, and *wikken* in Middle Low German and Middle High German ("to enchant," "to consecrate," and "to divine"), and *wicca* (pronounced "wee'cha") in Old English.

The earliest known record of the word *wicca* ("male sorcerer" or "wizard") in Old English dates back to the year 890 in the Common Era (CE hereafter—I prefer this scholarly term to the Christian term AD). The word *wicce*, meaning a "female sorcerer," was in use by the eleventh century CE. Other related words in Old English include *wiccian* (to practice sorcery), *wiggle* (divination), and *wiglian* (to divine).

In its modern usage, the word "wicca" is usually pronounced with a hard "c," as it would be in common English. It has no gender and can properly be used to describe both males and females. Some modern Wiccans, however, employ the original Old English usage: "Wicca" for a male and "Wicce" for a female practitioner. The words Wicca, Wicce, and Wiccan can each be used as a descriptive term for a Witch. Wiccans often refer to their faith as "the Craft" or "the Old Religion."

One of the most common misconceptions today is that male Wiccans are called "warlocks." The modern term "warlok" first appeared in Scotland before 1585 CE, with the spelling changing to the more familiar spelling, "warlock," in 1685 CE. Before this it was variously spelled "warlag," "warlau," or "warlo," going back to about 1400 CE. It is derived from the Old English expression *woer loga*, which means "traitor" or "oathbreaker" (*woer*, meaning "faith," "pledge," or "true," plus *loga*, an agent noun related to *leogan*, meaning "to speak falsely"), a term that dates back to 900 CE. "Warlock" was a term originally used by early Christians in a manner similar to the original use of the word "pagan," as an insult. Later "warlock" came to describe a male (non-Wiccan) Witch. The folklore surrounding the use of the word "warlock" ultimately influenced Anton LaVey, founder of the Church of Satan, to adopt the term in 1970 as the title of a male initiated into the second degree within his church. A male Wiccan, however, is properly referred to as a "Witch" or a "Wicca."

What confuses many is that groups other than Wiccans have been known to use the title "witch," thus making life difficult for both Wiccans and those attempting to learn about Wicca. In a series of articles that appeared in *The*

---

* Calvert Watkins, ed., *The American Heritage Dictionary of Indo-European Roots* (revised) (Boston: Houghton Mifflin, 1985). Initial asterisks are a standard linguistic convention indicating a hypothesized word in an extinct language.

Green Egg in 1976–1977 under the title "Witchcraft: Classical, Gothic and Neop-agan," Isaac Bonewits divided Witches into four categories, which are roughly as follows:

- *Classical Witches:* These are people whose ancestors were village herbal-ists, healers, and midwives. Many were believed to have psychic or magical powers. Their skills were passed down through their families in the form of an oral tradition. This type of individual can be found in most cultures. To some of them, religion is fairly irrelevant to the practice of their skills. Some religious Wiccans are also heirs to long family traditions, however.

- *Gothic or neo-Gothic Witches:* Few in number, these have picked up on the religious propaganda of past centuries and deliberately used the word "witch" to oppose themselves to Christianity. They would be more accu-rately classified as Satanists in the traditional sense and perform some of the practices invented by the Inquisition. This category also includes dab-blers who borrow rituals and beliefs from a variety of books, movies, and other sources and call themselves "witches" simply because they perform ritual magick or conform to Hollywood stereotypes. Such individuals are often not religiously motivated at all.

- *Feminist Witches:* Members of some radical feminist groups call themselves "witches" because they believe that the Inquisition was primarily anti-fe-male in nature. Some of them believe that being born a woman automati-cally makes one a Witch. Some of these individuals practice magick, but many do not. Many feminists *do* fall under the following category of neo-Pagan Witches, however.

- *Pagan or neo-Pagan Witches:* These are the vast majority of Witches and consist of those for whom Wicca or Witchcraft is a religion. It is this group that this book is partly about.

Wiccan Practice: a Comparison

In Wicca there is no scripture or dogma. Wiccans allow fellow worshippers an enormous amount of personal freedom in the practice of their religion. They are often eclectic and leave room for personal creativity and experience. Con-sequently, I can provide you with general guidelines for understanding Wicca, but it will be easy to find variations in ritual within the Wiccan community. To Wiccans such as myself, this is as it should be.

Earlier I showed you a table comparing and contrasting Christianity with neo-Pagan spirituality. The characteristics listed there all apply to Wicca, which is one of many neo-Pagan religions. The table below lists differences peculiar to Wicca.

Christianity	Wicca
Congregational: Clergy and congregation are separate.	Initiatory: All are a part of the priesthood.
No size restrictions on congregations.	Small groups (covens): Usually three to thirteen people, though may be larger.
Heaven (destination of Christian souls)	Summerland (resting place between incarnations)
Redemption/Atonement/ Confession	Karma/Threefold Law: All actions, for good or ill, are returned threefold.
Christening	Wiccaning (also known as Paganing or saining)
Hierarchical/Authoritarian	No hierarchy/Autonomous
The Bible (scripture)	No equivalent
No equivalent	Book of Shadows
Sabbaths and holy days based on biblical and Christian historical events	Seasonal Sabbats and lunar Esbats based on observance of natural cycles and tides and Pagan historical events
Marriage	Handfasting
Prophets/Saints/Messiahs	No equivalent
Generally daylight worship	Generally nocturnal worship
Churches/Temples: No size restrictions.	Circles are cast where convenient, usually no formal temple.
Ten Commandments	Wiccan Rede: "An it harm none, do what thou wilt."

Let's examine some of the characteristics of Wicca in more detail.

The Divine

The Wiccan concept of the Divine is shaped by what we see around us in the natural world. Unlike most denominations of Christianity, we see a connection between the mundane and the Divine (more on this in a moment). We conceive of Divinity as manifesting as both female and male, as this reflects what we see in our universe. Therefore, unlike Christianity, we are not monotheistic. Most Wiccans recognize a Goddess and a God, though they may use different aspects of each, with the aspects varying depending on the intention of the ritual being done. This practice often gives the outsider the impression that we are polytheistic.

Monism

Wiccans are monists. We believe that the Divine is immanent in everything around us. We do not separate the Divine from the everyday world as many Christians do, and instead assert that "the world is the garment that divinity puts on in order to be seen."[2] Everything around us is divine.

Equality

A natural and logical consequence of our duotheistic approach to the Divine is that men and women have an equal place in our religion. This has naturally attracted many women who found themselves excluded from other spiritual paths. There are some neo-Pagan traditions and groups that are for men only or women only. Such groups seem to have come about in order to explore themselves and their divinity from a single-gender viewpoint, but most do not oppose the duotheism of the larger Wiccan community.

Organizational Structure: Initiation/Wiccaning

Most Abrahamic religious groups operate on a congregational model: Professional clergy perform services for a separate group of lay followers. This elite minority dispenses spirituality. The clergy or prophets interpret spirituality and "the word of God" for the masses. People can be initiated as members of the group through a process such as baptism, but this does not make them clergy. In Christianity, children can be dedicated to the religion by their parents through a process called "Christening."

Wicca is traditionally not a congregational religion. All Wiccan coveners are essentially equal. There is no clergy that is separate from a group of lay followers. All Wiccans are initiated into the coven, becoming priests and priestesses. Wiccans experience Deity directly, not through intermediaries. We don't have prophets; if someone asks what the word of God/Goddess is, we teach them to listen for it. We all have equal access to Divinity. We just have to reach out for it.

Many Wiccan covens are "closed" (for initiates only). There are different levels of initiation (usually three) that define the amount of training an initiate has had, but these different levels don't separate an individual from the rest of the group. Ritual is participatory, and often the leadership of rituals will vary from one event to another. Those seeking initiation usually apprentice as novices for a year and a day before receiving their first-degree initiation.

Wiccans, once initiated, often choose ritual names, which are seldom revealed to the uninitiated. These private "magickal names" are sometimes changed. A Wiccan may choose a name that reflects a positive quality to be developed or a goal that he or she desires, then select a new name when he/she sets a new goal. Often, due to fear of persecution, they will adopt pseudonyms for use in public.

Wiccan parents may present their children to their deities and take oaths promising to raise and nurture these children properly and responsibly. This process is referred to as "Wiccaning" (also known as "Paganing," anointing, or saining). Other coven members usually assist the parents in this ritual. Wiccaning is usually done between an infant's third and thirteenth month, though the custom varies. Unlike in a Christening, the ritual does not involve an oath requiring the parents to raise the child to follow a particular religion. Rather, it is a protective ritual that is not binding on the child's future decisions regarding spirituality.

Covens

The term "coven" can be traced back to the thirteenth century CE. It is derived from the terms "covent" or "cuvent," which are found in the *Ancrene Riwle,* a monastic rule book for nuns. These terms were derived from the Old French terms "covenant" and *covenir,* in turn derived from the Latin *convenire* (to agree, to be of one mind, to come together). A coven, therefore, is a group of people who are of one mind and come together with a common purpose. The term "coven" first appeared in reference to "a gathering of witches" in 1662.[3] The word is usually used today to refer to a Wiccan group, though it is sometimes used by the press to describe groups of Satanists, probably due to popular Christian literature. Satanists do not use the term "coven" to describe their groups.

Wiccans traditionally meet in covens of thirteen members (six couples and a high priestess). This corresponds with the thirteen lunar months in a year. Covens may be larger, but as a rule are quite small. The area within three miles of a coven's meeting place is traditionally considered to be the "covenstead." This term dates back to a time when people walked to gatherings, but with most modern Pagans having vehicles and traveling much greater distances to attend gatherings, this term is no longer applicable. Wiccans often refer to coven meetings as "circling" or refer to fellow coven members as "people that I circle with." This is because covens worship within a consecrated Circle (more on this in a moment).

The leader of a coven is usually a high priestess; she may or may not share the leadership with a high priest. She has control only over her immediate coven (and in a few traditions, only during a ritual), and in some traditions, the coven members elect her. Members may leave at any time and join other covens or form their own covens elsewhere.

Often friendships and shared traditions are the only tie between covens. There is no hierarchy such as there is in authoritarian religions such as Christianity, although some traditions (e.g., Gardnerian and Alexandrian) maintain what might be termed a loose hierarchy. In some traditions, the high priestess wears a garter as a symbol of her position. Often buckles or ornaments on this garter will indicate how many other covens have been formed elsewhere as a result of her teaching.

In the Gardnerian tradition, a high priestess who has had three covens "hive off" from her teaching is accorded the title of "Witch Queen" by those covens. There is no such thing as a "Witch King." There have been, from time to time, individuals who have claimed such titles, mainly for egotistic purposes. Titles may boost sales of their books, but they don't win these people many friends within the Wiccan community. Such titles should be thoroughly checked out to determine if others accept them in the community.

In *Satanism: The Not So New Problem*, Lyle Rapacki properly identifies "coven" as a Wiccan term,[4] not mentioning Satanism in his definition at all. Rapacki includes this definition in a list labelled "Definitions of Satanic Terms," however, suggesting that Wicca is satanic, which it is not. The glossary of Watch Network's *Be Aware!* handbook describes "coven" practice this way:

> ... a group of six male and six female witches with a high priest or priestess. Satanic rites are parodies of Christian worship. One such rite is the Black Mass. Satanists practice a form of baptism and have their own corrupted kind of communion services. Sometimes human flesh and blood are used in this communion service. The Black Mass is celebrated over the body of a naked young woman. Satanists believe that all forms of perverted sexual indulgences are good.[5]

Wiccans do not celebrate the Black Mass, do not perform baptisms, and do not use humans as altars. The glossary in Johnston's *The Edge of Evil* defines "coven" this way: "Coven: Also called a clan, a coven is a group of satanists who gather to perform rites."[6] Johnston incorrectly thinks that Satanists and Witches are the same thing, judging from this definition. The 1734 Tradition of Wicca prefers the term "clan" to "coven," and some Druid groups also refer to themselves as clans. Satanists ordinarily organize themselves into grottos or pylons, not covens or clans. Wiccan covens have nothing to do with Satanists.

Reincarnation/Summerland

The Christian heaven is a place separate from the mundane world where followers are rewarded after they die. Some Wiccans believe that when we die, we go to a place called the Summerland. There, we rest for a time before returning to the mundane world in another form to continue the process of perfecting ourselves. Wiccans believe that they can use forms of divination to seek out details of past lives. A Wiccan's view of reincarnation in closely linked to the Threefold Law of Return (more on this in a moment).

Wiccan Rede

The traditional wording of the Wiccan Rede is "An it harm none, do what thou wilt." Some of our detractors have interpreted this to mean "Do whatever feels good," but this is incorrect. The Wiccan Rede is a serious responsibility, as it calls upon the Wicca to examine each and every one of their actions to determine the consequences to others. A more modern English translation of the first part of the Rede would be "Do nothing that may harm another." It calls for a high level of self-discipline from every Wicca.

In our society, people are accustomed to judging conduct against extensive sets of rules and laws, rather than using a more unstructured call to self-examination. The Wiccan Rede requires Wiccans to use their heads instead of someone else's list of rules. It asks us to take responsibility for our actions rather than relinquishing this responsibility to someone or something else. Wicca is not a dualistic system like some forms of Christianity, having extremes of light versus dark, good versus evil, right versus wrong. That sort of system requires no thought. It lacks shades of gray, and its morality is composed of long lists of rules and rigid codes. As Robin Wood points out in her book *When, Why ... If*:

> There are no gray areas here, no moral dilemmas, just right and wrong, simple and clear-cut. There are no natural consequences for your actions, no personal responsibility for any outcome, no reasoning, no thinking of any kind required; in short no ethics at all, just a list of things to be memorized, and a simple formula of repentance and forgiveness if you forget or decide to skip one.[7]

The theme of the prevailing system of commandments and laws in Western society is "Thou shalt not." By comparison, the theme of the Wiccan ethical system is "I will not." The Wiccan Rede is not a rule; it is a statement that counsels us to think. Personal responsibility is the basis of the Wiccan ethical system. We must take responsibility for our actions and think about what we are doing. Rules are for training young children to be adults; at some point, the child must grow up and understand the reasons for the rules. This understanding should replace the rules. For example: Wiccans don't steal, not because it is illegal, but rather because Wiccans understand that stealing hurts others and is therefore wrong.

Is it really possible to make it through life without harming someone or something? We eat to stay alive. We eat things that were alive. The death of living things brings us life. To survive cancer we must kill cancer cells. No matter how hard we try, we are bound to have an adverse effect on something in the world around us. Being present affects everything around us.

Remember how Wiccans are monists, treating everything around them as divine? To realize that everything around us is divine is to recognize that everything is worthy of respect. Wiccan priestesses Ashleen O'Gaea and Carol Garr put it this way: "When something dies so that we can continue to live, it's important to recognize that contribution, and to respect it, and honor the creature that makes it."[8] If a person believes that everything in the universe is divine, then violence will be contrary to his or her nature. People are less likely to harm someone or something that they respect.

Some people have challenged me to explain how I reconciled my job as a police officer (or as some people have put it, an "agent of the state") and the Wiccan Rede. Let me give two examples: First, let's say I saw a young woman working as a prostitute on a street corner. This activity is illegal. The law authorizes me to arrest her for engaging in such activity. I don't have to think about it; prostitution is illegal, so I arrest her.

But suppose I first went over and spoke to this young woman. Suppose I asked her why she was on that street corner prostituting herself. Perhaps she would tell me that her mother's fifth husband threw her out of the house. She is too young to collect welfare and has no job skills. Prostitution is the only option that she thinks that she has. I have the power to arrest her, but will arresting her solve her problem? Won't she just go right back out when she is released and do it again? How else is she going to feed herself? What choices does she have?

Do you see what I'm getting at? The Rede asks us to examine our actions carefully. It advises us to use our heads and solve the problem, rather than taking the easy way out. If I solve the problem, then hopefully the young prostitute won't end up back on the street. I can find social service agencies and resources to help her overcome this problem. I have many powers of arrest, but I use my common sense before I decide to apply them. This is how I apply the Rede to my police profession.

The second half of the Wiccan Rede seems equally simple: "Do what thou wilt." In modern English, we might say "Do what YOU will." It empowers Wiccans to be everything that they can be and to realize their full potential.

Karma/Threefold Law

In Abrahamic religious systems, transgressors are threatened with divine retribution: They tell you that God will whack you if you get out of line. In Wicca, however, as in some Eastern philosophies, one encounters the concept of karma. The word karma derives from a Sanskrit word meaning "action."[9] Karma is the totality of a person's actions determining their fate in this life and in other incarnations in the future. In other words, karma is the law of cause and effect.

The most common Wiccan equivalent of this principle is the Law of Threefold Return, which was established by one of the early founders of modern Wiccan practice, Raymond Buckland. Buckland's Law of Threefold Return states, "Everything you do comes back to you three times." He formulated this law as a public relations sound bite to help the public understand that Wiccans are harmless, not destructive cult members. As such, it was simple and effective. The original version, created by Wiccan founder Gerald Gardner, was a "twofold" law. It was in a later press interview that Buckland upped the ante to make it a threefold law instead. The threefold version stuck.

Basically, this law tells us that we get back three times whatever we put into life. If one does positive works, more abundant positive benefits will come in return. If a person does negative and destructive things to others, then that person will suffer even worse consequences to himself or herself. The trouble with this law is that it describes what in modern terms would be called a "feedback loop." If physicists or magicians had come up with proof that this system works so precisely in the past few centuries, you can be sure that you'd have heard about it.

It would be more accurate to use the concept of karma rather than the Threefold Law to describe how things happen in the real world. Wiccans believe that what you do gets passed forward by others and will eventually make its way back to you. As Sir Arthur Conan Doyle puts it, "Violence does, in truth, recoil upon the violent, and the schemer falls into the pit which he digs for another."[10]

Book of Shadows

Wiccans do not have a book of scriptures, such as the Torah, Bible, or Koran, as revealed religions do. Wicca is traditionally passed orally. Wiccans do keep a book listing their rituals and working notes called a Book of Shadows, however. This book is usually copied by hand from one Wiccan to the next. In the past, the books were often written in an unfamiliar script, such as Theban, Malachim, Runes, or Over the River. This is not as common today, as the technique was intended originally as a simple security measure. Ceremonial magicians (who call their books "grimoires") also use the same scripts.

A Wiccan Book of Shadows usually starts with a section called "The Ordains" or "Ardanes," which is a simple set of procedural rules for running a coven—a sort of *Robert's Rules of Order* for Wiccans.* The Gardnerian Book of Shadows includes 162 Craft Laws or "Ordains/Ardanes." Other Brit-Trad Wiccan groups may have more or less ordains/ardanes. The Ordains/Ardanes do not vary much from tradition to tradition, though some traditions have shortened the traditional Ordains/Ardanes. For example, some traditions no longer consider it necessary to keep the Craft secret, as they no longer fear persecution, and have deleted ordains/ardanes pertaining to secrecy.

NOTES

1. Kirschner & Associates, U.S. Government Publication #008-020-00745-5; *Religious Requirements of Certain Selected Groups- A Handbook for Chaplains* (Washington, DC, 1974).
2. Phyllis Curott, "Exploding Wiccan Dogma," lecture at Blessed Be and Merry Meet in DC conference in Washington, DC, October 14, 2000.
3. Robert K. Barnhart, ed., *Barnhart Dictionary of Etymology* (New York: H.W. Wilson), 228.
4. Lyle J. Rapacki, *Satanism: The Not So New Problem* (Intel, 1988), 56.
5. WATCH Network, *Be Aware!: A Handbook for the Purpose of Exposing Occultic Activity* (WATCH Network), 5.
6. Jerry Johnston, *The Edge of Evil* (Vancouver, BC: Word Publishing, 1989), 313.
7. Robin Wood, *When, Why ... If* (Livingtree Books, 1996), ii.
8. Ashleen O'Gaea and Carol Garr, *Circles Behind Bars: A Complete Handbook for the Incarcerated Witch* (unpublished, 2000).
9. *Webster's New Twentieth Century Dictionary*.
10. Sir Arthur Conan Doyle, "The Speckled Band," 1892, *Sherlock Holmes: The Complete Novels and Stories* (Bantam, 1986).

---

* *Robert's Rules* were created by Henry Martin Robert, an engineering officer in the army. Robert was asked to preside over a church meeting and apparently made a mess of it, as he had no experience in such matters. He further observed, in his transfers to various parts of the United States, that there were large variations in ideas about correct procedures for meetings. This motivated Robert to research the subject of parliamentary law. Eventually he wrote *Robert's Rules of Order*, which was first released in 1876. The tenth edition was printed in 2000, and it has become a standard reference for meeting rules worldwide.

Chapter Three

The Magick Circle

The power of the world always works in circle, and everything tries to be round.
—Black Elk (Hehaka Sapa), *Black Elk Speaks* (1961)

People in Western society are used to religions that utilize permanent temples. Christians have churches, Jews have synagogues, and Muslims have mosques. What makes these places of worship sacred is the belief of the people who use them. In other words, these places are holy because believers consciously choose to make them so. The sacred space is itself a symbol that takes on the meaning that we give it.

The average citizen may find it hard to grasp the idea of a religion like Wicca, which does not need permanent structures. Wiccans create their sacred space when and where they need it by casting a Circle. This underscores one of the two differences between sacred space as Wiccans use it and sacred space as it is usually used in the Abrahamic religions. Unlike the aforementioned permanent structures, the Wiccan Circle is portable; sacred space may be created anywhere at will. Wiccans are perhaps more conscious of the act of making a space holy than the followers of some other faiths, since Wiccans have to recreate their sacred space every time they use it.

Wiccans tend to use the term "circle" to refer to both the sacred space in which the rituals take place as well as to the ritual itself. To "circle" is to conduct a ritual. In the following descriptions, I am using the term to refer to the ritual itself.

Wiccan circles may be "closed" or "open." Many covens are now holding public rituals that are open to noninitiates. Such rituals are referred to as "open circles." Public circles are often referred to as "Pagan" rituals in order to differentiate them from "closed circles," or Wiccan rituals in which all of the participants are initiates.

A coven holding an open circle will often use somewhat different ritual forms than they ordinarily use in closed circles, but this is not always the case. Examples of situations where one would find an open circle are:

1. Major public Pagan festivals sponsored by various Wiccan and Pagan organizations. A few examples of such festivals are Dragonfest (Colorado), Spring Mysteries and Hecate's Sickle (Washington), Heartland Spiritual Festival (Kansas City, Missouri), Pagan Spirit Gathering (also known as PSG; Ohio) and Gathering of the Tribes (Georgia). These have proved to be very popular, some of them attracting over a thousand people. Open circles are usually held at such festivals so that people from a variety of traditions and beliefs can celebrate together. While many participants at festivals are relying on others to organize the events for them, such ritual is still not truly congregational in nature, since it is still intended to allow each individual to experience Deity personally, without mediation by clergy.

2. Where a candidate for initiation is allowed to participate to see if they can work harmoniously with the other coven members.

3. Where a visitor is invited to participate in the circle of a coven from a different tradition.

There are a number of urban legends concerning the Wiccan Circle. For example, Lou Sloat's *Texas Ritualistic Crime Information Network Occult Crime Manual* lists "circles" in an untitled list of symbols attributed to Satanism.[1] Definitions of "circle" that I've found in "occult crime manuals" over the years include:

- "Drawn on the ground at times with salt 8 feet in diameter. To enforce demons to appear [*sic*]."[2]
- "The satanic circle is well-known among witches and Satan-worshippers ... The point within the circle is the sign of Lucifer."[3]

Ceremonial magicians use the Circle as a psychic defense, meant to keep unwanted influences and spirits out. Ceremonial magick developed out of Abrahamic mythology and is performed by invoking or evoking spirits such as angels or demons. In the version described in the sixteenth-century magickal text *Lemegeton,* a triangle is drawn on the ground outside of this Circle and is placed in whatever quarter is appropriate to the spirit being evoked. Another variation, taken from *The Greater Key of Solomon*, has an inner Circle with a radius of nine feet, with second and third Circles having radii of ten and eleven feet respectively.

Satanists, borrowing much of their ritual from ceremonial magick, also usually use ritual Circles as a psychic defense. A notable exception to this is the Temple of Set, an organization that grew from Anton LaVey's Church of Satan.

Setians do not use any ritual Circle, as they believe that they are one with the forces they use and do not require protection from them.

In neo-Pagan religions such as Wicca, the Circle is both a defense and a container, meant to keep the energy that we raise in and unwanted influences out. A Wiccan Circle traditionally has a diameter of nine feet (not eight). In practice, a Wiccan Circle is often made larger, since a nine-foot Circle is a very small working area suitable for a solitary practitioner, not a group. Fitting thirteen people or more into a nine-foot Circle with an altar feels a bit like a high school prank where teenagers cram as many of themselves as possible into a phone booth.

To list all of the different Sabbat and Esbat rituals and all of their variations would take several volumes. Wiccans in some traditions encourage coven members to take turns writing their own rituals. Creativity and poetry are very much part of the Craft. Some traditions incorporate ritual drama into their circles, while others keep their circles very simple. One ritual, however, commences all Wiccan worship: This is the ritual of casting the magick Circle in which the Sabbat or Esbat takes place. Some of the words vary from one coven to the next, but the same basic elements of casting and, later, closing the Circle exist in all traditions.

In some traditions, the high priestess casts the Circle, but others may assist her. Sometimes a guest from another coven is given this honor. In traditions that share leadership between a high priestess and a high priest, the season or occasion might dictate whose duty it is to cast the Circle. Often the priestess leads from Beltaine to Samhain in the spring and summer months, while the priest rules the dark half of the year. One might view this symbolically as the male providing for the family or tribe in the winter as the hunter, while the female symbolically provides for the family or tribe in summer through agricultural pursuits.

Note the typical Circle in the accompanying diagram. It is oriented to the cardinal points of the compass. Note also that the four traditional elements of earth, air, fire, and water are represented on the altar and assigned cardinal points. Some traditions may vary in which element they assign to each particular cardinal point.

The ritual tools often found within a Wiccan Circle are described in the glossary. The most common is a ritual knife called an athame. Almost all Wiccans have one, and many Wiccan covens also have a sword. Some Wiccans prefer to use their wands or even their fingers instead of an athame. An athame usually has a metal blade, but this is not necessarily the case. I have seen many made of wood, stone, or plastic. Athames are used to trace the perimeter of the Circle during casting or to trace symbols in the air. They are usually not sharp. They don't need to be since they are only meant to "cut"

Circle Etiquette

In the course of an officer's duties, s/he may be called to investigate a gathering and come across a Wiccan Circle in progress. If the officer asks to speak to someone outside the Circle, then the Wicca that they are addressing may not leave the Circle without first drawing his or her athame and "cutting a door" through which to leave. This is habitual Circle etiquette to the Wicca involved, but to the uninitiated it may seem to be a threatening gesture, which is most certainly unintentional. This is a very important detail for a law enforcement officer. Most Wiccans have had little contact with law enforcement authorities and may not understand an officer's legitimate safety concerns without being told. If you are nervous about edged weapons, as any prudent police officer is likely to be, the best approach is to explain your concerns and ask the coveners present to please put their athames aside. There is no Craft rule that prohibits this; many traditions do this as a matter of course, placing their athames on the altar until needed. Any reasonable Wiccans will comply with this request if it is presented in an even-handed fashion, especially if you respect the Wiccans involved by not entering the Circle unless it has been opened for you or formally ended. Remember, it is an offense in most states (a criminal offence in Canada) to disturb the solemnity of a religious ceremony. Wicca is a recognized religion. The police officer walks a fine line between the legal execution of his or her duty and being accused of religious persecution.

air to symbolically separate the Circle from the mundane world during the casting ritual. They are not used as physical weapons, and they are never used to draw blood.

The coveners generally purify themselves before entering the Circle. This is normally accomplished by taking a bath in consecrated water containing a little salt and/or herbs. Once in the Circle, all Wiccans are expected to set differences aside and create an atmosphere of "perfect love and perfect trust." The bath helps the Wicca to purify negative thoughts and concentrate on the task ahead.

Almost all movement within the Circle is clockwise, which Wiccans call "deosil." A person wishing to cross the Circle will travel around its perimeter deosil rather than cutting straight across. Ordinarily, the only exception is when closing the Circle at the end of the ritual, when movement is sometimes counterclockwise or "widdershins."

The person casting the Circle will first consecrate the Circle with each of the four elements, including fire (usually a candle), air (incense), water, and earth (usually salt). Then the person casting will trace the perimeter of the Circle (deosil) with the sword, an athame, or a wand, depending on the tradition. If others are to enter later, this person will leave a gap in the northeast by raising the tool used as if tracing an arch or doorway.

Next, the person casting will go to each of the cardinal points and ask the gods (or guardians) to witness and protect the ritual. Often this person will trace an invoking pentagram in the air with an athame or the fingers. He or she will start in the east and work deosil around the Circle, then consecrate it by making a circuit with each elemental

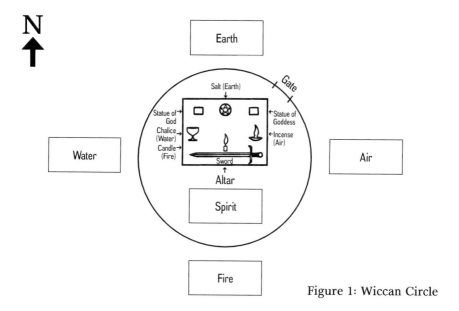

Figure 1: Wiccan Circle

representation in turn. Some traditions also invoke the center of the Circle, which represents the fifth element of spirit.

If the coveners are not already in the Circle, they now enter through the "doorway" left open earlier. After everyone has entered, the person casting seals this "door" by drawing a line across it with his or her ritual tool to complete the Circle, sometimes adding a pentagram. If for some reason a participant has to leave the Circle during the ritual, this doorway will be reopened by redrawing the door with an athame. Sometimes two people do this, starting at the apex of the "arch" and working outwards, then leaving their athames on the ground at either side of this door until it is to be closed. The doorway is then closed in the reverse direction, raising the athames back to the apex. Leaving the Circle during a ritual is a rare occurrence in most covens, as it is usually thought to diminish the power of the Circle.

After the casting, the ritual to be performed begins, its content depending on the nature of the Sabbat or Esbat being celebrated. Afterward, a thanksgiving ceremony is performed in which cakes and wine are consecrated and shared. This ceremony is not to be confused with the Christian ritual of transubstantiation. Wiccans do not transform the cakes and wine; we merely share them to give thanks for the bounty of the harvest and the gifts of Mother Earth.

When the ritual work is completed, the person who cast the Circle will open or "ground" the Circle. This is often done by making a widdershins (counterclockwise) circuit, starting in the north, thanking the gods (or guardians) at each cardinal point, and finishing in the east. Some traditions do this circuit deosil, starting in the east, and may trace a banishing pentagram in the air at each cardinal point. Most Wiccan Circles end with words such as "The Circle is open, but never broken. Merry meet, merry part, and merry meet again!"

Lunar Esbats

Wiccans conduct full and new moon rituals called Esbats. Erroneous definitions of "esbat" that I've found in "occult crime manuals" include "a weekly or biweekly meeting of witches"[4] and "a meeting of witches to accomplish an evil act."[5]

The Egyptologist Margaret Murray first used the term "esbats" to describe mundane gatherings of Witches. She derived the term from the Old French *esbatment*, which means "to divert oneself" or "an amusement." Today, Wiccans use it to describe a ceremony occurring during a full moon. These are regular meetings where Wiccans worship, discuss business, perform tasks such as healing, and enjoy each other's company. Occasionally, Wiccans may also meet during the new moon for "dark moon" ceremonies, or even during the first quarter (called "Diana's bow") or the last quarter (called "Hecate's sickle"), depending on the kind of work they wish to accomplish. For example, the period of the waning moon is considered by Wiccans to be a good time to work on banishing negative influences. Of course, the full moon comes along every twenty-eight days, so the lunar calendar is not in sync with the solar calendar. Esbats are not weekly meetings.

Magick

In occidental (i.e., Western) ceremonial magick and modern neo-Pagan religions such as Wicca, magick is spelled with a *k* to differentiate it from legerdemain or sleight-of-hand stage magic. Interestingly, when the term appeared in Chaucer's *House of Fame* (circa 1380), it was spelled "magik." In this context, the meaning was the same as the modern "magick," so "magick" may represent a return to an earlier spelling and meaning. The term can be traced back through Old French (*magique*) to Latin (*magice*) and ultimately to Greek (*magikos*).

In its original Greek usage, magick was the art of the Magi.* Many modern Wiccans would define it as "the art of changing consciousness and achieving

---

* Magi (var. maga, mage, magus, magician): "Mage" first appeared in the English language before 1350 CE. Circa 1200 CE, a "magy" was a person skilled in magick and astrology in the *Ormulum*. Deriv. Latin *magus* and its plural *magi*, derive from the Greek *magos* ("one of the Magi" or "Magians", members of the Medean tribe, who were considered to be enchanters). A *maga* is the feminine equivalent of a magus. Pliny (in his *Natural History*), Herod, Porphyry, and other ancient historians reported that the Magi or Magians were a Persian priestly caste, in charge of rites, dream interpretation, and magic for the Medean tribe. There is a reference to an enchanter of this tribe named Simon Magus in Acts 7:9–24 in the Bible.

other goals at will, through disciplines and systematic use of the mind and natural forces."[6] Other definitions include:

- "Magic is a joyous exceptional experience which leads to a sense of well-being."[7]
- "Magic is the science of the control of the secret forces of nature."[8]
- "Magic is a comprehensive knowledge of all nature."[9]
- "Magic is the art of affecting changes in consciousness at will."[10]
- "Effective magick works like this: The Middle Self chooses a purpose in harmony with its True Will; it communicates this purpose to the Younger Self in a special way, at the same time raising power; the Younger Self 'boosts' the power and channels it to the Higher Self, along with a clear image of the goal; and the Higher Self uses the power to manifest the desired result. Middle Self experiences the result, and the circle is complete."[11]

I've devoted whole books to the subject of magick (see Bibliography), and I don't wish to lengthen this one by going into the subject in detail. Suffice it to say that the first rule of magick for some Wiccans is "You create your own reality." Wiccans don't leave things to fate; they use their abilities and skills to take charge of their lives and steer them in the direction they want. That's magick.

Summary of Wiccan Beliefs

A good summary of Wiccan beliefs can be found in the following Principles of Wiccan Belief, formulated by the Council of American Witches, which met on April 11–14, 1974 in Minneapolis:

> The Council of American Witches finds it necessary to define modern Witchcraft in terms of the American experience and needs.

> We are not bound by traditions from other times and other cultures and owe no allegiance to any person or power greater than the Divinity manifest through our own being.

> As American Witches we welcome and respect all Life Affirming teachings and traditions, and seek to learn from all and to share our learning within our Council.

> It is in this spirit of welcome and cooperation that we adopt these few principles of Wiccan belief. In seeking to be inclusive, we do not wish to open ourselves to the destruction of our group by those on self-serving power trips, or to philosophies and practices contradictory to those principles.

In seeking to exclude those ways contradictory to ours, we do not want to deny participation with us to any who are sincerely interested in our knowledge and beliefs, regardless of race, color, sex, age, national or cultural origins or sexual preference.

1. We practice Rites to attune ourselves with the natural rhythm of life forces marked by the Phases of the Moon and the Seasonal Quarters and Cross-Quarters.

2. We recognize that our intelligence gives us a unique responsibility toward our environment. We seek to live in harmony with Nature, in ecological balance offering fulfilment to life and consciousness within an evolutionary concept.

3. We acknowledge a depth of power far greater than that apparent to the average person. Because it is far greater than ordinary, it is sometimes called "supernatural," but we see it as lying within that which is naturally potential to all.

4. We conceive of the Creative Power of the Universe as manifesting through polarity—as masculine and feminine—and that this same Creative Power lives in all people, and functions through the interaction of masculine and feminine. We value Sex as pleasure, as the symbol and embodiment of life, and as one of the sources of energies used in magical practice and religious worship.

5. We recognize both outer worlds and inner, or psychological, worlds—sometimes known as the Spiritual World, the Collective Unconscious, the Inner Planes, etc.—and we see in the interaction of these two dimensions the basis for paranormal phenomena and magical exercises. We neglect neither dimension for the other, seeing both as necessary for our fulfilment.

6. We do not recognize any authoritarian hierarchy, but do honor those who teach, respect those who share their greater knowledge and wisdom, and acknowledge those who have courageously given of themselves in leadership.

7. We see religion, magick, and wisdom-in-living as being united in the way one views the world and lives in it—a

worldview and philosophy-of-life which we identify as Witchcraft, the Wiccan Way.

8. Calling oneself "Witch" does not make one a Witch—but neither does heredity itself, or the collecting of titles, degrees and initiations. A Witch seeks to control the forces within him/herself that make life possible in order to live wisely and well, without harm to others, and in harmony with nature.

9. We acknowledge that it is the affirmation and fulfillment of life, in a continuation of evolution and development of consciousness, that gives meaning to the Universe we know, and to our personal role within it.

10. Our only animosity toward Christianity, or toward any other religion or philosophy-of-life, is to the extent that its institutions have claimed to be "the only way" and have sought to deny freedom to others and to suppress other ways of religious practice and belief.

11. As American Witches, we are not threatened by debates on the history of the Craft, the origins of various aspects of different traditions. We are concerned with our present, and our future.

12. We do not accept the concept of "absolute evil," nor do we worship any entity known as "Satan" or "The Devil" as defined by the Christian tradition. We do not seek power through the suffering of others, nor do we accept the concept that personal benefit can only be derived by denial to another.

13. We acknowledge that we seek within Nature for that which is contributory to our health and well-being."*

A fellow Wiccan and police officer once summed up Wicca as follows: "Wicca is a nature religion. Wicca is also ... a manifest religion, as opposed to a revealed religion such as Christianity or Islam. Wicca holds that the God and Goddess are manifest in all of nature, and are accessible to all. In a revealed religion, a prophet or messiah receives what purports to be the word of God and reveals this to the less spiritually adept faithful. Wicca has no prophets or

---

*   Margot Adler, *Drawing Down the Moon* (Boston: Beacon Press, 1986), 101–103. It should be pointed out that there is no hierarchy of Witches, and that the Council of American Witches became moribund before holding a second such meeting due to internal disagreements.

messiahs."[12] Each Wiccan, then, has a personal relationship with Deity.

Wiccan author Phyllis Curott wrote one of the best summaries of Wicca in fifteen words: "Wicca is the indigenous shamanism of Northern Europe and has nothing to do with Satanism."

Some people have suggested that Wicca must be anti-Christian, simply because it isn't Christian. This belief is exclusivism: the idea that there can only be one true faith. The same individuals who make this suggestion usually accuse *any* faith or Christian denomination other than their own of being anti-Christian or satanic. Wicca is not Satanism. A Satanist must, by definition, believe in the Christian mythos. We Witches do not believe in the Christian God *or* the devil, so the whole question of Satan is outside of our religion. Like Hindus and Buddhists, we believe in good and evil. We have ethics and believe that there is right and wrong. But we do not have a forces-of-light versus forces-of-darkness concept such as many Christians and Satanists do. We are not anti-Christian. We are simply different.

Wiccans believe in an individual's right to choose his or her own religious path, and for this reason, we do not proselytize. There are many Wiccans like myself who have suffered physical and verbal abuse from intolerant Christians. Regrettably, as a result of this treatment, some Wiccans have ill feelings toward the *entire* Christian community. The vast majority of Wiccans, however, have had positive contact with Christians and recognize that our problems stem from a group of Christians that are a minority.

Some Wiccan traditions are still very secretive about their ceremonies, and their coven members have taken oaths not to reveal this information to the uninitiated. This secrecy relates to folklore concerning the deadly serious precautions taken in the days of the Inquisition. Regrettably, religious persecution still makes secret worship necessary in some parts of North America. Elsewhere, secrecy can still be useful, as a priest or priestess can often verify someone's claim to being an initiated Wiccan based on that person's knowledge (or

The Body Is Sacred

Many a thrill-seeker has approached a Wiccan coven looking for orgies and licentiousness, as they have heard that the covens engage in the ancient practice of ritual nudity. These individuals are invariably disappointed, as they find no such activity. Wiccans have no concept of original sin, as most Christians do. To a Wiccan, the body is a sacred thing and worthy of respect. I have always been amazed by those Christians who find nudity sinful, perverted, and/or pornographic, but also state that human beings were made in God's image. How is it that God's image could be corrupt? A Wiccan also believes that women and men were created in the image of the God/Goddess and reveres the body as such. As a re-creation of older fertility religions, Wiccan ritual is full of sexual symbolism. What thrill seekers fail to appreciate, however, is that we do not view this sexual symbolism through a Christian lens. We view it as Wiccans, for whom there is nothing sinful about the body.

lack thereof). Since 1949, when Gerald Gardner wrote his novel *High Magic's Aid*, however, literature has detailed many previously secret rituals. Today, Wiccans are generally much more open, making it quite easy to obtain information on any of the Wiccan traditions.

Some British Wiccan traditions (such as the Gardnerian and Alexandrian traditions) normally worship in the nude, which is called "going skyclad" (that is to say, clad only by the sky). Not all traditions go skyclad, with climate often being a factor. In many Wiccan traditions, the celebrants wear simple robes. Some Wiccan traditions use a colored cord or sash (cingulum) around the waist, which may give an indication of their rank or degree. These colors vary from one tradition to the next. Robe colors vary from one tradition to another, and may be black. This color is no more satanic than it is when worn by a Jewish rabbi or a Christian minister or nun.

The high priestess often wears a crescent moon crown or circlet on her head during rituals. The high priest may wear a helmet or headdress with horns or antlers. The wearing of horns is an ancient practice relating to the God as Lord of the Hunt, and has nothing to do with Satanism.

NOTES

1. Lou Sloat, *Texas Ritualistic Crime Information Network Occult Crime Manual*, 28.
2. *Colorado Bureau of Investigations Questioned Documents Examiner's Occult Guide*, 4–35.
3. Texe Marrs, *Mystery Mark of the New Age* (Westchester, IL: Crossway Books, 1988), 107–108.
4. Lou Sloat, *Texas Ritualistic Crime Information Network Occult Crime Manual*, 18.
5. WATCH Network, *Be Aware!: A Handbook for the Purpose of Exposing Occultic Activity* (WATCH Network), 5.
6. The Center for Non-Traditional Religion, "Wicca and Paganism: A Rebirth of the Religion of the Mother Goddess," 4.
7. Sybil Leek, *The Complete Art of Witchcraft* (New York: Signet, 1971).
8. Aleister Crowley, *Magick in Theory and Practice* (New York: Castle Books), xii.
9. Francis Barrett, *The Magus* (New York: University Books, 1967), 13.
10. Isaac Bonewits, *Real Magic* (Berkeley, CA: Creative Arts Book Company, 1970), 28.
11. Amber K, *True Magick* (St. Paul, MN: Llewellyn Publications, 1990), 63.
12. Letter to the author from Sean Watson, November 1988.

Chapter Four

What Wicca is Not

The fear of the Devil, evil spirits and witches can be seen at the back of many omens and superstitions.
—Philippa Waring, *A Dictionary of Omens and Superstitions* (p. 260)

Partially because a great deal of the nonsense in circulation about the occult is described as "Witchcraft," and partially because Wicca is one of the better-known and larger neo-Pagan spiritual paths, I've devoted separate chapters to some of the major urban legends in circulation about Witchcraft.

The Great God Samhain Myth

Some so-called experts claim that the Wiccan Sabbat called Samhain (which I describe in Chapter Eight) is named after a Celtic "god of death." In *Schemes of Satan*, Michael Warnke claims that the Druids sacrificed humans at Samhain to appease the great god Samhain, and that they threw their victims into raging fires. Later Warnke states that Samhain is cognate with the name Satan.[1] Bill Schnoebelen writes that October 31 was named after "Saman [*sic*], god of the Dead"[2] and lists Wade Baskin's *Dictionary of Satanism*[3] and Barbara Walker's *Woman's Encyclopedia of Myths and Secrets*[4] as his sources.

Barbara Walker claims that the Celtic festival of Samhain was "named for the Aryan Lord of Death, Samana, 'the Leveller,' or the Grim Reaper, leader of ancestral ghosts ... the Irish used to call the holy night the Vigil of Saman."[5] I believe that this is a mistaken assumption based on the partial similarity of the two names. The Celtic gods of death were Gwynn ap Nudd for the British, Bile or Donn for the Irish, and Beli/Belenus or Arawn for the Welsh. One would think if the intention was to use the name of a god of death, then the Celts would have named their festival after one of these gods. Schnoebelen seems unaware that Wiccans call October 31 "Samhain," not "Saman."

It is likely that the idea that Samhain was named for a god of death was taken from Ray Bradbury's 1973 short story "The Halloween Tree." In it, Bradbury invents a god of death named Samhain. Bradbury's book demonstrates a grasp of what the Samhain festival represented to the ancient Celts, but he obviously named his character after the festival rather than the other way around.

In fact, there is a Celtic god named Samhain. He was a minor god of cattle, but neither a god of the dead nor a title of Satan. He is a lesser Irish deity, one of the Tuatha Dé Danaan (people of the Goddess Dana). Samhain's story can be found in the *Leabhar Gabhala Eireann* (*Book of the Conquest of Ireland*), more commonly known as the *Book of Invasions*, a compendium of folklore compiled in the eleventh century. Samhain (sometimes translated as "Sawan") is the brother of Cian, a healer god (father of the solar god Lugh Lamfada and son of the god of medicine, Diancecht), and Goibhniu, a blacksmith god. As is typical with many Celtic deities, we know very little about Samhain. In the *Leabhar Gabhala Eireann*, Cian owns a cow named Glas Gaibhnenn, which he leaves in the care of his brother Samhain. The evil Fomorii leader Balor appears to Samhain as a little redheaded boy and tricks Samhain into parting with the cow, then takes it to his fortress on Tory Island. Cian pursues Balor and rescues the cow. In the process, Cian seduces Balor's daughter Ethlinn, who later gives birth to the Sun God Lugh. There is no evidence in this story or elsewhere to suggest that Samhain was a Lord of Death or the afterlife, particularly considering that we know who the Celtic gods of the dead were.

Is it still possible that the festival was named after the god Samhain as described in the *Leabhar Gabhala Eireann*? We cannot say for sure, but I have a theory: Cows were used by the early Celts as a currency, the worth of things being measured in head of cattle. For this reason, much of Irish Celtic mythology concerns cattle raids, like the classic stories "Tain Bo Culaigne (The Cattle Raid of Cooley)" and the "Tain Bo Fraoch (The Cattle Raid of Fraoch)." The festival of Samhain was the time that the pastoral Celts culled the herds, slaughtering all the cattle except those essential for next year's breeding, then salting the meat to see them through the winter. It is possible that Samhain, as a guardian of cattle, was considered an appropriate deity to name this day after.

Muck Olla

Muck Olla is a legendary boar of enormous size who was said to have been slain by one of the Geraldines in County Cork in Ireland. At Ballycotton in County Cork, a Samhain procession was led by a man called the *Lair Bhan*, who dressed in a white sheet and carried or wore a mask like a mare's skull.*

---

* The basic texts of these stories are found in the eleventh century *Leabhar na h-Uidhre* (*Book of the Dun Cow*) and the twelfth century *Leabhar Laighnech* (*Book of Leincester*).

Instead of saying "trick or treat" as children nowadays do in North America today, members of the procession would demand gifts in the name of Muck Olla.

No one can say precisely how old this custom is, but the boar (or pig) was a sacred animal to the Celts and provided meat for the feasts of the otherworld or Summerland. A sow is the symbol of the goddess Cerridwen, while a mare symbolizes the goddess Epona or Rhiannon.

In Wales, people used to light bonfires on hilltops at Samhain. They would dance, sing, and roast potatoes and apples to eat, and when the fire burned down, they would leap over it. As the flames burned down, the celebrants would suddenly dash off down the hill, crying, "May the tailless Black Sow take the hindmost!" This saying was a reference to the *hwch ddu gwta*, the tailless black sow that was a symbol of Cerridwen in her Crone aspect.

I have seen several references to Muck Olla as the "Celtic god of the dead" or as a "Sun God" in recent texts. As you can see, however, Muck Olla is a name clearly related to several Celtic goddesses, not to any god.

The "Black Mass of Witchcraft" Myth

The Black Mass, also known by its French name, Le Messe Noir, is a mockery of the Roman Catholic Mass in which a parody of the Mass is read and Catholic ritual objects are defiled. The alleged practices of Satanists were invented by the demonologists of the Inquisition, but some of the ideas incorporated into their descriptions were derived from far earlier practices. As early as 681 CE, the Council of Toledo prohibited the "Mass of the Dead," which was a Mass said for a deceased person. It had come to the attention of the Church that certain priests were saying the Mass of the Dead for living persons in the hope that this would cause their deaths. This Mass of the Dead is the root from which the Black Mass grew.[6] It has no place in Wiccan worship.

In fifteenth-century France, Gilles de Rais (the original Bluebeard) was the Marshall of France (and may have been a personal escort of Joan of Arc). According to the story told during his trial, de Rais squandered his fortune and then fell in with an alchemist named Prelati, who promised to help him turn his fortunes around. The rituals prescribed by Prelati involved the sacrifice of children to Satan (or in some accounts, to a particular demon). The victims were either abducted or purchased from peasant families as "farm workers." In 1440, de Rais' wife informed the authorities of her suspicions, and authorities found a chapel in his premises complete with inverted crosses, black candles, and statues of Satan. In one room, they found neatly labeled vessels of blood, each bearing the name of its victim, as well as a freshly slaughtered child. De Rais was subsequently burned at the stake. The account of de Rais' activities provided many ideas that found their way into modern portrayals of Satanism.[7]

In the sixteenth century, J. G. Sepulveda's *De Vita Aegidii Albornotti* described a renegade order of Franciscan monks called the Fraticelli, who practised indiscriminate sex at night. Sepulveda claimed that babies produced by these sexual unions were burned, the ashes being mixed into the sacramental wine. This would develop into the modern myths about satanic "breeders," women who have children for the specific purpose of providing sacrificial victims.[8]

By the end of the sixteenth century, the format of the Black Mass was beginning to take shape. It began as a diversion for the aristocracy, looking for thrills. In 1590, Henri Boquet described a Mass at which the priest put water in the chalice instead of wine, used a slice of black turnip instead of a wafer, and turned his back to the altar.

It was not until the seventeenth century in France that the Black Mass took the stereotypical form we may recognize today. This version of the ritual involved the mistress of Louis XIV, the Marquise de Montespan; a Catholic priest, the Abbe Guiborg; and a clairvoyant, Catherine Deshayes. De Montespan attempted to use the Black Mass and assassination through poisoning to eliminate rivals for the king's affection. Guiborg conducted a parody of the Catholic Mass, culminating in the sacrifice of a child by cutting its throat and collecting the blood in a chalice. A wafer was made from blood and flour. De Montespan acted as the living altar, lying on the altar naked while Guiborg performed the sacrifice over her. Finally, the king ordered an inquiry, the Chambre Ardente. Deshayes was burned at the stake, Guiborg died three years later in prison, and de Montespan was allowed to go free.[9] Authors such as Russell Hope Robbins have suggested that this ritual heavily influenced the writings of the Marquis de Sade, who popularized similar hideous practices in his novel *Justine*.

In the eighteenth century, a number of "hellfire clubs" sprang into existence, the most famous being at West Wycombe in the 1750s, organized by Sir Francis Dashwood. These were primarily an excuse to engage in sexual orgies and other outrageous behavior and did not involve the sacrifices practised in the Black Mass. Toward the end of the century, they died out.

The nineteenth century saw a resurgence of interest in the Black Mass. Abbe Boullan, a defrocked priest who claimed to be a magician, performed such rituals with a former nun, Adele Chevalier. In 1859, they founded the Society for the Reparation of Souls, which specialized in exorcisms. These exorcisms involved force-feeding consecrated communion hosts mixed with feces to the "possessed" and the performance of a Black Mass. Boullan reportedly sacrificed his own bastard son at one of these Masses. He later left the Society and associated with an outlaw Catholic prophet named Eugene Vintras, who held "White Masses." Before his death, Boullan bizarrely preached that the way to salvation lay in having sexual intercourse with angels!

The final step in the development of the Black Mass was the fictional book by J. K. Huysmans, entitled *La Bas* (1891). Huysmans seems to have based it on knowledge of Boullan. In it, the character Canon Docre holds Black Masses in a deserted chapel. Black candles and hallucinogenic incense are used, and Docre wears a red, horned biretta and a red chasuble. During the ritual, the priest throws the communion host on the floor and lets the congregation trample it. Docre also performs a Mass of Saint Secaire, in which a triangular black host is used and the sacramental wine is water in which an unbaptized baby has been drowned.[10] The idea that the Black Mass involves the reading of the Catholic Mass backward is a common urban legend. While some modern Satanists have adopted this practice, the "traditional" version from this novel is a parody of Matthew 6:9 (The Lord's Prayer).

Aspects of the Black Mass have inspired some of the rituals of modern Satanists, although they do not perform sacrifices of any sort. Modern Satanists are, for the most part, nonviolent, and allegations of ritual abuse are urban legends with no basis in reality.

Neo-Pagans such as Wiccans do not perform Black Masses. Pagans are not anti-Christian and do not have any reason to belittle or pervert Christian ritual. For example, the Black Mass often involves the desecration of a communion host stolen from a church. Catholics believe that this host becomes the body of Christ through transubstantiation, just as the sacramental wine is supposed to become his blood. Anglicans call this consubstantiation. Anti-Christians may covet these relics in order to use them in their ceremonies; as Christian objects, they may have some value to them. A Wiccan is indifferent to these items, as we do not believe in Christian transubstantiation. I don't mean to ridicule this Christian ceremony, which can be a very effective ritual drama, but I don't believe that a Catholic priest can make anything other than a meal out of his hosts and wine. Wiccans are not going to commit criminal acts to obtain something that is meaningless to them. If I want crackers and wine, I'll go to the supermarket.

Cornu/Mano Cornuto/Horned Salute

The horned salute is a hand gesture that has been misinterpreted as a satanic recognition signal in many books on the "occult" and Satanism. Michael Warnke refers to this gesture as a recognition signal for "the Brotherhood" in *The Satan Seller*. The *cornu* gesture is prominently displayed on the cover of John Frattarola's *America's Best Kept Secret*. Mary Ann Herold lists it twice in *A Basic Manual on the Occult for Law Enforcement Agencies*. A cornu, also described as an "Italian horn," is listed as a "demonic symbol" on the Madrak's Demonbuster website.[11] The glossary of the Watch Network's *Be Aware!* handbook defines "horned hand" as "the sign of recognition between those who are in the occult."[12] Thomas Carder's ChildCare Action Project/Christian Analysis of American Culture website defines the horned hand or the *mano cornuto* this way: "This gesture is the satanic salute, a sign of recognition between and allegiance of members of satanism or other unholy groups. It is also called the Il Cornuto."[13]

The cornu or horned hand shows up in several police manuals. Lou Sloat's *Texas Ritualistic Crime Information Network Occult Crime Manual* lists the cornu as a "horned hand sign" in an untitled list of symbols attributed to Satanism.[14] Other examples include:

- "A satanic salute or sign among members; represents devil's horns. Often used innocently by adolescent heavy metal groupies without knowing its alternate meaning."[15]
- "Originally used by Pseudo-Satanists as a secret hand sign to gain access to rituals, the sign is now widely used by Self-styled Satanists to indicate that they are in league with Satan."[16]

The cornu, mano cornuto, or horned hand salute is made by raising the hand with the index and little fingers extended and the other fingers and thumb folded against the palm. In different contexts, this gesture has several meanings, including the following:

- In Wicca, some traditions use the horned hand as the sign of the Horned God. Warnke may have been aware of this, as he mentions it in reference to what he describes as "witches."
- Some Native American traditions use the horned hand as the sign of the buffalo.
- Anton LaVey adopted the horned hand as a satanic salute in the 1960s and 1970s, resulting in it being advertised as such in anti-Satanist books.
- The Piru (Bloods) gang members in Los Angeles use the horned hand as a recognition symbol.
- Football fans use the horned hand to support the Texas Longhorns football team.
- In American sign language, the horned hand is a slang expression for "bullshit."

This last interpretation of this hand sign disproves the claim that the horned hand is always a satanic symbol. Incidentally, the image of the hand with the eye in the palm that Carder refers to is a common image in Tibet and in the art of Native American mound builders, both of which predate the Christian belief in Satan.

White/Grey/Black Witches

Many ill-informed people suggest that Wiccans organize themselves into categories of "White Witches," "Black Witches," and, sometimes, "Grey Witches." The idea is that if you do no evil, you're a "White Witch," and if you do evil, you're a "Black Witch." This simplistic system was borrowed from the Witch hunts in Tudor and Stuart England,[17] and it was invented by outsiders who don't understand what Wiccans believe. To claim there are White and Black Witches makes as much sense as claiming there are 'White Christian' priests and 'Black Christian' priests. I've never heard anyone call a Satanist a 'Black Christian'—a Satanist is not a Christian at all, nor would a 'Black Witch' be considered a Wiccan. The Wiccan community feels that those who violate the Wiccan Rede to "harm none" do not deserve to be called Wiccans. The idea of powers of "light" versus powers of "darkness" is an ancient Zoroastrian concept, which the early Christian Church adopted. It is a concept foreign to Wicca. Wiccans believe in a balance of positive and negative forces, similar to the Yin/Yang concept of some Eastern religions. A Wiccan is more likely to define evil as a loss of interest in balance and harmony, a situation that is bound to be destructive.

Ritual Sacrifice Myths

Wiccans do not sacrifice any living thing. This would not only violate our Wiccan Rede, but also offend our sense of affinity with all creatures. Many Wiccans are ardent environmentalists and are fiercely protective of their children. Myths about Witches using unbaptized babies for various nefarious purposes are in the same category as earlier ones accusing Jews of the same atrocities—complete fiction. These myths originated during the Inquisition, when "confessions" extracted under torture were considered "proof" of such crimes. It is interesting to note that early Christians were also accused of being "cannibals," probably because of a misunderstanding of the communion ceremony, in which the "body and blood" of Christ are consumed. Although there is little to no evidence proving that child sacrifice has systematically taken place at any time in history, these myths persist, and accusations of such atrocities continue to be leveled against minority groups. Similarly, despite the overwhelming evidence that most reports of cattle mutilations are mistaken observations of predator damage, certain 'experts' and organizations continue to cite these cattle deaths as "proof" of ritualized animal abuse.

Commonly Misunderstood Groups

Those who disseminate misinformation about Pagan practices often attempt to link Pagan religions to myths surrounding various other metaphysical organizations and lodges that have existed throughout history. A working knowledge of the common spurious claims made against these minority religious groups, as well as the facts about these organizations, can be very useful when investigating an accusation or when defending oneself against religious persecution.

Minoan Brotherhood

A few years ago, I attended a presentation on "Satanic crimes" for police officers in Vancouver. The presenter was Eric Pryor, who claims to have once been a satanic priest. Pryor also claimed that "a Minoan is a gay occultist" and that "all great Pagan leaders were at one time in the Minoan Brotherhood." The Minoan Brotherhood is a gay men's tradition of Wicca; however, there is no requirement for Pagan leaders from other traditions to have been Minoans, as Pryor suggests.

The Minoan Brotherhood was founded by Edmund ("Eddie" or Ed) M. Buczynski (also founder of the New York Welsh and Wica* Traditions), Carol Bulzone (the founder of the Enchantments store in New York), and Lady Rhea (of the Magickal Realms store in the Bronx). These three wanted to create a place for gay and lesbian Pagans to celebrate in peace, though heterosexuals were not excluded from their celebrations. Buczynski (who used the Craft name Minos Gwydion-Hyakinthos) established Knossos Grove in New York in 1975. In the same year, Bulzone (Lady Miw) and Lady Rhea set up the Minoan Sisterhood, which seems to have remained a New York phenomenon. The Minoan Tradition has since expanded to three branches with groups in New York; Boston; San Francisco; Salem, Massachusetts; New Orleans; Sarasota; Dallas; Toronto; Columbus; and Miami: the Minoan Brotherhood, the Minoan Sisterhood, and the Cult of the Double Axe/Cult of Rhea. The Cult of the Double Axe is the common ground between the brotherhood and the sisterhood. As their name suggests, they incorporate Minoan mythology into rituals based on Gardnerian practices.

Order of Melchizedek

Bill Schnoebelen, author of *Wicca - Satan's Little White Lie*, also claims to have been a satanic priest. Schnoebelen once made a presentation to some Canadian church groups. I possess an audio copy of this presentation, in which Schnoebelen claims that the priesthood of Witchcraft is called the "Order of Melchizedek." "[H]e's this kind of mysterious fellow who pops up in the book

---

* Different from Gardner's original Wica.

of Genesis, brings out offerings of bread and wine," he said. According to Schnoebelen, "the problem is that many occult orders and many secret societies like, like the Masons and even the Mormons of course claim to have a Melchizedek priesthood. And so do Witches ..."[18]

Melchizedek is a prototype for the Messiah who appears later in the Bible, but the concept of a messiah is foreign to Wiccan religion. Melchizedek is an old Canaanite name variously translated as "My Name is [the God] Sedek" or "My King is Righteousness."* Melchizedek appears as the King of Salem in Genesis 14:18. Later in the Bible, Salem is identified as Jerusalem (Psalms 76:2). Genesis describes Melchizedek as a "priest of God Most High," in this case the Canaanite God Elyon. Elyon was the name of God used by the Zadokite sect; whereas, the Levite sect that Abram (Abraham) belonged to used the Caananite name Yahweh (Jehovah). Melchizedek appears before Abram and gives him wine and bread, and Abram then gives him a tithe.

Melchizedek next appears in Psalms 110:4, a psalm of David, in which the Lord calls David "a priest forever after the order of Melchizedek." This references a future messiah in the Davidic line. Later in Hebrews 5:6, God tells Christ, "Thou art my son, today I have begotten thee ... Thou art a priest forever after the order of Melchizedek ... being designated by God a high priest after the order of Melchizedek." And in Hebrews 6:20 to 7:3:

> Where Jesus has gone as a forerunner on our behalf, having become a high priest forever after the order of Melchizedek. For this Melchizedek, king of Salem, priest of the Most High God, met Abraham returning from the slaughter of the kings and blessed him; and to him Abraham apportioned a tenth part of everything. He is first, by translation of his name, king of righteousness, and then he is also king of Salem, that is, king of peace. He is without father or mother or genealogy, and has neither beginning of days nor end of life, but resembling the Son of God he continues a priest forever.

The Melchizedek priesthood is an order within the Church of Jesus Christ of Latter Day Saints, otherwise known as the Mormon Church. At the age of twelve, young Mormon males become deacons in the "Aaronite priesthood," later graduating at age eighteen to the "Melchizedek priesthood." There is no "priesthood of Melchizedek" in Wicca as Schnoebelen claims, however, as Wicca does not come from the biblical tradition.

---

*   All Bible verses are from the King James Version.

NOTES

1. Michael Warnke, *Schemes of Satan* (Victory House, 1991), 122.
2. Bill Schnoebelen, "Saints Alive In Jesus," *Halloween: Tis The Season To Be Evil* (1990), 3.
3. Wade Baskin, *Dictionary of Satanism* (Philosophical Library, 1972), 285.
4. Barbara Walker, *The Woman's Encyclopedia of Myths and Secrets* (1983), 372.
5. Ibid.
6. Arthur Lyons, *Satan Wants You: The Cult of Devil Worship in America* (New York: The Mysterious Press, 1988), 51.
7. Lyons, 52.
8. Ibid.
9. Ibid.
10. Ibid.
11. Stanley Madrak, "Wicca - Satan's Little White Lie," http://www.moodymanual.demonbuster.com/witchcr1.html.
12. WATCH Network, *Be Aware!: A Handbook for the Purpose of Exposing Occultic Activity* (WATCH Network), 9.
13. Thomas Carder, *Back To School Special*, ChildCare Action Project: Christian Analysis of American Culture, http://www.capalert.com/backtoschool/backtoschool.htm.
14. Lou Sloat, *Texas Ritualistic Crime Information Network Occult Crime Manual*, 28.
15. Sgt. Edwin C. Anderson Jr., *Law Enforcement Guide to Occult Related Crime* (California State University Police), 40.
16. William Dubois, *Occult Crime*, 46.
17. A. D. J. MacFarlane, *Witchcraft in Tudor and Stuart England* (London: Routledge and Kegan Paul Ltd., 1970), 67.
18. Toronto, circa 1990.

Chapter Five

Wiccan Symbols

Ex umbris et imaginibus in veritatem. (From shadows and symbols into the truth.)
—Epitaph for John Henry Cardinal Newman (1801–1870) at Edgbaston

A list of symbols is usually included in law enforcement guides to "occult"-related crimes. The trouble with this is that symbols have a specific meaning for the group that uses them. Another group may use the same symbols to represent something completely different. An example of this is the Afro-Diasporan Santeria faith, which uses Catholic saints to represent Nigerian (Yoruba) tribal gods.

Wiccans traditionally use certain symbols in their practice. Some of them have been borrowed by other religious groups, just as other religions have borrowed magical, Qabbalistic, and Christian symbols, changing the meanings to suit their own purposes. Below I'll give the Wiccan meanings of some common symbols and any alternate meanings that other groups who use the same symbols may attribute to them.

Pentacle

In Wiccan usage, a pentacle is a flat, round disk with a pentagram or hexagram in a circle engraved on it, representing the element of earth. In neo-Pagan religion, the pentacle is used as a plate to distribute cakes during ritual (also spelled "pantacle" in this usage). It is traditionally made of wood, although I have seen metal, ceramic, and glass pentacles/pantacles as well.

SPIRIT

AIR

WATER

EARTH

FIRE

Pentagram

The five-pointed star, with one point uppermost. Also known as Solomon's Seal, though other texts assign the name Solomon's Seal to the hexagram instead. Pythagoras referred to this symbol as the pentalpha, since it represents the Greek letter *alpha* (the letter *A*) in five different positions.

The ancient Greeks regarded the pentagram as a talisman that protects from danger, and they inscribed it on the thresholds of doorways. Early Christians used it as a symbol of the five wounds of Christ. Regardie, in his *Complete Golden Dawn System of Magic*, refers to it as the Signet Star of the Microcosm, representing the operation of the spirit and the four elements under the presidency of YHSHVH (Yesheshuah or Yeheshuah), one of the names of God. Regardie and the Hermetic Order of the Golden Dawn associated this symbol with Mars and with the Hebrew letter *Heh*. The Golden Dawn called it the Flaming Pentagram or the Star of the Great Light.

In modern times, the pentagram has become a symbol of Wicca. Each of the five points of the pentagram represents one of the five traditional elements: spirit, air, fire, water and earth. As spirit is the topmost point, the pentagram is said to represent the dominion of spirit over the other four elements and the supremacy of reason over matter.

'Inverted'—that is, with two points uppermost—it has multiple meanings. Within some traditions of Wicca, the inverted pentagram is a symbol for the second degree of initiation. The Order of the Eastern Star, a Masonic women's organization, uses the inverted pentagram as its symbol. It also appears on the highest decoration for valour in the United States, the Medal of Honor.

Satanists have also used the inverted pentagram as a symbol of their beliefs. They interpret the four points of the elements over the point of spirit as representing the domination of matter over reason. The inverted pentagram also resembles a goat's head with two horns uppermost, though this is probably a recent interpretation. A symbol of LaVey's Church of Satan is an inverted pentagram on a circular field with a goat's head superimposed, which they refer to as the sigil of Baphomet.[1] The Temple of Set has also adopted the inverted pentagram against a circular field as their official symbol. The color of the background field indicates the degree of initiation of the wearer: white for Setian, red for adept, black for priest or priestess of Set, blue for magister/magistra, purple for magus, and gold for ipsissimus.

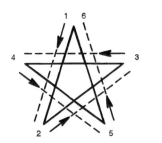 

Figure 2: Invoking (L) and banishing (R) pentagrams

Invoking and Banishing Pentagrams

Many magickal traditions, including Wicca, trace the symbol of the pentagram in the air during rituals as part of invoking the elements. As a general rule, the practitioner begins the drawing by tracing toward the point of the pentagram that represents the element being invoked, then later traces away from that point to make a banishing pentacle that dismisses the element.

In some traditions, Wiccans may bless themselves by using a pentagram sign as follows: fingers to forehead, then to right breast, then to left shoulder, then to right shoulder, then to left breast, then back to forehead.

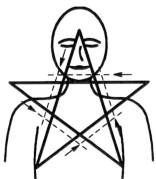

Myths About Pentagrams

The literature of satanic conspiracy myth disseminators, such as Texe Marrs in *Mystery Mark of the New Age,* claims that the pentagram is "known universally as the sign of the Devil among Satan-worshippers and witches."[2] Marrs goes on to say that you will find

> ... the pentagram ... on display in the lodges of Freemasons and the ladies of The Order of the Eastern Star. As evangelist John Barela's research proves, the pentagram has "a place of honor and prominence at the Mormon Temple in Salt Lake City." This is not surprising considering the Luciferian and Masonic roots of the Mormon Church and its

founders. Another New Age group with an occult orienta-
tion, the Order of the Golden Dawn, which reportedly has
an official membership of some 40,000, conducts two rituals
using the pentagram ... The wicked occultic pentagram has
a long, infamous history. Celtic priests called it the witch's
foot. In the Middle Ages it became known in Britain and elsewhere in Europe as the goblin's cross, devil's sign, and the
wizard's star. Among the druids of Great Britain, it was the
blasphemous sign of the Godhead. 'In ancient times,' symbolism expert Rudolf Koch has written, "it was a magical charm
amongst the people of Babylon." The pentagram was also
used by the Babylonians as a healing device and as a medium
for bringing good fortune.*

Neither the Freemasons, nor the Order of the Eastern Star, nor the Mormons, nor the Order of the Golden Dawn are Satanists. Some Christian authors, such as Marrs, list Luciferians as an international satanic cult, using this
title as a synonym for Satanists.

The Luciferians of the past were founded by Lucifer Calaritanus, the fourth-
century bishop of Cagliari, Sardinia. He ardently opposed Arianism, a Christian
doctrine put forward in the early fourth century CE by the Alexandrian presby-
ter Arius. Arianism held that Christ was not divine, since God is self-existent,
immutable, and unique. The Roman Emperor Constantius II, himself an Arian,
opposed Lucifer. As a result of two councils, one in Arelate, Gaul (later Arles,
France) in 353 CE and the second in Milan in 355 CE, the Luciferian's chief
bishop, Saint Anthasius the Great, was condemned, and Lucifer Calaritanus
was exiled to the east. He continued to write tracts opposing the emperor.

When Constantius II died in 361 CE, Lucifer returned by permission of
Constantius' successor, Julian the Apostate. He went to Antioch, where two
factions were struggling over who would be the rightful bishop. Lucifer Calaritanus consecrated one of the candidates, Paulinus, as bishop. Lucifer's rival,
Meletius, opposed his actions. When Anasthasius held a council in 362 CE
that pardoned former Arians who renounced their views, Lucifer Calaritanus
founded the Luciferians, who promulgated his opinion that all former Arians
should be deposed and any bishop accepting them should be excommunicated.
We know of the Luciferians partially from Saint Jerome's criticism of them in
his *Altercatio Luciferiani et Orthodoxi* (*The Dispute of the Luciferian and the
Orthodox*).

The Luciferians were never a large group, and they died out by the fifth century CE. Marrs, then, is incorrect on many counts. Neither the Freemasons, the

---

* Texe Marrs, *Mystery Mark of the New Age*, 94. Marrs cites Manly P. Hall's *The Secret
Teachings of All Ages*, Kathryn Paulsen's *The Complete Book of Magic and Witchcraft*,
and Paul Huson's *Mastering Witchcraft* as sources of this information.

Order of the Eastern Star, the Mormons, nor the Order of the Golden Dawn are connected to these long-dead Christian Luciferians. Their use of the pentagram has nothing to do with either Luciferians or Satanists. Further, Celtic priests/Druids did not call the pentagram the "witch's foot," and in fact did not use the pentagram as a symbol at all. Neither could Druids have used it to blaspheme the Judeo-Christian God—it's hard to blaspheme a religion you don't even know exists. The expressions "witch's foot," "goblin's cross," "devil's sign," and "wizard's star" are all titles assigned to the pentagram by Inquisitional demonologists, not by those who used it as a religious symbol.

Mary Ann Herold lists the pentagram as a "Satanic symbol" in *A Basic Guide to the Occult for Law Enforcement Agencies*. Frattarola states that the pentagram "may be used in both Black and White Magic"[3] in *America's Best Kept Secret*. Even though it appears in a list of "Demonic Symbols" on the Madrak's Demonbuster website, the "upright Pentagram" is described there as a "symbol of Wicca (white or good witchcraft)."[4] "Pentigrams [*sic*]" are listed as "Identifiers of Occult Relations" in Alford's *Occult Crimes Investigations*.[5] The *Southwest Radio Church* newsletter states that "the Pentagram is the major symbol for witchcraft covens and occult activities. So it is not surprising that within the Pentagon, meditation groups are increasing and the peace shield is the symbol of their New Age activities."[6] Of course, a pentagram (a five-pointed star) and a pentagon (a five-sided figure) are not the same symbol, but this doesn't prevent the *Southwest Radio Church* people from making this illogical leap.

Christian author Phil Phillips claims, "When witches want to talk to demons they often will stand within a pentagram. Then the demon will appear within a hexagram."[7] Wiccans don't believe in demons, and they practice their Craft in Circles, not pentagrams. In occidental ceremonial magick, the magician invokes entities such as angels and demons while standing in a Circle, which may or may not have a pentagram drawn in it, and the magician uses talismans with pentagrams and/or hexagrams inscribed on them to control these spirits. The spirit supposedly appears in a triangle outside of the Circle, not in a hexagram. The grimoires describing these rituals are still in print. Ceremonial magick is not 'satanic'; in my view, it comes from a Christian context, and ceremonial magicians are Christians.

Thomas Carder's ChildCare Action Project/Christian Analysis of American Culture website states, confusingly, "I have found contradiction surrounding its use, so there will be seeming contradiction herein."[8] Carder then lists many of the possible interpretations of the pentagram by various groups, but then states that no matter how you present it, "it is not from or of God."[9] "Used primarily as a tool in witchcraft for conjuring evil spirits," Carder tells us the pentagram/pentacle is also is used [*sic*] the mean "Morning Star": a name claimed by Satan; a name claimed in mockery because it is also one of the names Jesus uses: [Rev. 22:16] ... While some believe the circle around the five-point star is symbolic of focusing the power of Satan, I suspect the pentagram/pentacle is also symbolic of the wishes of occultists and satanists to confine the power of the true Morning Star.[10]

The glossary of the Watch Network's *Be Aware!* handbook contains the same misinformation, stating that the pentagram "symbolizes the morning star, a name that Satan has taken. This symbol is used within witchcraft and in occultic rituals in the conjuration of evil spirits." On page fifty-six they add, "It is worn by witches involved in black witchcraft."

Carder is correct about the contradictions; we've looked at quite a few here. The name Lucifer is derived from the Latin *lucis* (light) and *ferre* (to bear). Thus it means "bringer of light." It first appears in the Bible in Isaiah 14:12: "How art thou fallen from heaven, O Lucifer, son of the morning! How art thou cut down to the ground, which didst weaken the nations!" The original word translated as "Lucifer" in the Bible was "Helel" in the Hebrew texts. Some scholars argue that the name is, in fact, a reference to the King of Babylon, who was compared to the morning star.[11] Others point out that the story of Helel, a Canaanite deity, is similar to the later story of Satan. Christians have mythologized Lucifer as a rebellious angel who fell from grace and took the name Satan. There is no direct connection between Lucifer and the pentacle, however.

Pentagrams are included on Pat Pulling's "Profiling, Symptoms and Investigative Clues for Juveniles Involved in Fantasy Role Playing Games." Pulling's list is subsequently reproduced in Sloat's *Texas Ritualistic Crime Information Network Occult Crime Manual*. The manual also includes the pentagram in its list of occult terms and on an untitled list of symbols attributed to Satanism.[12] The manual depicts a pentacle with a different symbol on each of its five points. The pentacle is captioned:

> This is a duplicate of an actual pentacle worn by a 16 year old "apprentice." This 16 year old resides in El Paso, Texas. It is believed that this 16 year old was recruited in the school by a teacher. The pentacle is worn at all times, but is not worn outside of the clothing. There are the element symbols, the top point holds a symbol that means mind control. The symbol [here they show a stylized letter *h* with a cross bar on the top of the vertical stroke] is actually the cross of confusion. Note the direction of the moon—purely black.[13]

In fact, all of the symbols at the five points are elemental symbols, including the top one, which represents Spirit, not mind control, as this source suggests. The symbol that they believe to be the "cross of confusion" is the astrological symbol for the planet Saturn. Since there is no moon depicted in the diagram, I must assume that the comment about the moon refers to the curved portion of the Saturn symbol. This crescent shape is the only thing that resembles a moon in the diagram. Presumably their comment "purely black" refers to their belief that this represents "black magic." A few pages later, another pentagram with different symbols for the five elements is depicted. Sloat has them in the wrong order: water-east, fire-south, earth-west, air-north, spirit-center. The correct order in most Wiccan traditions is air-east, fire-south, water-west, earth-north, spirit-center.

Gangs, Groups, Cults: An Informational Aid to Understanding, the San Diego County Sheriff's Association manual, states: "This inverted star points downward toward Hell and Satan. It is a popular symbol but has no other meaning than a satanic one."[14] As I have shown, there are many other meanings that are not satanic at all. Elsewhere in the same manual they describe *The Key of Solomon* as follows: "The pentagram is used with a circle surrounding it when any conjuring takes place. The symbol is drawn on the ground, generally with two circles around the pentagram."[15] Circles formed with concentric circles is an aspect of ceremonial magick, not Wiccan ritual. In all the years that I've been practicing Wicca, I've never seen a ritual done in a Circle with a pentagram drawn on the ground.

In the glossary at the end of *The Edge of Evil,* Johnston states:

> The pentagram, or without the circle, the pentacle is used in most forms of occult magic. A spirit conjured within the pentagram cannot supposedly leave the circle without permission. Witches generally conjure spirits from outside the pentagram while satanists can submit to possession by the spirit by standing within the pentagram while calling up a demon.[16]

There is no form of traditional magick that conjures any kind of spirits into pentagrams. In Western ceremonial magick, a pentagram may be drawn inside the magick Circle, but entities are called into a triangle outside the Circle, as it is not considered to be a safe practice to invite entities into the Circle itself. Witches, however, don't conjure spirits as Western ceremonial magicians do.

As you can see, there are plenty of myths surrounding the pentagram and its use. Now let's look at some other common symbols used in Wicca.

Symbols of Degrees of Initiation

Most traditions of Wicca have three degrees of initiation. The first is the new initiate; the second is that of priest/ess; the third degree is that of elder. While some traditions may have more degrees or none at all, the traditions having three use the following symbols for each degree:

First Degree

Second Degree

Third Degree

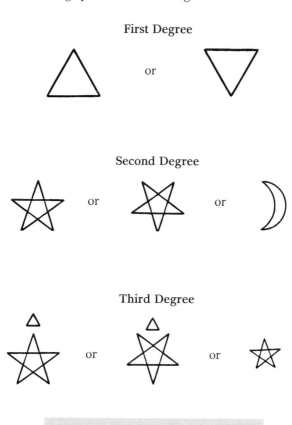

The inverted pentagram here is *not* a satanic symbol. Satanists do commonly use an inverted pentagram as a symbol of their faith, but to Wiccans it has a different meaning.

Symbols on Wiccan Ritual Tools

The following symbols are often found engraved on Wiccan ritual tools:*

The Eightfold Path (represents the Sabbats—the "Wheel of the Year")

Ritual scourge

Sign of the Goddess (represents the waxing/waning moon)

Arrow of magick issuing forth

Sign of the God (also the astrological symbol for Taurus)

Perfect couple

Name of the Goddess

Kiss

S

Name of the God

---

* In a Wiccan's Book of Shadows, the names of the Goddess and God used by their particular coven will often not be written. The original British traditions of Wicca, which emerged in an era when there was a great deal of misunderstanding and intolerance, kept their practices secret. Their coven members would write their Book of Shadows using cyphers or magickal scripts like Theban and use the above symbols for the names of the Goddess and God. These names vary from one tradition and coven to the next, but the symbols representing the names generally do not. These names are known only to the groups involved and are only spoken in ritual. Other names will be used in public.

FFFF

FFF or 777

This is an acronym for the Old Saxon blessing "Flag, Flaex, Foddor, Frigg" (Flags, Flax, Fodder and Frigg). FFFF is a blessing upon the house (flagstones of the hearth), possessions (flax representing clothing), food (fodder), and from the Goddess Frigg or Freya. A short form is FFF for Flags, Flax, and Fodder. It is commonly used by Wiccans.

Authors of popular literature about Satanism in modern times have interpreted the shortened version of this acronym as being synonymous with the number of the Beast, 666, in Revelation 13, with *f* being the sixth letter of the English alphabet.

- In *America's Best Kept Secret*, Frattarola lists the number 666 next to the letters FFF, followed by "different ways which refer to the 'mark of the beast' or Satan. Note that the letter 'F' is the sixth letter of the alphabet."[17]
- On Madrak's Demonbuster website, the "disguised 666, 666 FFF" is listed as a "demonic symbol."[18]
- FFF shows up in Dubois' *Occult Crime*.[19]
- In the Appendix of *The Edge of Evil*, Johnston incorrectly lists FFF as a version of 666 in Revelation.[20]
- Lou Sloat's *Texas Ritualistic Crime Information Network Occult Crime Manual* lists FFF in an untitled list of symbols attributed to Satanism.[21]
- Detective Don Rimer's *Ritual Crime and the Occult: The New Youth Subculture* includes FFF in its list of "Satanic symbols."
- Anderson's *Law Enforcement Guide to Occult Related Crime* defines FFF as: "Three sixes [is] The 'sign of the beast' as described in the Bible ... Sometimes written as 'FFF' ..."[22]
- The Pennsylvania State Police Missing Persons Bulletin, "Satanism: The Law Enforcement Response," defines FFF as "Mark of the Beast (Rev. 13:16–18)."[23]

In *Mystery Mark of the New Age*, Marrs claims that "to discover the secrets behind the mysterious number 666, we can go to two valuable sources of information. First, there is the ages-old practice of numerology. Second, we can profitably look at the very roots of the number 6, examining its dark origins."[24] Marrs then quotes extensively from Barbara Walker's *The Woman's Encyclopedia of Myths and Secrets*. Walker states in her book that the word "hex" was derived from the Greek word *hex* and the Latin word *sex*, which Walker tells us both mean the number six. Walker then says that they are cognate with the Egyptian word *sexen*, which she says translates as "to embrace, to copulate."[25] From this, Walker launches into a discussion of how the number six is related to sexuality. Marrs expands on her theory, stating:

> The religion of Babylon was primarily the worship of the Mother Goddess, who was later pictured in Revelation 17 as the great whore of Babylon, Satan's last-days world religion—a revived form of Babylonianism. In this religion six was considered the number symbolizing sacramental sexual ecstasy in which the participants achieved union with the divine universe and with the Mother Goddess. A triple 6—666—was the magic number of the Goddess Ishtar, also called the "Triple Aphrodite," because in her personage was the unholy trinity of Mother-Father-Son.[26]

Walker's book is popular amongst some feminists, but I take issue with its scholarship. Walker's etymology for the term "hex" is not correct. The Greek word for the number six, *hex*, though having a similar spelling, is an unrelated term. The English word "sex" is derived from the Middle English *sexe*, from the Old French *sexe*. This term derives from the Latin *sexus* or *secus* from the Latin *secare* ("to cut" or "to divide"). Etymologist John Ayto reports that the first person to use the word "sex" to refer to sexual intercourse in English literature was D. H. Lawrence[27]—a usage that is quite recent, dating back only to the beginning of the twentieth century. The number "six" in the English language came to us from the Indo-European *seks* through Anglo-Saxon and Middle English. The Latin *sex*, meaning "six," comes from the same root, as does the Greek *hex*, Welsh *chwech*, German *sechs*, Dutch *zes*, Swedish and Danish *sex*, and Russian *shest*. The English word "hex" did not come from the use of the hexagram, nor is the hexagram used to curse someone or necessarily used to call entities. It comes from the German word *hexe*, which means "witch."[28]

FFF ≠ 666

Rev. 13:18 certainly gives the number 666 as the number of the Beast: "Here is wisdom. Let him that hath understanding count the number of the beast: for it is the number of a man; and his number is Six hundred threescore and six." The Bible makes no connection between the number six and the letter *f* in this passage, however. Revelation was written in Greek, not English; *f* is only the sixth letter of the alphabet in English.

Now that we've introduced you to Wicca, let's move on to examine another Pagan religion: Druidism.

NOTES

1. Anton LaVey, *The Satanic Bible* (New York, NY: Avon Books, 1996).
2. Texe Marrs, *Mystery Mark of the New Age* (Westchester, IL: Crossway Books, 1988), 94.
3. John Frattarola, "Passport Magazine Special Edition: America's Best Kept Secret," insert "A Look At Modern Day Satanism," 2.
4. Stanley Madrak, "Wicca - Satan's Little White Lie," http://www.moodymanual.demonbuster.com/witchcr1.html.
5. Clifford Alford, *Occult Crimes Investigations*, 41.
6. Southwest Radio Church, *The Gospel Truth*, Southwest Radio Church (1998), 1.
7. Phil Phillips and Joan Hake Robie, *Halloween and Satanism* (Starburst Publishers), 86.
8. Thomas A. Carder, "Back To School Special, ChildCare Action Project: Christian Analysis of American Culture," http://www.capalert.com/backtoschool/backtoschool.htm.
9. Ibid.
10. Ibid.
11. Barnhart, 613.
12. Lou Sloat, *Texas Ritualistic Crime Information Network Occult Crime Manual*, 28.
13. Ibid., 65.
14. San Diego County Sheriff's Association, *Gangs, Groups, Cults: An Informational Aid to Understanding*, 114.
15. Ibid.
16. Ibid., 314.
17. Frattarola, 1.
18. Madrak, "Wicca - Satan's Little White Lie."
19. William Dubois, *Occult Crime* (South Orange, NJ: USCCCN), 48.
20. Jerry Johnston, *The Edge of Evil* (Vancouver, BC: Word Publishing, 1989), 313.
21. Sloat.
22. Sgt. Edwin C. Anderson Jr., *Law Enforcement Guide to Occult Related Crime* (California State University Police), 42.
23. Pennsylvania State Police Missing Persons Bulletin, Bureau of Criminal Investigation-Missing Persons Unit, vol. 3, no. 3, "Satanism: The Law Enforcement Response."
24. Marrs, 63–64.
25. Barbara Walker, *The Woman's Encyclopedia of Myths and Secrets* (San Francisco, CA: Harper Collins), 400–401.
26. Marrs, 118.
27. John Ayto, *Arcade Dictionary of Word Origins* (Arcade Publishing; Ltr. Prtg ed.), 470.
28. *Webster's Unabridged Dictionary*, second edition (New York: Random House, 2001).

Chapter Six

Druidism

*This is the forest primeval. The mumuring pines and the hemlocks stand
like Druids of old.*
—Henry Wadsworth Longfellow, "Evangeline, l.1" (1847)

As far as we know, the Celtic peoples did not have a name for their religion. The identity of the founder of Druidism, if there was only one such
individual, is lost in the mists of time. This sets it apart from most other
religions of the world; most religions can name their founder. Like Wicca,
modern Druidism is derived from Celtic customs and mythology and has no
fixed canon of scriptures. Like the Brahmin caste in Indian society, the Druids
were the teachers, priests and priestesses, physicians, historians, and judges in
law. The Druids supervised the rites of the Celtic tribes, just as the Brahmins
supervise Hindu rites. Their function was to make sure that the rites were performed correctly, and their presence lent spiritual authority to the proceedings.
The Druids were subdivided into the bards (keepers of stories and genealogies,
satirists), ovates (healers, seers), and Druids (clergy, counselors, and judges).[1]

Interest in the Celts was rekindled in the 1600s by the British Antiquarian
movement. In 1659, the proto-archaeologist John Aubrey attributed the building of Stonehenge to the Druids. We now know this claim to be false, yet this
belief in the connection between the Druids and Stonehenge persisted for the
next three hundred years. Stonehenge was actually constructed by Neolithic
peoples between 3000 and 1500 BCE, long before the Celts existed in Britain.[2]
In 1717, in a London pub called the Apple Tree Tavern, the antiquarian scholars John Toland and William Stukeley founded a Druidic group called the
Universal Druid Bond. The modern Order of Bards, Ovates & Druids (OBOD)
grew out of this organization. The United Ancient Order of Druids (UAOD),
another fraternal order, also began in the 1700s. The UAOD borrowed the
name and image of Druids for their ceremonies and performed their rituals in
stone circles, including Stonehenge.

In the eighteenth century, the stonemason Edward Williams (who went by the Welsh name Iolo Morganwyg) wrote *The Barddas*. Williams claimed that *The Barddas* contained ancient Bardic and Druidic knowledge from Wales, based on an ancient text that he had found (but never showed to anyone). Groups based on these efforts flourished and promoted Druidism as a nature philosophy. Most incorporated sacred geometry or geomancy in a pantheistic context, making their practices seem more liberal Christian or deistic in nature than Pagan. The UAOD still exists today, doing social and charitable work.

In 1963, a group of students at Carleton College in Northfield, Minnesota founded the Reformed Druids of North America. The group was originally meant to protest the college's religious attendance rule, but took on a life of its own. They pasted together ideas of an Earth Mother with various Celtic deities, guided meditations, and bits of ceremony from other religions. Participants from this group later scattered across North America, spawning offshoots such as the Orthodox Druids of North America, the New Reformed Druids of North America, the Schismatic Druids of North America, and the Hasidic Druids of North America. Well-known Pagan author Isaac Bonewits (1949–2010) created the last three.

In 1983, Bonewits founded Ár nDraiocht Féin: A Druid Fellowship, which is thriving today. Ár nDraiocht Féin (ADF) currently has about one thousand members in North America, with most of these being in the US.[3] Half of these are solitary practitioners unaffiliated with any grove. Currently there are fifty-four active ADF groves or proto-groves, with fifty of these in the United States. In 1987, the Henge of Keltria hived off of the ADF as an exclusively Celtic group.

The Independent Order of American Druids, which changed its name to Ord Draiochta na Uisnech (Druid Order of Uisnech or ODU) in 2001, has similar liturgy to the aforementioned Keltrian tradition. The Triune Council is the governing body of the Ord Draiochta na Uisnech, and consists of the *ceann* (chief), *ardfaidh* (high seer) and *ollamh* (doctor of poetry). Other members of the council include the *seanchai, breitheamh, Priomh-Droi* (Arch-Druid), and the various grove leaders and elected officers known as *uasal.*

Meanwhile, in Britain, an offshoot of the aforementioned Ancient Order of Druids sprung up: the Order of Bards, Ovates & Druids (OBOD). Ross Nichols (along with Wiccan founder Gerald Gardner) is often credited with creating the eightfold year used by this order. Ross wrote most of *The Book of Druidry* before his death in 1975. Philip Carr-Gomm, a psychotherapist and author of several books on Druidism and Celtic studies, took over as chief of the order in 1988. Therafter, under Philip's guidance, the order gradually evolved into a more neo-Pagan organization.

Etymology of "Druid"

The term "Druid" appears as *druydan* in *Barclay's Ship of Fools* in 1509. It appears as "Druid" in Golding's translation of Caesar's *Gallic Wars* in 1563, while in Latin, it was *druidae*. The word also appears to have been a Gaulish (mainland Celtic) term, *Druides*. In Old Irish Gaelic, the word for wizard is *drui* (plural: "Druid"). "Druid" may derive from the old Celtic words *dru*, meaning "very" or "assuredly," and *wid*, meaning "wise" or "all-knowing" (from the Indo-European root *wid*, meaning "to know"). Thus, the name Druid likely means "very wise," and not "men of oak," as John Todd suggests.

"Druidism" is the preferred term used by Druids who see their beliefs as a revival of an ancient religion. "Druidry" is the term used by organizations such as the UAOD and OBOD, who see Druids as individual philosophers and mystics. *Druidecht*, the Irish Gaelic word for both magick and the activities of ancient Druids, is used by modern Druids whose interest is in magical aspects of their path, such as Searles and Deborah O'Dubhain, founders of the online School of Celtic Studies at the Summerlands website.[4]

Misinformation about Druids

There is a great deal of nonsense written about Druids. In an earlier chapter, I mentioned Christian author Michael Warnke's claim that the Druids sacrificed humans to appease the great god "Samhain."[5] This is typical of the bizarre claims that some ill-informed individuals have made about Druidism. John Todd, who has made spurious claims about being a former Druid priest and a member of the Illuminati, describes the Druids as follows:

> Way over in the British Isles, Scotland and Ireland, in that area, was one of Satan's strongholds. The most evil people living in this horrible darkness were the Druid priests (known as "men of oak"). They demanded human blood sacrifices. These men were so filled with demons that some had strange, frightening powers. People lived in terror of the Druids. Male slaves or Roman soldiers would be burned alive in cages over barren (solid) ground. The Druids would call forth Elvin fire out of the earth to consume the victims, and it did! In the Background the Druid musical beat could always be heard.[6]

Todd doesn't know enough about the Druids to come up with a plausible-sounding story.

The Druids and the Celtic tribes to which they belonged were not found just in the British Isles. On the mainland of Europe, they were known as the Gauls, and at the height of Celtic culture, these tribes spread all the way east

---

* A detailed description of the claims and activities of John Todd can be found in my online article "Warlocks," http://www.witchvox.com/whs/kerr_warlocks1.html.

to the Middle East: The Galatians mentioned in the Bible were a Celtic tribe. Todd's assertion that the Druids called "Elvin fire" out of the earth is a fantastic creation of his own overactive imagination, and his apparent suggestion that the word "barren" is a synonym for "solid" is simply confused.

In *The Dark Side of Halloween*, David Brown asks the question:

> Who were the DRUIDS? They were occult practitioners, witches of sorts. In the century preceding the birth of Christ, Caesar conquered the Britons and he records very carefully the account of the DRUID PRIESTS (early witches): "All Gallic nations are much given to superstition...they either offer up men as victims to the gods, or make a vow to sacrifice themselves. The ministers in these offerings are the Druids, and they hold that the wrath of the immortal gods can only be appeased, and man's life redeemed, by offering up human sacrifice, and it is a part of their national institutions to hold fixed solemnities (Ceremonies) for this purpose."[7]

It is curious that Brown is so willing to accept the Caesar's account of Celtic religion, given that the same Romans accused early Christians of being cannibals. Caesar's accounts were highly slanted to justify his military conquests in Gaul. Other contemporary historians without Caesar's agenda, such as Strabo, and Diodorus Siculus (both of whom get their information from a lost writer, Posidonius), do not corroborate these reports.[8] Brown's claim that the Druids were Witches is also confused; the Druid and Wiccan faiths, while sharing common roots, differ in significant ways.

Brown goes on to claim that "you will still find Druids meeting at Stonehenge this Halloween symbolically carrying out their grotesque sacrifices. Although they claim no longer to practice human sacrifices they are one group responsible for keeping the occultic celebration of Halloween before the media."[9] As I mentioned earlier, Stonehenge predates the Druids by many centuries.* Some have suggested that the Druids used this preexisting structure in ancient times, but there is no evidence that the ancient Druids ever used Stonehenge; usage of this site by modern Druids dates back to the late nineteenth century.[10]

In *Satanism: The Not So New Problem*, Lyle Rapacki claims that the Druids were "Celtic priests in pre-Christian Britain and Gaul. Very powerful and dangerous—still active today."[11] While some Druids carried out Celtic religious functions, others specialized in unrelated fields such as music and law.

---

* Stonehenge was started as a wooden structure around the fourth millennium, and stones were erected at that site beginning about 2100 BCE and continuing until 1500 BCE (Ronald Hutton, *The Pagan Religions of the Ancient British Isles: Their Nature and Legacy* [Oxford: Basil Blackwell Ltd., 1991]), 15. The Celts emerged in the first millennium and were firmly established by the sixth century BCE (Peter Beresford Ellis, *Dictionary of Celtic Mythology* [London: Constable, 1992]), 59.

Druid Sacrifice Facts

Fragments of ancient records refer to Druids performing sacrifices. These records indicate that criminals or prisoners were used and even describe these victims being burned in massive wicker structures. Artifacts such as the Gundestrup Cauldron* and archaeological finds such as the Lindow Man (a body discovered in an English bog near the border of Wales in 1984) provide evidence that ancient Druids practiced human sacrifice. We do not know the reasons for this ancient practice, or whether it was religious or punitive in nature—it may have been equivalent to our capital punishment. The current Druid orders, however, date back to no earlier than the 1700s, and modern Druids do not engage in animal or human sacrifice.

Druid orders have been recreated in today's world, but they are small, and they certainly aren't dangerous. Satan is the personification of evil in the Christian mythos, and not something that Druids believe in. In the glossary of *The Edge of Evil*, Johnston agrees with Rapacki that Druids are "very powerful and very dangerous—still active today."[12] Active? Yes. Dangerous? No.

The Druid Worldview

Druids recognize three worlds. Some orders list these as the heavens, the midworld, and the underworld, though the ODU lists them as the realm of sea (underworld), the realm of land (middleworld), and the realm of sky (otherworld). These worlds are known in many Druid traditions as the vertical axis. The Shining Ones (deities) reside in the heavens. The midworld is the mundane world that we live in and the abode of the nature spirits. The underworld is the place of the dead and of the chthonic deities. The sea is often considered to be part of the underworld, as the Isles of Youth and Isles of the Blest are beyond the Western Sea. The midworld is often divided into the three realms: land, sea, and sky. These realms are known as the horizontal axis.

The Nemeton or Nyfed

A Druid grove is usually called a nemeton, though some Welsh groups use the ancient term *nyfed*. Unlike Wiccan Circle casting, the ritual of consecrating the nemeton is not a process of cutting the sacred space away from the mundane world. Druids do not separate sacred space from the midworld. This sacred space is fully in the mundane world as well as in the otherworlds during ritual. People can come and go from Druid rituals without cutting "doors," as is done in Wiccan ritual. Some Druids set up permanent ritual spaces.

---

*   Miranda Green, *Dictionary of Celtic Myth and Legend* (Thames & Hudson, London, 1992), 108–109. This cauldron was found in the Raevemose peat bog at Gundestrup in Jutland. It dates to between the 4th and 3rd centuries BCE.

Sonoran Sunrise Grove, ADF, Arizona

In the nemeton, one finds symbolic representations of the well, fire, and tree (the hallows). The well corresponds to the underworld and the sea. The fire corresponds to the heavens and the sky. The tree dwells in the midworld, and grows to connect the three worlds. It corresponds with the midworld and the land. Thus, when Druids consecrate the well, fire, and tree, they connect all the worlds and realms.

The center of the worlds, the sacred center, is where these worlds intersect and where the gates to the otherworlds may be opened. Unlike Wiccan sacred space, the Druid sacred space has a central reference point, called the gateway. This gateway acts as a link between the mundane world and the otherworld. It is through this gateway that the offerings are directed and through which the energy returns. When Druids enter the grove, nemeton, or nyfed, they typically walk in a circle to define the sacred area. Then the priests purify themselves and all of the participants and perform ritual to further mark the area as sacred space.

Awen

British Druids use a symbol called *awen* to represent themselves and their beliefs. It consists of three vertical lines, with a vertical center line and the lines to either side leaning in toward the center (/|\). This is sometimes accompanied by three circles above or three concentric circles around the lines.

Awen is a principle referred to in Druidic ritual and writings. In his *Barddas,* Morganwg explains the symbol as representing three light rays. The first recorded reference to awen, however, occurs in Nennius' *Historia Brittonum,* a Latin text written around 796 CE and based on earlier writings by the Welsh monk Gildas. After referring to King Ida of Northumbria, who reigned from 547 to 559, Nennius says, "Then Talhearn Tad Awen won renown in poetry."[13] The so-called Four Ancient Books of Wales: the *White Book of Rhydderch*, the *Red Book of Hergest*, the *Black Book of Caermarthen*, and especially the thirteenth century *Book of Taliesin* all contain a number of poems which refer to awen.

The feminine noun *awen* has been variously translated as "inspiration," "muse," "genius," or even "poetic frenzy." The word itself is formed by combining *aw* (a fluid, a flowing) and *en* (a living principle, a being, a spirit, essential), so *awen* may be translated as "a fluid essence" or "flowing spirit." *Awen* is called "the Holy Spirit of Druidry"[14] by some Druids and "the name by which the universe calls God inwardly"[15] by others. Some in Welsh traditions hold that the awen represents the letters *OIU*, from which all the others are obtained. The letter *O* relates to the perfect circle of Gwynvyd, the letter *I* to the mortal world Abred, and the letter *U* to the cauldron of Annwn. This triad relates to earth, sea, and air; body, mind, and spirit; and love, wisdom, and truth. Other Druids see the three foundations of *awen* as understanding, love, and truth. Druid author Brendan Cathbad Byers describes *awen* as "the 'light' of enlightenment that shines from the primordial source of being, the spiritual realms that exist 'above' us in the starry heavens."[16] The word *awen* also means "inspiration" and "soul."[17]

The World Tree or Bilé

In Druid practice, the world tree is honored in a manner reminiscent of Ásatrú (which we will discuss later, in Chapter Twelve). Many Druids have permanent places of worship with a tree in the middle to represent the world tree. If such a tree is not available, or if the ritual is to occur indoors or at a site not usually used, a bell branch is typically used. The Henge of Keltria altar depicted in the photo below has a bell branch representing the world tree in the center of the altar.

Henge of Keltria altar

Another alternative is a pole representing the world tree, erected within the nemeton, often in the middle of the central altar. This pole is called the *bilé* (pronounced 'bee-lah').

Bilé of Red Oak Grove, New Jersey   Bilé of Sassafras Grove, Pittsburgh, PA

The Ritual Area

Druid altars will incorporate the traditional four elements (earth, air, fire, and water) in some form. Typically this will involve incense for air, stones and/or crystals for earth, candles or lanterns for fire, and a cauldron or grail of water. Typically they will also involve symbols of the three worlds: the sacred tree, the sacred well, and the sacred fire.

There are variations on this, such as the arrangement found in the General Welsh Liturgy of the Red Oak Grove.[18] The central altar is placed in the center of the nyfed. The altar is covered in a white cloth, and the bilé is erected through its center. God and Goddess lamps are hung on the bilé, along with a bell. On the altar, a chalice is set on the east edge, a sword on the south edge, a sickle on the west edge, a wand on the north edge, sacrificial oil and liquor in the northeast corner, and seeds in the northwest corner. Goblets are placed east and west of the bilé. There are three cauldrons, one each for earth, water, and incense. They are placed north, west, and east of the bilé respectively. A bottle of whiskey is placed north of the bilé, along with mistletoe and oak tinctures. A cauldron representing Brighid's* well is filled with charged water and placed northwest of the central altar with a ladle. A fire urn is set northeast of the central altar. Four subsidiary altars are also set up: Brighid's altar at the edge of the nyfed in the east, an altar for Llew (a Celtic Sun God) at the edge of the nyfed in the south, an altar for Modron (a Goddess whose name means "Divine Mother"; she is the mother of Mabon, for whom the autumnal equinox is named) at the edge of the nyfed in the west, and an altar for Cernunnos (a

---

*   Brighid is the Celtic goddess of healing, crafts, and poetry.

God of nature whose name means "Horned One") at the edge of the nyfed in the north. Each of these four altars is decorated with items symbolic of the deity it represents.

This focus on the cardinal directions by Red Oak Grove is not typical; most Druids do not acknowledge the cardinal points of the compass as Wiccans do. While in Celtic mythology, there were the five directions of Ireland and Wales (based on the five provinces), they usually only get passing mention, if any, in Druid ritual.

Divinity

In Judeo-Christian rituals, a person often supplicates God, asking for blessings to be bestowed as a reward for faith or an act of mercy. In a manner similar to Ásatrú practices (see Chapter Thirteen), the Druid approaches the gods as partners. Both Druid and God have parts to play in life. The Druid believes that tradition, knowledge, and experience will lead to his or her ritual acts producing certain expected results. Like Wiccans, Druids believe that all of nature is divine and that we are inseparably connected to the world around us. The Druids honor three categories of beings in ritual: gods and goddesses, nature spirits, and the ancestors. These are referred to by some Druid groups as "the Powers" and by others (with Norse influence) as the three Kindreds. Druids use Celtic deities in their rituals.

Druid Ritual

Some Druids consider ritual as having three principal aspects: ritual, sacrifice, and trance. Sacrifice refers to making things sacred through offerings of words, songs of praise, food, drink, and precious objects. As I mentioned earlier, modern Druids do not sacrifice live animals or humans, as some fundamentalist extremists would have you believe. Trance is a state of deep relaxation facilitating connection with the otherworld. Ritual, as one might expect from a group with such bardic heritage, is full of song, storytelling, and ritual drama. Keltrian Druids would say instead that the three foundations of ritual are honoring the ancestors, revering the nature spirits, and worshipping the gods and goddesses of the tribe. Trance and sacrifice are considered elements of the ritual, but not principal aspects.

Druids, like Wiccans, typically use a phrase to conclude pronouncements of desire or blessing, much as Christians use "Amen." In Wicca, the phrase is "So mote it be." Druids using Irish Gaelic use the phrase *Bíodh sé* ("be it," pronounced "BEE-uh SHAY") or *Bíodh sé amhlaidh* ("so be it," pronounced "BEE-uh SHAY OW-lee"). The Scottish variation is *Bitheadh e mar sin* ("so be it," pronounced "BEE-uh ma-SHEEN"), and the Gaulish is *Buetid Ita* ("so be it," pronounced "Boo-AY'-tid EE'-ta"). In Druid ceremonies with Welsh influence, the most common expression is *Gadael hi bod* (Let it be) or *Felly y bydded* ("so be it," pronounced "VEH-khlee uh BUH-thed"). Some groups used the variation *Bydded felly* (pronounced "BUH-thed VECH-ly").

Druid ritual is normally held outdoors in good weather, in as natural an environment as possible. If the weather is foul, the ritual is held in a cave or in some setting that reminds the participants of the natural world. The altar is set up in or near the center of the grove. Arrangements are made for some sort of fire in the center of the grove.

There are many variations and interpretations of ritual within Druid practice. This stands to reason in a tradition that reveres poetry and bards. In a typical ritual, participants will often gather in advance of the ceremony to be briefed on the event and to learn the songs or chants to be used. They then parade to the nemeton or grove where the ritual will take place. The Druid presiding announces commencement of ritual by blowing a conch horn, sounding a gong, or chiming a bell. This varies from three sounds[19] to nine.[20] The participants are often purified through asperging with water and/or smudging with incense or sage as they enter the ritual area.

Some groves have more elaborate purification ceremonies. In one grove, a Druid pours water over each person's hands so that they can be ritually washed, and another Druid follows with a towel for drying. The first Druid then pours water around the periphery of the grove. Some Druid groves wait until after the well, fire, and tree are consecrated before purifying the space and people.

Having entered the nemeton, the participants may go through a process of grounding and meditation. There is often an announcement of purpose or "ritual precedent" to those present, but in some rituals, it may occur later in the proceedings.

Next, a bard will make an invocation, calling for awen or inspiration in the ritual. This invocation is known as *imbas* in Irish rites, and it is often directed to the goddess Brighid and accompanied with offerings. Often there is a meditation on the purpose of the ritual and/or on the world tree. Words are then spoken to honor the Earth Mother and/or a patron deity.

The sacred grove or sacred center is then established with the three key symbols of the grove. Some groups refer to this as "establishing group mind." Many groups consider these three symbols to be the tree (bilé), the fire, and the well: The well represents the well of Segais, a source of mystic inspiration in Celtic myth. Others use the bilé, stone of destiny and Holy Mound. There are two stones of destiny in Celtic legend, both known as the *lia fáil*: One resides on the Holy Mound at the sacred site of Tara in Ireland, and the other was used by the Dal Riada kings of Alba. Both were said to roar when the rightful king set his foot on it. Thus, the stone of destiny represents sovereignty and the Holy Mound, the *axis mundi* or center of the universe. The sacred fire is kindled, and incense is burned. Silver is placed in a well or in a receptacle such as a cauldron representing the well, and water is poured from this receptacle into a blessing cup. Often the blessing of the water god Nechtan is invoked as this is done. The bilé is then dressed and censed.

The Druids then make an offering to entities known as the "outsiders" or "outdwellers," usually a coin, along with a request that they not interfere with the ritual. This gift to the outdwellers protects the space and explains why Druids don't need to cut their sacred space off from the mundane world as is done in Wiccan ritual and ceremonial magick. Some groves make an offering to a guardian deity for protection instead of to the outdwellers (or in addition to them).

A gate opening ceremony is then performed in which a god is invoked as the keeper of the gateway to the otherworld, with the phrase "Let the gates be open" in Irish, Welsh, Scottish, or Gaulish.* This is typically Manannan Mac Lir (Manawydan Map Llyr in Welsh rites) or Ogma (in Irish rites). Offerings are made to the three Kindreds. Offerings made to the sidhe (nature spirits) often include beans, corn kernels, or cornmeal scattered about the edge of the nemeton.

Next, a particular deity or spirit related to the purpose or date of the ceremony is honored. The names and lore of the deity are announced and appropriate offerings made. In some cases, the terms *a Bhantiarna* (O Lady) and *a Thiarna* (O Lord) are used instead of naming specific deities, but this isn't common practice. General praise offerings are made to the three Kindreds. During these praise offerings, an item of seasonal significance is passed around the grove to be charged by the participants with energy or intention. For example, at Samhain gatherings a wreath is typically passed. Participants tie black ribbons to it in remembrance of family members who died in the past years. This wreath or object is then offered as the main sacrifice. Unused portions of offerings may be gathered into one vessel for a final offering to a deity such as Danu. Final offerings are poured into the ritual shaft at the base of the bilé.

Following the main offering or sacrifice, omens are read or "taken." Some Druid groups refer to this part of the ritual as "reciprocity."[21] A ceremony is then performed for the blessings of the deities and spirits. The Druid presiding typically raises the blessing cup high and gives blessings to the spirits, asks blessings for the waters, and asks for inspiration and vitality. The blessing cup is then passed around, and the participants drink from it. The blessing cup may contain water or whiskey, which is referred to as the "waters of life." I've seen examples of rituals where two chalices, one with whiskey and one with water,

---

* Irish: *Osclaítear na geataí* (OS-kluh-TEER na GA-thay)
  Welsh: *Bydded y Pyrth ar Agor* (BUH-thed uh PEERTH ar uh-GOR)
  Scottish: *Fosgailtear na geataichean* (FOS-ge-tir na GA-ti-kun)
  Gaulish: *Badentir Duorica* (BAH'-den-TEER' Doo-or-EE'-ka

were circulated.[22] In small group gatherings, the blessing cup is passed sunwise (clockwise). Each person may drink from either or both, or may pour a little liquid onto the ground or into the sacred fire as a libation. Each participant says, "Behold! The waters of life!" before passing the cup to the next person. Some groves pass the cup around four times, and each person may recite a blessing, sing a song, or play a tune, similar to the sumbel ritual of Ásatrú (which we'll discuss later, in Chapter Thirteen).[23]

In a large group ritual, passing the cup around the circle may take a long time, so the ritual may be modified to speed this process up. For example, the circle of people may be split in half and one cup may go in each direction (one clockwise, one counterclockwise).

At this stage in the ritual, Druids announce new members or install officers for the coming seasons. Thanks are then given to the Kindreds and spirits, their names followed by the Celtic thanks: *Go raibh maith agait!* (a singular thank you, pronounced "Gora mah ahgit"; *Go raibh maith agaibh* is the plural form, pronounced "Gora mah ahgeev").

Grounding and unwinding ceremonies follow, and then a closing statement is made to close the gates, with the expression "Let the gates be closed" in Irish, Welsh, Scottish, or Gaulish.* A recessional parade takes the participants out of the grove.

Handfasting

Like Wiccans, Druids call their wedding ceremonies "handfastings." The term handfasting is derived from the Middle English *handfasten* or *handfesten* (circa 1200 CE). There is a similar Icelandic word: *handfesta* (*hond* [hand] and *festa* [to fasten or pledge]). This archaic word is now a modern term for weddings in neo-Pagan religions such as Wicca, Druidism, and Ásatrú. The photo below depicts a Druid handfasting at Stonehenge.

---

* The expression "Let the gates be closed" is similar in the different traditions:
- Irish: Dúntar na geataí (DUN-tar na GA-thay)
- Welsh: Bydded y Pyrth ar Gau (BUH-thed uh PEERTH ar GAI)
- Scottish: Dùintear na geataichean (DUN-tir na GAH-ti-kun)
- Gaulish: Clausontir Duorica (CLOW'-sun-TEER' DOO'-or-EE'-ka)

Summerland or Tech Duinn

Like Wiccans, Druids believe that the soul of the deceased goes to a place of rest called the Summerland or Tech Duinn (the name of the House of the Dead) before being reincarnated. Druid funeral ceremonies involve decorating the ancestor shrine with apples (symbolic of the Summerland), favorite foods and beverages of the departed ancestor, a picture of the deceased, and an article of their clothing and jewelry.[24] An empty seat is placed for the ancestor among the seats for his or her descendants. The ritual follows the normal druidic pattern, with a processional leading the participants into the nemeton. The tree meditation typically features an apple tree rather than an oak. A descendant presents a eulogy and lights the ancestor fire in the southwest, then the gatekeeper is invoked as a psychopomp.* Often a feast is held, and a plate of food for the ancestor is placed in front of the fire or candle on the ancestor altar. Afterward, the food is disposed of in a cemetery or in water.[25]

Initiation

The initiation of a new Druid is a simple rite. Some Druid groves have a period of probation for new members. In such organizations, this initiation binds the new member for a year and a day. A more binding initiation may be entered into after this probationary period. Other Druid groves believe that as they are a public religion that welcomes all, this probationary period is too restrictive.

The new initiate is called forward to the bilé and asked to take an oath. The initiate places their hand upon the world tree, states the name that he or she is to be known by, and swears an oath. A typical oath reads: "I, _____, swear before the gods and the folk, to work for and with this grove, for as long as I am a member, in return for being counted among the folk. Thus do I swear by all I hold sacred!"[26]

The new member is dressed in her or his tabard, censed, and asperged.[27] A talisman signifying the bond between the new member and the grove may be presented.[28] The first Druid then welcomes the initiate, followed by each member of the grove. One at a time, the members come forward, put their hands on the new member's shoulders, and look into his or her eyes and say, "You are of my folk. Welcome." Music and drumming follow.[29]

NOTES

1. Brendan Cathbad Myers, PhD, *The Mysteries of Druidry* (Franklin Lakes, NJ: New Page Books, 2006), 34.
2. Stuart Piggot, *The Druids* (Thames and Hudson, London, 1975), 133–145.
3. E-mail to the author from David Foster, Administrator of Ár nDraíocht Féin, March 14, 2005.
4. School of Celtic Studies (Scoil an Léinn Cheiltigh), http://www.celt.dias.ie/.

---

* A psychopomp is a person who conducts spirits or souls to the otherworld.

5. Michael Warnke, *Schemes of Satan* (Victory House, 1991), 122.
6. Edward E. Plowman, "The Legends of John Todd," *Christianity Today* (February 2, 1979), 19.
7. David L. Brown, *The Dark Side of Halloween*, 7.
8. Miranda Green, *Dictionary of Celtic Myth and Legend* (Thames & Hudson, 1992), 86.
9. Ibid., 8.
10. Ronald Hutton, *The Pagan Religions of the Ancient British Isles: Their Nature and Legacy* (Basil Blackwell Ltd., 1991), 141.
11. Lyle J. Rapacki, *Satanism: The Not So New Problem* (Intel, 1988), 57.
12. Jerry Johnston, *The Edge of Evil* (Vancouver, BC: Word Publishing, 1989), 313.
13. Greywolf, "Awen - The Holy Spirit of Druidry," http://web.archive.org/web/20070208035536/http://www.druidorder.demon.co.uk/awen.htm.
14. Ibid.
15. Katinka the Broc'h, "The Awen," http://www.druidry.org/obod/druid-path/awen.html.
16. Brendan Cathbad Myers, *The Mysteries of Druidry* (Franklin Lakes, NJ: New Page Books, 2006), 112.
17. Katinka the Broc'h.
18. Red Oak Grove, General Welsh Liturgy, http://www.adf.org/rituals/celtic/general/genwelsh.html.
19. Anthony R. Thompson, "A Solitary Celtic Ritual Template," http://www.adf.org/rituals/celtic/general/sol-template-art.html and "Rite of Ancestral Healing," http://www.adf.org/rituals/celtic/general/ancestral-healing.html; Erika Brown, "Full Moon Rite," http://www.adf.org/rituals/celtic/general/fullmoon.html; "Sonoran Sunrise Grove Samhain 2003," http://www.adf.org/rituals/celtic/samhain/ssg-samhain-03.html.
20. "1999 SCG Claiming and Saining," http://www.adf.org/rituals/celtic/samhain/scg-samhain-99-saining.html; Ian Corrigan, "Rite of Claiming and Hallowing," http://www.adf.org/rituals/general/claiming-and-hallowing.html and "Rite of Offering," http://www.adf.org/rituals/general/offering.html.
21. Erika Brown, "Imbas Liturgy," http://www.adf.org/rituals/celtic/general/imbas.html.
22. "Mother Grove Gaelic Rite," http://www.adf.org/rituals/celtic/general/mg-gaelic.html.
23. Ibid.
24. Erika Brown, "Summerlands Funeral Rite," http://www.adf.org/rituals/celtic/general/funeralrite.html.
25. Ceisiwr Serith, "Ancestor Ritual," http://www.adf.org/rituals/general/ancestors.html.
26. Paul Maurice, "Welcoming to the Grove," http://www.adf.org/rituals/general/grove-welcome.html.
27. Ibid.
28. Emerald Dragyn, "New Member Welcoming," Grove of the Midnight Sun, http://www.adf.org/rituals/general/gotms-welcoming.html.
29. Paul Maurice, "Welcoming to the Grove," http://www.adf.org/rituals/general/grove-welcome.html.

Chapter Seven

Wiccan and Druid Deities

Drunk with fire, toward Heaven advancing,
Goddess, to thy shrine we come ...
—Johann Christoph Friedrich von Schiller, "Ode to Joy," st.1 (1785)

Wiccans work with deities from any number of pantheons in their rituals. I've seen Wiccans honoring Greek, Roman, Egyptian, Celtic, and Norse deities, to name but a few. British Traditionalists use Aradia and Cernunnos in their basic rituals.

Aradia is a Goddess of Witches who first appeared in the book *Aradia: Gospel of the Witches* in 1899. Charles Leland, a lawyer and soldier of fortune, wrote this book. It is allegedly a description of traditional Tuscan Witchcraft as related to Leland by a Witch named Maddelena, as well as a translation of their "gospel," called the Vangelo. *Aradia* bears a striking resemblance to Jules Michelet's earlier book *La Sorciere* (circa 1862; the English translation is entitled *Satanism and Witchcraft*). The name of the Goddess in Leland's book is identical to that in Michelet's book: Herodias.

Michelet accepted a theory advanced by Jarcke, Mone, Murray, and others that there had been a large, organized "Witch cult" or Pagan religion that spread across Western Europe as resistance to a Christian ruling class. Michelet believed that the name of the Goddess of this ancient religion was Herodias. This is also the name of a wicked woman who appears in the Bible, in Matthew (14:3, 14:6), Mark (6:17, 6:19, 6:22), and Luke (3:19). In the tenth century, the Catholic Church issued the Canon Episcopi, which claimed that literal belief in Witchcraft was folly because it was an illusion inspired by Satan. The Canon, reenacted several times until the Council of Treves in 1310, gave the name Herodias as the name of the leader of the Wild Hunt, the nocturnal procession of the Goddess of the Hunt and her retinue. Michelet seems to have accepted this as a factual account, rather than the speculation of Church theologians.

Leland's use of the name Herodias suggests that he is borrowing from Michelet, the Canon Episcopi, or the Bible. Once rendered into Italian, "Herodias" became "Aradia."[1] Leland's claims are weak because no historian or folklorist has found any evidence of the Tuscan Witch cult described by Leland, or any evidence of a Goddess named "Aradia." The language of the Vangelo, the Witch "gospel" allegedly recovered by Leland, is unmistakably nineteenth century, not fourteenth century as Leland asserts. Nevertheless, Gerald Gardner, who used Leland's *Aradia* as one of his source books, assigned the name "Airdia,"[2] a modified form of "Aradia," to the Goddess in Wiccan religion. Many Wiccans still use it.

Druid groups primarily use Celtic deities in their rituals. Focusing on their Celtic roots, many Wiccan traditions also tend to use them today. The Celts were spread across Britain, southern Europe (Gaul), and into Turkey (the Galatians) at the height of their influence in the years before Julius Caesar invaded their lands. The following is a short list of some of the principal Celtic deities of that age:[3]

Celtic Deities

Anu: (Anna, Anoniredi): Irish Mother Goddess. Appears to be cognate with Anna in Britain, and Anoniredi in Gaul. It is uncertain whether the name Anu is cognate with Danu.

Aengus Og: (Angus, Aonghus, Oengus, Oenghus): The Irish god of love and death, son of the Dagda and Boann. Because it was believed that he was conceived at the break of day and born between daybreak and evening, Aengus was believed to have power over time. Tradition has it that his palace is the Brugh Na Boinne at New Grange by the river Boyne. His name appears to be cognate with the Welsh Mabon and the Gaulish Maponos.

Arawn: The Welsh god of the underworld, Annwn (the land of the dead). His Irish equivalent is Donn, and his British equivalent is Gwyn ap Nudd. He also is the god of the dark half of the year, who battles annually with Hafgan (whose name means "summer white").

Arianrhod: Welsh stellar goddess who rules Caer Sidi, a magical otherworld castle in the North where poets learn wisdom and the dead go between incarnations. She is a goddess of time, space, and energy who weaves the lives of people and the matter of creation. She is the mother of the magical twins Llew and Dylan.

Badbh: Also known as Bodua (war fury). The Irish goddess of death and battles, whose name also means "rage" and "violence." Like the Morrigan, her symbol is the raven, and in this form she was known as Cathubodha or Badbh Catha (battle crow). She forms a trinity with the goddesses Nemain and Macha, who together are the Morrigan. Some legends have her married to Neit.

Banbha: An Irish goddess of sovereignty, wife of Mac Cuill, son of Ogma. She forms a trinity with Fódla and Ériu.

Belenus: His name means "brilliant" or "bright." A Gaulish god cognate with Bel, Beli, Belinos, and Bile. A solar god who brings light and healing, he was identified with Apollo by the Romans.

Beli: A Welsh god of death, the husband of Don. Cognate with the Irish Bile (see below), he appears to be a later form of Bel. See *Belenus*.

Bile: An Irish god of death and husband to Danu, who gathers the souls of the dead and takes them to the otherworld. His name is cognate with the Welsh Beli.

Boann: An Irish water goddess, also known as Boand. Her husband in some tales is Nechtan, another water deity. In others, she is the wife of Elcmar and has an affair with the Dagda, resulting in the birth of the god Aengus Og. The river Boyne is named after her.

Bodua: (Translates as "war fury.") An alternate name for Badbh (q.v.).

Bran: Also known as Bendigeidfran (Bran the Blessed). An early Irish god of the underworld, who is the son of Lir and brother of Manannan, mentioned in the *Book of Leinster*. Appears in Welsh myth (in the second branch of the Mabinogi) by the same name and with the same parentage (Llyr) and brother (Manawydan).

Brennus: Gaulish equivalent of Bran.

Brigantia: (Literally "the high one.") She is the Goddess of the Celtic Brigantes tribe and is cognate with the Irish goddess Brigid. She is a goddess of water and pastoral activities. Brigantia may be the Goddess that Caesar identified with the Roman goddess Minerva. (See below.)

Brighid: (Bride or "Breed," Brigit, or Brigid): The goddess of healing, smiths, fertility, and poetry. Daughter of the Dagda, her festival is Imbolg (Feb. 2). Saint Brigid (450–523 CE) later took on most of her traditions within the Catholic Church.

Cailleach: (Cailleach Beara, Cailleach Bolus, Cailleach Corca Duibhne, Cailleach Bui): The Old Woman or Hag of Beara. In her Cailleach Bui aspect, she is the wife of the Sun God, Lugh. She is related to the goddess Cerridwen (see below).

Cerridwen: Welsh goddess of inspiration, she owned a cauldron of knowledge. She is an initiatory aspect of the Cailleach.

Cernunnos: A God of animals and the underworld whose name means "the Horned One." This God of nature is found in both Britain and Gaul, where he is often equated with the Dis Pater. He appears to correspond in many ways to the Dagda in Ireland.

Dagda, the: Irish father of the gods. His name means "the Good God." He is also known as Eochaidh Ollathair (All Father), Aedh (fire), and Ruad Rofessa (Lord of great knowledge). Appears to correspond with the Gaulish Dis Pater. He is the son of the goddess Dana. The Dagda has three magick implements: a club with one end that kills and one that heals; a magick harp named Uaithne ("Oak of Two Greens" or "the Four Angled Music"); and a cauldron, named the "undry" or Uinde (act of beholding), from which no one goes unsatisfied. The Dagda's club is so large that he has to drag it on a set of wheels. His horse is named Acein (ocean).

Danu: Also known as Anu or Dana. An Irish Mother Goddess from whom the Tuatha De Danaan (people of the Goddess Dana) take their name. The Dagda is her son.

Diancecht: The Irish god of medicine and healing.

Don: Welsh equivalent of Dana. She is remembered in the stars as the constellation Llys Don, now known as Cassiopeia.

Donn: The Irish god of the dead. He is said to live at Tech Duinn (the House of Donn) on an island southwest of Ireland.

Elcmar: Husband of the river goddess Boann. See *Boann*.

Ériu or Éire: One of the tutelary goddesses of Ireland, along with her sisters Banba and Fódla. Ireland is named for her.

Epona: ("The divine horse") One of the most important Gaulish goddesses. The only Celtic goddess to have been worshipped in Rome.

Fódla: (Fótla, Fódhla, or Fóla): One of the tutelary goddesses of Ireland, along with her sisters Banba and Ériu.

Gofannon: Welsh god of smithcraft, artistry, and handicrafts. Corresponds to the Irish god Goibhniu.

Goibhniu: Irish god of smithcraft, artistry, and handicrafts. Corresponds to the Welsh god Gofannon. He has two brothers, Cian and Samhan (Samhain).

Grannus: Also appears as Grannos. A popular Gaulish Sun God, associated with Apollo by the Romans. His worship was known in Rome itself.* Usually paired with the Goddess Sirona.

Grian: An Irish Goddess of the sun whose home is in Pailis Greine (now County Limerick). The Goedelic word for sun is *grian*.

Gwyn ap Nudd: Lord of the otherworld where the dead reside in the legend of Culhwch and Olwen (see *Arawn*).

Hafgan: ("summer white") The rival of Arawn, king of Annwn. Hafgan and Arawn battle annually, representing the seasonal change at summer and winter.

Herne: A British antlered psychopomp, who to this day is said to haunt Windsor Great Park.

Lir: The Irish god of the ocean. His name is cognate with the Welsh god Llyr. His son Manannan Mac Lir later took over as god of the sea.

Lleu Llaw Gyffes (Llew): A Welsh solar god, cognate with the Irish Lugh (see below).

---

*   When the Romans invaded Gaul, they incorporated many Celtic deities into their pantheon, including Grannus.

Lugh: Irish god of the sun and of arts and crafts. The festival of Lughnasad (Aug. 1) is named for him. He is cognate with the Welsh Lleu and the Gaulish Lugus.

Mabon: Son of the goddess Modron. His name means "son," as Modron's means "mother." Corresponds to Maponos.

Macha: (Personification of battle) One of the Irish triune goddesses of war, along with Badb and Nemain. She is supposed to have built Armagh (Ard Macha or "Macha's Height"), a city in county Armagh in Ireland. Her husband, Nuada, is the ruler of the gods.

Manannan mac Lir: (Manannan, son of Lir): Son of the Irish god of the sea, Lir, Manannan succeeded his father. On the Isle of Man, he is known as Manannan Beg or Mac Y Leirr. In County Galway, he is known as Oirbsen.

Manawydan mab Llyr: (Manawydan, son of Llyr): Son of the Welsh god of the sea, Llyr. Manawydan succeeded his father.

Maponos: (The Divine Son) His mother was Matrona (the Divine Mother). The Romans equated him with Apollo, and he corresponds to the Welsh Mabon and the Irish Aengus Og.

Morrigan: (Great Queen) Also known as Morrigu. The Irish goddess of war, death, and sex. She is often viewed as a combination of the triune goddesses Badb, Nemain, and Macha. Her favorite shape is the raven.

Néit (Net): A Celtic god of war, whose wife is Nemain (see below).

Nemain: (Venomous) Also known as Nehain (frenzy). One of the Irish triune goddesses of war, the others being Macha and Badb. In some legends, she married the god Neit.

Nemetoma: (goddess of the sacred grove) A Gaulish goddess of war, probably cognate with the Irish goddess Nemain/Nehain.

Nuada: Also known as Nuada Argetlamh (Nuada of the Silver Hand). Supreme leader of the Tuatha Dé Danaan. He lost his hand at the first battle of Magh Tuireadh against the Fir Bolg, but the healer god Diancecht replaced it with a silver hand. Married to the war goddess Macha. He is cognate with the Welsh Nudd.

Ogma: Also known as Grianainech, Cermait (honeyed mouth). Irish god of poetry and eloquence. He is a warrior god who conveys the souls of the dead to the otherworld. Son of the Dagda. He is credited with the invention of the Ogham alphabet, which is named for him.

Ogmia: The British equivalent of the Irish god Ogma, with additional solar attributes.

Ogmios: The Gaulish equivalent of the Irish god Ogma. The Roman Lucan equated Ogmios with Heracles.

Rhiannon: An otherworld goddess in Welsh mythology who is equivalent to Epona. Her name may be derived from the Celtic phrase *Rig Anona* (Great High Queen).

Sucellus: (The Good Striker) Usually depicted as carrying a mallet and accompanied by a drinking vessel or cask. Often accompanied by a dog. Usually appears with the goddess Nantosvelta. A Gaulish god identified by Caesar as "Dis Pater." Unfortunately, Caesar did not record this god's Gaulish name, but evidence strongly suggests that Dis Pater was Sucellus. Some scholars say that he appears to have been the Gaulish equivalent of the Dagda, while others make him the equivalent of the Irish god Donn.

Taranus: (The Thunderer) The Gaulish god of thunder and the wheel of the year. Appears in Welsh myth as Taran.

Teutates: A Gaulish god of the arts, journeys, and commerce. He appears to have originally been a Germanic tribal god. Caesar equated him with the Roman god Mercury. The name Teutates comes to us from the writings of the Roman Lucan, and may not have been his original name. It comes from a Goedelic root word *teuta* meaning "the people," so it translates as "the God of the people." The Celts referred to their Germanic neighbours as "Teutons," a name still used to refer to Germanic peoples.

NOTES

1. Ronald Hutton, *Triumph of the Moon: A History of Modern Pagan Witchcraft* (Oxford University Press, 1999), 144–149 and Jeffrey B. Russell, *A History of Witchcraft: Sorcerers, Heretics and Pagans* (London: Thames and Hudson, 1980), 148–153.
2. Doreen Valiente, *The Rebirth of Witchcraft* (London: Robert Hale Ltd., 1989), 53 and Hutton, 234.
3. R. J. Stewart, *Celtic Gods, Celtic Goddesses* (Blandford, London, 1990); Peter Beresford Ellis, *Dictionary of Celtic Mythology* (Constable, London, 1992); Miranda J. Green, *Dictionary of Celtic Myth and Legend* (Thames and Hudson, London, 1992).

Chapter Eight

Wiccan and Druid Festivals

Dance for the Sun in glory
Dance for the Oak King's passing,
Dance for the Holly King's triumph
Dance, Lady, dance ...
—Janet and Stewart Farrar, *Eight Sabbats for Witches*

Wiccan and Druid festivals are based on Celtic festivals that date back over four thousand years. There are eight of these during the cycle of the year: four fire festivals interspersed with four solar festivals. Druid author Philip Carr-Gomm associates the four solar festivals with four key functions or processes: inspiration, reception, expression, and recollection.[1] In most cases, the dates of these eight festivals or Sabbats correspond with Christian festivals due to the old Christian practice of adopting existing Pagan festivals as Christian holy days.

The early Christians found that the followers of the older Pagan religions continued to celebrate their festivals despite their proselytizing efforts and laws that made Church attendance mandatory. Eventually, clergy such as Saint Augustine decided to rededicate Pagan temples as Christian churches and convert Pagan festivals to Christian festivals. An example of this is Christmas (Yule). Initially, both were celebrated on the winter solstice, originally December 25. But during Pope Gregory's papacy (January 7, 1502–April 10, 1585), the year was recalculated at 365 1/4 days rather than 365. When Pope Gregory adopted the Gregorian calendar, replacing the older Julian one and correcting this problem, the solstice and Christmas were separated.[2] The winter solstice now occurs around December 21, which is when Wiccans and Druids celebrate Yule. Another example is All Souls' Day, which was moved from May 13 to November 2 in the ninth century in order to coincide with Samhain (Halloween). Most of the older Pagan festivals were absorbed into the Christian system in this fashion.

Sabbats

Wiccans refer to these eight seasonal festivals as Sabbats. The term "Sabbat" is derived from the Hebrew term *shabbath* (rest).* This later became *sabbaton* in Greek, *sabbatum* in Latin, and ultimately *sabat* in Old English (circa 950 CE). The Wiccan use of the term Sabbat derives from Margaret Murray's work, published around 1920. Murray used "sabbats" to refer to the major celebrations of Pagans who were persecuted as Witches during the Inquisition. Murray borrowed the term from the works of early demonologists, who used it to describe alleged meetings of Witches. The term was chosen for anti-Semitic reasons, because the same demonologists held Judaism to be the antithesis of Christianity. Modern-day Satanists also use the term Sabbat to describe their ritual meetings.

The four Celtic solar festivals (the two equinoxes and the two solstices) are Lesser Sabbats. The Greater Sabbats or fire festivals, which Wiccans refer to as "cross-quarter" days, fall halfway between the solstices and equinoxes. Beginning at the new year, the Wiccan Sabbats are Samhain (October 31), Yule (winter solstice), Imbolc (February 2), Eostre (spring equinox), Beltaine (April 30), Litha (summer solstice), Lughnasad (August 1), and Mabon (autumnal equinox). In accordance with Celtic tradition, Wiccans normally consider the day as beginning at sundown and ending at the following sundown. Hence, Samhain runs from sundown on October 31 through sundown on November 1. The dates of the Lesser Sabbats are approximate because the exact dates of the equinoxes and solstices vary by two days on either side of the twenty-first. The exact dates are easily found in an ephemeris, calendar, or newspaper.

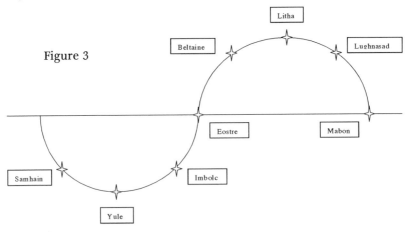

Figure 3

---

* In Christianity, the Sabbath is a day of rest, being the seventh day after the creation of the world, according to the Bible. In Judaism and some Christian sects, the Sabbath is Saturday, but in most Christian denominations it is Sunday.

The ancients noticed that on the cross-quarter days the length of the days began to change; they either began shortening or lengthening at a much faster rate (for example, after August 1 or February 2), or shortening or lengthening at a much slower rate (for example, after October 31 or April 30). As you can see in Figure 3, the graph of the amount of light per day (i.e., the length of the days) over the span of the year makes a sine curve. The cross-quarter days were much more easily recognized astronomical events than the equinoxes and solstices, around which the length of the days changes at a hardly perceptible rate. It may be because these cross-quarter days were so noticeable that they became Greater Sabbats.

Misinformation Concerning Sabbats

There is a great deal of misinformation about the term "sabbats." Erroneous definitions of "sabbat" that I've found in police occult crime manuals include

- "[a] meeting of witches and satanists to bring in new members";[3]
- "… other meetings satanists and witches hold, however, these are more like festivals or holidays. … These festivals consists of beating for those who had failed at tasks, meals including cannibalism, dancing, chanting, promiscuous intercourse, and other perverted activities [sic]. Sacrifices of different kinds may also occur";[4]
- "Witches Sabbath [is a] Meeting of a witches' coven held in order to perform magical rites and ceremonies. A large number of witches and warlocks who would gather around a bonfire or cauldron, lighting black candles and performing sacrifices. The sabbath would culminate in a sexual orgy";[5]
- "Seasonal assembly of witches in honor of the archfiend";[6]
- "Seasonal assembly of witches in honor of the Archfiend. A quarterly or semi-quarterly meeting of witches for celebration or for observance of Black Mass [sic]"[7]
- "Pagans, Witches and Satanists share 8 common Sabbats during the year."[8]

In his handbook *Symptoms Characterizing Occult Ritual Abuse*, Detective Rimer lists the eight Wiccan Sabbats as "occult holidays." The implication is that all occult groups worship on these days, which is not the case. Followers of Satanism and of African diasporan religions do not. Rimer repeatedly refers to "Sabbots [sic] and Festivals" on his list. Not only has he misspelled Sabbat, but he seems unaware that "festival" is the meaning of the term Sabbat. In a fashion typical of such handbooks, Rimer claims that orgies are a part of Sabbats. Rimer also lists the Sabbats in the wrong order, starting the Wiccan calendar at February 2 instead of October 31.[9]

In his book *Schemes of Satan*, Michael Warnke tells us that "historically, the worship of the moon as goddess predates the worship of the sun god; therefore, the four most significant holidays of witchcraft are taken from the lunar calendar."[10] Of course, there are a number of examples of ancient solar goddesses: Amaterasu and Wakahiru-Me (Japan), Brunissen (Provencal), His-Ho (Chinese), Igaehindvo (Cherokee), Knowee (Australian), Nahar (Syrian), Sapas (Phoenician), Shapash (Sumerian/Canaanite), Wurusemu (Hittite), and the Yatudhanis (Hindu). Secondly, the "four most significant holidays of witchcraft" are Samhain, Imbolc (Oimelc), Beltaine, and Lughnasad, all of which are seasonal events with fixed dates that are set according to a solar calendar.

The bizarre descriptions of activities at Witches' Sabbats are fanciful propaganda borrowed from Inquisitional demonologists. Regular meetings of Wiccans to "perform magical rites and ceremonies" are called Esbats, not "sabbaths." Neither Esbats nor Sabbats involve sacrifice or orgies. This is simply inquisitional nonsense.

Druid Festivals

Like the Wiccan ritual calendar, the Druid wheel of the year is marked by eight festivals, consisting of four fire festivals and four solar festivals. Druids do not refer to these as Sabbats, nor do they consider the solar festivals to be lesser festivals. Like the Wiccan calendar, the Druid year commences at Samhain. Beginning at the New Year, the Druid festivals are Samhain (October 31), La Ceimbroadh (winter solstice), Imbolc (February 2), An Earraigh (spring equinox), Beltaine (April 30), Grianstod (summer solstice), Lughnasad (August 1), and An Fhomhair (autumnal equinox).

NOTES

1. OBOD'S "Druid Festivals," http://www.druidry.org/obod/intro/festivals.html.
2. Started to be adopted in 1582. Bernard Grun, *The Timetables of History*, 3rd ed. (Simon and Shuster, London, 1991), 241.
3. WATCH Network, *Be Aware!: A Handbook for the Purpose of Exposing Occultic Activity* (WATCH Network), 5.
4. Shane Westhoelter, *General Information Manual With Respect to Satanism and the Occult* (National Information Network, 1989), 113.
5. Lyle J. Rapacki, *Satanism: The Not So New Problem* (Intel, 1988), 61.
6. *Colorado Bureau of Investigations Questioned Documents Examiner's Occult Guide*, 7.
7. Lou Sloat, *Texas Ritualistic Crime Information Network Occult Crime Manual*, 22.
8. Ibid., 58.
9. Don Rimer, "Symptoms Characterizing Occult Ritual Abuse," http://www.ogia.net/oklahoma%20gang%20investigators'%20association/occult/htm.
10. Michael Warnke, *Schemes of Satan* (Victory House, 1991), 130.

Chapter Nine

Samhain Misinformation

There are more strange urban legends connected with this festival than with any other in the Celtic calendar:

- In *America's Best Kept Secret*, Frattarola claims that Halloween is a four-day celebration: "DATE: Oct. 29–Nov. 1, CELEBRATION: All Hallow Eve (Halloween), TYPE: Blood, Sexual, USAGE: Sexual climax association with the demons, AGE: Any age (male or female)."[1]

- In *Schemes of Satan*, Warnke has a section entitled "The Mysteries of Stonehenge" in which he states: "Ancient Celtic priests known as Druids used Stonehenge as their special site for the observance of their pagan religion. They celebrated a major holiday—the Vigil of Samhain—there on October 31. Samhain was their god of the dead, and his special holiday forms the basis of our modern day celebration of Halloween."[2]

- Warnke's coauthor and associate, David Balsiger, doesn't even get the date correct in his satanic calendar: "May 13: Friday the thirteenth ... Samhain. Old celebration date until 8th century."[3]

Friday the thirteenth has no religious significance, and this claim on Balsiger's part is simply triskadecaphobia (fear of the number thirteen). The actual date of Friday the thirteenth changes from year to year.

There are many theories about the origins of the belief that Friday the thirteenth is unlucky. Christian mythology holds that Friday was the day that Adam and Eve were expelled from Eden, the day that Noah's flood started, and the day that Christ was crucified. There were also thirteen people at the Last Supper. In Norse mythology, there were twelve guests at a feast in Valhalla when an unexpected thirteenth guest showed up, the god of deceit. The Knights Templar were rounded up and arrested on the order of the Pope on

Friday, October 13, 1307. Any or all of these things may have combined over the years to give Friday the thirteenth an evil reputation.[4]

Balsiger is only partially correct about May 13 being the "old date" of Samhain. Samhain has always been observed on October 31. It is the Christian Feast of All Souls that used to be on May 13. This Feast of All Souls was moved to November 2 by the Church in 835 CE to make it coincide with Samhain and give the people a Christian alternative. Later, Balsiger attempts to link further dates to Halloween with these entries:

- "October 22–29. Sacrifice preparation.
- "October 29 ... October 30. Satanist High Holy Day. Related to Halloween. Human Sacrifices."[5]

Reachout Trust repeats the popular fundamentalist Christian myth that Halloween is the "ancient Celtic festival of Samhain, the god of the dead."[6] They warn us that Halloween "has always been associated with the Devil and his supernatural realms."[7] It has, but only by Christians such as the ones writing for *Reachout!* The authors claim that "it was felt that this was a good evening to invoke the Devil's help concerning marriages, health, etc., by means of divination."[8] They are correct about Halloween being a popular time to divine the future, but the Celts weren't calling on the devil to do this for them.

John Todd gives a highly inaccurate description of the history of Halloween customs: "Their big night was Halloween, in the occult it is called Samhain, October 31st. All the little kids going from door to door yelling 'Trick or Treat' had its origin with the Druids. It's fun for the kids today—but in the times of the Druids it was a night of horror. On Halloween the Druids and their followers went from castle to castle and serf to serf playing trick or treat."[9] This scenario wasn't possible, as there were no castles in the days of the Druids. Castles weren't constructed until centuries after the Celtic empire had dissolved. Serfs were a class of people that existed in the Middle Ages, which was also centuries after the time of the Druids.

Former-Wiccan-turned-evangelical-Christian Tom Sanguinet claims that "the modern holiday we call Halloween has its origins in the full moon closest to November 1, the witches' New Year."[10] Samhain always occurs on October 31 (or, to follow the ancient practice precisely, from sunset on October 31 to sunset on November 1) and is in no way related to the phases of the moon. Sanguinet doesn't know this fact because he was trained by the Frosts' Church and School of Wicca, which does many things differently from the rest of the Wiccan community. The Church and School of Wicca "requires that sabbats and eshbats [*sic*] be held at the full of the moon."[11] Therefore, unlike the rest of the Wiccan community, members of this group will hold their Samhain at the full moon closest to October 31. Note how the Frosts even spell the term Esbat differently.

Sanguinet also claims that

> Samhain is the time that the Druids (pagans who lived in Northern France) used to demand their yearly sacrifice from the countryside... The Druids would go to a castle or a house and would demand a female for sacrifice and upon receiving their demand, would leave a jack-o'lantern there as a sign of good luck for the year... The price of refusing to give in to the Druid's demands was high. They would leave a hexagram on the door and usually someone would die. It was either give up a common female or lose your firstborn son... The tradition is carried on in present Halloween practices.[12]

This statement about the Druids being "pagans who lived in Northern France" in castles is the same nonsense that we saw Todd spreading earlier. The Druids were an integral part of the Celtic peoples who inhabited the British Isles, much of Europe, and part of what is now Turkey, not just Northern France. There is no evidence that Druids demanded sacrifices or cursed those who did not comply. This is pure fantasy.

Caryl Matrisciana's 1991 movie *Halloween: Trick or Treat* describes Halloween as follows:

> All of today's seemingly innocent Halloween customs and symbols have their origins in the ancient Celtic Day of the Dead. For example, the practice of trick or treat is from Celtic tradition where people gave food in return for blessings from spirits of the dead. Failure to supply treats would result in demonic retaliation. Jack O Lanterns grew out of the Celtic tradition of carving the faces of demonic spirits on turnips, and later, on pumpkins. *The World Book Encyclopedia* says the apparently harmless lighted pumpkin face of the jack-o'-lantern is actually an ancient symbol of a damned soul. Candle-lit pumpkins, or skulls, at a home signified that the occupants were sympathetic to Satan, and would therefore receive mercy by spirits and trick-or-treaters on their Halloween rounds. Perhaps the most sickening of all Druidic New Year practices were the human sacrifices, which occurred at midnight. Adults and children alike would be thrown into huge fires while the celebrants danced around them in demonic fits of abandon. By mornings light only ashes and bones would remain. These were called "bone fires," which is where we get the tradition of bonfires today. The Druids believed that black cats were reincarnations of the evil dead and

> were possessed with supernatural powers and knowledge. ...
> By understanding the Pagan origins of Halloween, we can no
> longer claim ignorance. As parents, we are called to a sense
> of responsibility and must decide whether to allow our chil-
> dren to participate in a Celtic celebration which glorifies the
> powers of darkness.

The custom of bonfires did not originate in the fashion that Matrisciana
suggests. It was once customary for farmers to collect the bones of livestock
slaughtered for food and burn them at festivals such as Samhain, the fires being called "bone fires" and later "bonfires."

Author Hal Lindsey appears in Matriciana's film, saying:

> Halloween seems to be the high holy day of the Satanist
> and the occultist. Halloween is the time when, all across the
> country, in secret little places, in the dark, there will be little
> babies sacrificed to Satan. You don't believe it? I know it's
> hard to believe myself, but there has been such an accelera-
> tion of worship of Satan that we believe that these sorts of
> things are happening, and we have evidence that they are.

This illustrates one of the common tactics used by disseminators of misinformation on the occult: They make a statement about it being "hard to believe"
but urge you to accept their word as experts, even though the evidence is entirely absent or contradictory.

David Brown's book *The Dark Side of Halloween* (and the tract bearing the
same name, which is an abbreviated version) states that

> the origin of Halloween is the Celtic Festival of Samhain,
> lord of death and evil spirits. Long before Christ (at least 2000
> years) Druids in Britain, Ireland, Scotland, France, Germany
> and other Celtic countries observed the end of summer by
> making sacrifices to Samhain. ... They believed Muck Olla,
> their sun god was losing strength and Samhain, lord of death,
> was overpowering him. Further, they believed that on Octo-
> ber 31st Samhain assembled the spirits of all who had died
> during the previous year. These spirits had been confined to
> inhabit animal's bodies for the past year, as punishment for
> their evil deeds. They were allowed to return to their former
> home to visit the living on the eve (Oct 31) of the Feast of
> Samhain. Druid priests led the people in diabolical worship
> ceremonies in which horses, cats, black sheep, oxen, human
> beings and other offerings were rounded up, stuffed into

wicker cages and burned to death. This was done to appease Samhain and keep spirits from harming them. It is clear to see that HALLOWEEN HAS ALWAYS BEEN A CELEBRATION OF DEATH... [13]

There is that "Muck Olla, the Celtic Sun God" myth that I described earlier. The Celts had totem animals, but they represented certain deities and were not considered to be the abode of departed souls. While Brown is closer to the mark with his suggestion that Halloween is a time of year when the Lord of one half of the year is beginning to give way to the Lord of the other half, his timing is incorrect. The turning point for this solar myth is Yule (December 21), when the days begin to lengthen again, not Samhain. While there is evidence that the Druids conducted religious sacrifice—as did many of the religions of that era—Brown's description of Druid sacrifice here is pure speculation, based on sensational accounts such as in films like *The Wicker Man*. Brown further claims that

> Druid priests and people would go from house to house asking for fatted calves, black sheep, and human beings ... Hence we have THE ORIGIN OF TRICK OR TREAT. "Trick or Treat" is a re-enactment of the Druidic practices. The candy has replaced the human sacrifices [*sic*] of old, but it is still an appeasement of those deceptive evil spirits. The traditional response to those who do not treat is to have a trick played on them. When you give out Halloween candy, you are, in essence providing a sacrifice to false gods. You are participating in idolatry, says the former high priest of Wicca, Tom Sanguinet. [14]

This is the same misinformation that we read from Sanguinet earlier. Brown also buys into the myth about "Samhain, the God of death":

> ... [I]t began long before Christ among the ancient Celtic peoples (Briton, Gauls, Scots, Irish). They observed the end of summer with sacrifices to SAMAN (Shamhain). He was "the lord of death and evil spirits". ... Depending on your source material, the Druid lord of death and evil spirits was called Saman, Samana, Shamhain, or Samhain. His "holiday" was called "The Vigil of Sama" or Samhain (pronounced so-wein). You probably have seen a modern day version of SAMAN without even knowing it. This pagan god was shown as a ghostly, skeleton holding a sickle in his hand. He later came to be known as THE GRIM REAPER ... Ralph Linton in his

book *Halloween Through the Centuries* says: "The American celebration (of Halloween) rests upon Scottish and Irish folk customs which can be traced in a direct line from pre-Christian times. The earliest celebrations were held by the Druids in honor of Shamhain, lord of death, whose festival fell on November 1st."[15]

The prototypical image of the grim reaper isn't modeled after Samhain; it is a representation of the Greek god of time, Cronos. It should be noted that Ralph Linton's book has no bibliography, and it is therefore impossible to see where Linton got his information. Brown goes on to say:

> Owen Rachleff amplifies this when he wrote: "Halloween can be, and to many is, a deadly serious affair. ... All Hallows' Eve predictably became a time of spells, curses, and horrors for those who did not believe, but for the Satanists, particularly the witches, it was a joyous festival and major sabbat. So it remains in a diluted form, ironically celebrated by Christian society far more vigorously that All Saints' Day."[16]

Rachleff, the fundamentalist Christian author of the books *The Secret of Superstitions: How They Help, How They Hurt* and *The Occult Conceit: A New Look At Astrology, Witchcraft, and Sorcery*, contradicts himself here. First he says that Samhain was an ancient Celtic festival and that early Christians created All Saints' Day to coincide with these rites. Actually, All Souls' Day had been celebrated for centuries. Then Rachleff says that Satanists reversed the Christian practices to create Halloween. Rachleff therefore has two different groups inventing the same celebration! He can't have it both ways. In fact, it was members of the Christian community who created the demonic myths surrounding Halloween that Satanists then seized upon.

Brown first contradicts Rachleff, saying that "in AD 800 the Roman Catholic Church moved 'ALL SAINTS DAY' from May to November 1st. The new day was called All HALLOW'S DAY and it soon became ... HALLOWEEN."[17] In the first paragraph, however, he says that "the Celtic Festival of Samhain" predates Christ by "2000 years." Brown then contradicts himself by quoting Rachleff. He cannot seem to make up his mind whether Samhain predates Christ, or when it became known as Halloween. Brown then quotes Sanguinet:

> Halloween is a "religious day" but it is NOT a Christian day. Tom Sanguinet, former high priest in the Celtic tradition of Wicca (witchcraft) said, "The modern holiday we call Halloween ... has its origins in the full moon closest to November 1, the witches' New Year. It was a time when the 'spirits' (demons) were supposed to be at their peak power and revisiting the earth planet.' He went on to say, "Halloween is purely

and absolutely evil, and there is nothing we ever have or will do that would make it acceptable to the Lord Jesus."[18]

Samhain always occurs on October 31, and as I mentioned earlier, it is in no way related to the full moon. Brown tells us over and over that "Halloween accentuates mutilation, murder, blood, guts and gore. It even glorifies it!"[19] and that "HALLOWEEN IS HARMFUL BECAUSE OF THE EMPHASIS ON FEAR."[20] Yet it is Brown (and people like him) who accentuate fear and carnage. The hysteria they create perpetuates these myths.

In Lieutenant Larry Jones' *File 18* newsletter, we find Brown quoting fundamentalist Christian author Texe Marrs:

> Noted New Age Researcher Texe Marrs said this about the activities of witches on Halloween: "Our own research confirms that on this unholy night [Halloween], witches' covens meet, drink, dance, spit out curses and spells, conjure up spirits, engage in sexual orgies, induct new members, and offer up animal and human sacrifices. (Witches have become expert at covering up these sacrifices by use of cremation ovens and the use of privately owned land preserves for disposal of bodies in deeply dug graves) ... Somewhere in America in the week prior to this coming Halloween, children will be kidnapped by witches and become statistics as "missing children." ... While chances of your children being snatched may be remote, never the less we believe caution and good judgment is in order.[21]

Here you see how the misinformation from one author is used as a reference by another in an attempt to shore up their assertions. The impression that they give is that this must be a real problem, because there are so many 'experts' talking about it.

In *Halloween and Satanism*, Christian co-authors Phil Phillips and Joan Hake Robie assume that since Christians moved All Souls' Day to November 2, the earlier Pagan festival was "a celebration of death."[22] They also repeat the myth that "the Name of the Celtic sun god was Muck Olla"[23] and that "Samhain" was the name of the "Lord of the dead."[24]

Phillips continues to demonstrate his total misunderstanding of Samhain when he suggests, "An alternative to a Halloween party might be to have a 'Harvest Party.' "[25] This is no alternative, but precisely what the celebration of Samhain was to the ancient Celts: a festival following the end of the harvest. Of course, Phillips wants the people at his "harvest party" to dress up as Bible characters.[26] Phillips suggests that during his party "parents may wish to have a Prayer Meeting"[27] in order to [pray] "for the youth as well as rebuking Satan and the witches in the area."[28] Phillips suggests renaming this day "Holy-ween"[29] and using it to "bring other youths to a saving knowledge of Jesus Christ."[30] He continues: "What could be more crushing a blow to Satan than to have others won to Jesus on Satan's holiday! ... Halloween is not just fun and games. It is serious business."[31] Here is that same message again: We believe that they're indoctrinating your kids. They're using the fear of mysterious cults to scare you away from Pagan groups. In fact, what they are trying to do here is use this to scare you into signing up for their religion so that they can indoctrinate you instead.

In *Like Lambs to the Slaughter*, Johanna Michaelsen presents the usual (erroneous) history of Halloween, complete with the ubiquitous and nonexistent "great God of Death Samhain." Michaelsen attacks Halloween in the chapter "Pagan Playday" in *Your Kids and the Occult*. She claims that "the Feast of Samhain was a fearsome night, a dreaded night, a night in which great bonfires were lit to Samana the Lord of Death, the dark Aryan god who was known as the Grim Reaper, the leader of the ancestral ghosts."[32] There are those urban legends about "Samhain/Samana the Lord of Death" and "grim reapers" again. Michaelson goes on to make other incredible allegations in this chapter:

> [Halloween] is most assuredly the night set aside for the glorification and worship of idols, false gods, Satan, and death. The son of God appeared for this purpose, that He might destroy the works of the devil! ...
>
> Terror can kill. When my husband was a teenager, the family next door to him lost their toddler one Halloween when the little one opened the door to trick-or-treaters. Their hideous appearance and shrieks so traumatized the child that he literally dropped dead on the spot.[33]
>
> And even colder, darker creatures filled the night: evil Witches flying through the night, hobgoblins, and evil pookas
> ...
> Their rituals of necromancy often go far beyond that of the Witches and mediums in the horror and perversion in which these people specialize.[34]

Typically, Michaelsen gives no details about names, dates, or places that may be used to verify her allegations about a child being frightened to death by trick-or-treaters. She is using the very fear tactics that she condemns to further her own agenda. She concludes her chapter with the following statements:

> So ... should your family participate in the traditional Halloween celebrations? Absolutely ... if you and/or your

children are Witches, Satanists, Humanists, atheists, or anything other than born-again Christians (or Orthodox Jews).
For a true Christian to participate in the ancient trappings of
Halloween is as incongruous as for a committed cult Satanist
coming from a blood sacrifice on Christmas Eve to set up a
creche in his living room and sing "Silent Night, Holy Night"
with heartfelt, sincere devotion to Baby Jesus ...[35]

Halloween is a day in which virtually everything that God
has called **abomination** is glorified.[36]

Michaelsen complains that "since God and Jesus have been banned from
Christmas and Easter and Thanksgiving celebrations in most of our schools,
why should the Witches and Satanists get free promotion on Halloween from
those same institutions?"[37] While I would agree that schools should not be
promoting any particular religion, I am amazed at the suggestion that Halloween, as it is commonly practiced in North America today, is a promotion of
Witchcraft. Halloween festivities typically depict Witches in the most uncompli-
mentary terms: green-faced, wart-nosed, pointy-hatted figures on brooms. This
is hardly what I would call a promotion for Wicca or Paganism. Michaelsen
continues by stating, "One thing that Halloween should *not* be for the Christian is a time for fear."[38] Her remarks certainly look like fearmongering to me,
however.

Detective Don Rimer's *Symptoms Characterizing Occult Ritual Abuse* includes a section on Halloween. Some of the information in his description of
Halloween customs is relatively accurate. For example, he correctly identifies Halloween as a modern celebration based upon the old Celtic holiday of
Samhain. Rimer states, however, that the Celts believed that "all persons who
had died in the previous year assembled to choose the body of a person or
animal that they would inhabit for the next 12 months"[39] and that "to frighten
the roving spirits away, Celtic family members dressed as demons, hobgoblins,
and witches."[40] Also, Rimer's calendar describes October 31 as "HALLOWEEN
Great Sabbot [*sic*] High Holly Day."[41]

The 1991 issue of *Freedomlight Report* joins the ranks of fundamentalists
who have bought into the myth concerning the "god of death Samhain":

Before halloween there was a Celtic holiday to celebrate
the new year and honor Samhain, who was the Celtic god of
the dead. ... Halloween, which is also called All Hallow's Eve,
then became a pagan festival to honor all the deities with a
special emphasis on Samhain ... A common druidic belief
was that barriers between the worlds of the gods and mankind were broken down on this night. Because of this, fires,

animal and even human sacrifices were common in some
areas. The festival has traditionally been Satanic, or at least
associated with witchcraft practices ... to modern Satanists,
Samhain is one of the highest holidays of the year. It is a
night of sacrifices, rape and rituals.[42]

The writers go on to claim that "halloween is often a time when Satanists
and witches look for converts. Often they will hold what appear to be harmless celebrations of halloween. People from outside the group are invited to
bonfires or other activities and they look for those who are unduly interested
in the occult activities."[43] Wiccans do not proselytize as suggested here. The
Samhain celebration is meant to honor the ancestors, not to recruit followers.

In their *Handbook of Today's Religions: Understanding the Occult*, Christian
co-authors McDowell and Stewart claim that on Halloween "it is believed that
on this night Satan and his witches have their greatest power ... The celebration honored their god Samhain, lord of the dead ... Having turned their backs
on the God of the Bible, they invoke the help of Satan, fallen from God's favor
and relegated to darkness."[44]

Here McDowell and Stewart are assuming, incorrectly, that ancient Pagan
beliefs must be satanic because they aren't Christian—a variation on the old
Christian adage that if you aren't with me, you must be the enemy.

Christian author Russ Parker offers a somewhat more reasonable description of the history behind Halloween than most of the satanic conspiracy myth
supporters. This apparently reasonable tone doesn't last long, however. Next,
he says:

What really lies at the heart of Halloween, however, is a
desire to placate the forces of evil. It is a christianized version of the ancient Celtic ritual of Samhain, which was held
on October thirty-first. It marked the end of the summer and
so formed the Celtic New Year's Eve. Bonfires were lit to
frighten away evil spirits. Samhain did not attempt to get in
touch with evil forces but was considered a necessary ritual
to ward off any harm that may come. It was also seen as a
good time for divination about death, health, marriage and
luck. It is not surprising, then, that it lent itself to the practice
of other occult activities.[45]

Parker then tells an anecdote about his first ministry. He reports that he
found children putting up cutouts of Witches. "I explained to the play-group
leaders that Halloween makes evil appear fun," Parker tells us. "Much damage
is done by Christians who mix up Christianity with the occult by encouraging
this practice, which is pagan at heart."[46] I counter that much damage is done

by extremist Christians spreading falsehoods about Halloween and what it represents.

Parker then quotes the Association of Christian Teachers pamphlet on Halloween: "If we suppose that witches and spirits are nonsense, why then, encourage children to celebrate their mythical frolics and perhaps take them seriously? Paganism is hardly a cultural mainstay of all that is best in our country."[47] I believe we should encourage children to celebrate mythology because the supposition of this Christian organization is false. Witches are real people with a real religion. As for cultural mainstays, I'll support the values that Pagans stand for up against the domination, hatred, and destruction that some extremist Christians advocate any day.

Parker continues:

> Suppose that in our folklore, witches and demons merely represent moral evil. Halloween then tends to celebrate evil in the ascendant by the reversal of moral standards. If Nazi figures were regularly presented for children's admiration and affection there would soon be a public outcry. But loveable little witches are brought out every autumn. This disturbs the polarization of good and bad, right and wrong, in children's minds ... Hallowe'en does in fact encourage an interest and fascination in the occult and this invariably leads to more serious involvement and damage to the individuals concerned.[48]

The things that damage individuals are the falsehoods being spread by Christian propaganda pamphlets such as this.

In Johnston's *The Edge of Evil* is a section entitled "The Satanic Calendar of Brainwashing Ritual." In it, Johnston claims that

> [t]he high point of the satanic calendar is Halloween. ... Samhain was worshipped as the Celtic god of death about 2,000 years ago in what is now northern France, Britain and Ireland. The Celtic year began November 1, and since these tribes began their 'day' in the evening, the night of what the Romans dated October 31 was the festival of Samhain.
>
> ... Some legends have it that the souls of the wicked dead of the preceding year had been condemned to live in animals throughout the 12 months, and food set out in honor of Samhain would free these spirits from their condemned status. If a spirit returned to his home and found no offer of food, an evil spell would be cast over the house—sort of a macabre prototype of 'trick or treat' I would guess.

The October 31 celebrations were orchestrated by the teacher-priest Druids. Huge bonfires of sacred oak branches were kindled to burn sacrifices of crops, animals and apparently humans in honor of the god of death. The people dressed in animal skins and wore animal headdresses as the priests predicted the coming year's fortunes by examining the remains of the sacrifices.[49]

Johnston includes that "Samhain, God of the Dead" myth again. The Celts, not the Romans, celebrated Samhain on October 31. No substantial evidence exists to substantiate Johnston's claims about human sacrifice.

In his *File 18* newsletter, Lt. Larry Jones describes Halloween as "most likely to include ritual sacrifices to Satan; ritual altar in circle faces Northwest."[50] Wiccans don't believe in Satan, we don't practice ritual sacrifice, and we place our altar in the north of the Circle, not the northwest. This newsletter places the altar in a different position for each of the eight Sabbats—an interesting concept, but not a common Wiccan practice.

The modern custom of trick or treat is derived from the custom of "souling" (which I will describe in the next section). You'd never guess this connection from books like *The Dark Side of Halloween*, in which Brown states:

What about COSTUMES? They originated with these terrible Druid death rites also. As people and animals were screeching in agony while being burned to death the observers would dress in costumes made of animal skins and heads. They would dance, chant and jump through the flames in hope of warding off the evil spirit. It is obvious that Halloween is a pagan day rooted in the worst kind of pagan rituals and worship. ... Halloween is the devil's day![51]

Brown also comments on jack-o'-lanterns:

... In [Rachleff's] book *Occult Conceit* the author says on page 190, "The candle lit pumpkin or skull served ... as a signal to mark those farms and homes that were sympathetic to the Satanists and thus deserving of mercy when the terror ('trick or treat') of the night began." Further, an old edition of *The World Book Encyclopedia* says, "The apparently harmless lighted pumpkin face of Jack O'Lantern is an ancient symbol of a damned soul."[52]

John Todd claims that at Halloween "the treat from the castle demanded by the Druids would be a princess or some woman for human sacrifice. If the treat pleased the Druids they would leave a Jack O'Lantern with a lighted candle made of human fat to protect those inside from being killed by demons that night."[53] Bill Schnoebelen claims that the jack-o'-lantern is a symbol of "the Lord of the Dead, a 'god,' just like a Buddha—in short *an idol*"[54] and that its "fearsome face represented the god, Saman [*sic*]."[55] None of this information concerning jack-o'-lanterns is accurate. I'll give you the true story in the next chapter.

NOTES

1. John Frattarola, "Passport Magazine Special Edition: America's Best Kept Secret," 7.
2. Michael Warnke, *Schemes of Satan* (Victory House, 1991), 121.
3. David Balsiger, *1988 Witchcraft/Satanism Ritual Calendar*, 3.
4. Philippa Waring, *A Dictionary of Omens and Superstitions* (1978), 98, 224; http://all-sands.com/History/originscommons_ssd_gn.htm.
5. Ibid.
6. Reachout Trust, "Halloween," *Reachout Quarterly*, autumn 1998, no. 53, 13, www.reachouttrust.org/pdf/quarterly/Quarterly53.pdf; "Hallowe'en Is Here Again," Reachout Quarterly, autumn 2007, no. 77, 3, www.reachouttrust.org/pdf/quarterly/Quarterly77.pdf.
7. Ibid.
8. Ibid.
9. Edward E. Plowman, "The Legends of John Todd," *Christianity Today* (February 2, 1979), 19.
10. Quoted in Keith Morse, "Questions and Answers on Wicca: A Christian Perspective on Witchcraft," *Personal Freedom Outreach Newsletter* 3.4 (Oct. to Dec. 1983), 6.
11. Gavin Frost, *The Witch's Bible* (Los Angeles: Nash Publishing, 1972), 173.
12. Keith Morse, 6.
13. David L. Brown, *The Dark Side of Halloween*, 1. Emphasis in original.
14. Ibid. Emphasis in original.
15. Ibid. Emphasis in original.
16. Ibid., 9.
17. Ibid., 11. Emphasis in original.
18. Ibid., 2.
19. CCIN Inc., *File 18 Newsletter* vol. 3, no. 6:3.
20. Ibid. Emphasis in original.
21. Ibid., 9.
22. Phil Phillips and John Hake Robie, *Halloween and Satanism* (Starburst Publishers), 17.
23. Ibid., 26.
24. Ibid.
25. Ibid., 57.
26. Ibid.
27. Ibid., 58.
28. Ibid.
29. Ibid.
30. Ibid.
31. Ibid.
32. Ibid., 39.
33. Ibid., 38.

34. Ibid., 37–42.
35. Ibid., 42. Emphasis in original.
36. Ibid., 43. Emphasis in original.
37. Ibid., 45.
38. Ibid. Emphasis in original.
39. Don Rimer, "Symptoms Characterizing Occult Ritual Abuse," http://www.ogia.net/oklahoma%20gang%20investigators'%20association/occult/htm.
40. Ibid.
41. Ibid.
42. *Freedomlight Report* 1:3 (Oct/Nov 1990), 1.
43. Ibid., 4.
44. Josh McDowell, Stuart McDowell and Don Stewart, *Handbook of Today's Religions: Understanding the Occult*, 175.
45. Russ Parker, *Battling the Occult*, 34.
46. Ibid., 35.
47. Ibid.
48. Ibid.
49. Jerry Johnston, *The Edge of Evil* (Vancouver, BC: Word Publishing, 1989), 211–212.
50. CCIN Inc., *File 18* newsletter 3, no. 6:3.
51. Ibid. Emphasis in original.
52. David L. Brown, *The Dark Side of Halloween* (Logos Communication Consortium, 1998), 2.
53. Edward E. Plowman, "The Legends of John Todd," *Christianity Today* (February 2, 1979), 19.
54. Bill Schnoebelen, *Halloween: Tis The Season To Be Evil* (1990), 8. Emphasis in original.
55. Ibid, 4.

Chapter Ten

The Real Samhain

Samhain (pronounced "sow-in") is the Celtic New Year's Eve and was celebrated from sunset from October 31 to sunset on November 1. Some Druid groups refer to it as Samhuinn, the Welsh call it Calan Gaef or Nos Galan Gaeof, and it is still celebrated today as Halloween, All Hallow's Eve, or Hallowmas.

Samhain was the end of the summer season and the beginning of the winter season for the Celts. At this time, the Celts culled their herds, slaughtering cattle and salting or drying the meat. Only breeding cattle were left to be fed over the winter. This custom is one of the reasons that Samhain is associated with death and spirits. To the Celts, Samhain was the turning of the year, a time during which the barriers between the worlds of life and death were believed to be as thin as veils. For this reason, it was believed that spirits of the departed could return, to be welcomed by their kin and celebrate with them. It was a time to honor those who have gone before us, not to fear them. It was also a time of truce for the Celtic tribes, when councils were held, legal judgments passed, and agreements made.

The Feast of Samhain marks the end and beginning of the sacred year for both Wiccans and Druids. It marks the last harvest and is a time for remembering our ancestors. It is a Feast of the Dead, with offerings made to the Lord of the House of the Dead, to the Queen of Phantoms, the gods, the dead, and the sidhe. In "We offer to Donn the Dark One," Ian Corrigan writes, "the Antlered God who offers hospitality and peace to those bound for the Ancestors' Country. We offer to Morrigan, the Great Queen of Battle and Sorcery; the Old Woman of Death and the Cauldron of Rebirth. In this Season of Death we honor the Holy Dead as the ancients did, and we seek the Seed that will wait in the Womb of Winter."[1]

Both Wiccan and Druid Samhain rites are concerned with making contact with the spirits of the departed, who are seen as sources of guidance and inspiration. The dead are honored and celebrated as the living spirits of loved ones, and as guardians who hold the root-wisdom of the tribe. Offerings are also left for the gods. Some Druid groups offer silver or precious stones to the offering bowl, oil or whiskey to the fire, horn or feathers at the foot of the World Tree or bilé, while offerings of apples, pork, and hazelnuts are made to the ancestors. Another common Druid practice involves passing a wreath among the participants. Those who wish may tie a black ribbon on the wreath in commemoration of departed relatives. Later, this wreath is given to the fire during the "Prayer of Sacrifice." A variation of this custom involves passing a basket into which each person can make an offering or simply add energy. The basket is then offered to the dead.[2] Divination is performed by tossing apples and nuts into the fire.

With the coming of Christianity, this festival became Hallowe'en (October 31), All Saints/All Hallows (November 1), and All Souls (November 2). Here we can see most clearly the way in which Christianity built on the Pagan foundations it found rooted in the British Isles. Not only does the purpose of the festival match with the earlier one, but also the unusual length of the festival is the same. In the seventh century CE, the Church established a Feast of All Saints, which was originally celebrated on May 13. They moved it to November 1 in 835 CE to coincide with the festival of Samhain, probably with the purpose of giving the people a reason to celebrate that was more palatable to the Church. In 988 CE, the festival was expanded to November 2 in order to include a commemoration of the dead, which was called "All Soul's Day"." This was later shortened to "All Souls" in Scotland in 1745.[3]

Samhain is one of the two great fire festivals of the Celtic peoples, the other being Beltaine. Bonfires were lit all over Britain at Samhain. In many parts of Britain, these fires were known as *teanlas*, *teanlay*, *tindles*, or *tandles*. Farmers would take pitchforks of flaming straw, burning splinters, or smouldering brands from these fires and carry them around the fields to bless them.

Samhain also marks the rising of the constellation of the Pleiades, which is to be found in the constellation Taurus. The setting and rising of the Pleiades are occasions for festivals celebrated in diverse cultures all around the world, as they mark the beginning and end of the fishing and hunting seasons.

An ancient custom still practiced in Ireland and Scotland is guising, the forerunner of the current trick-or-treat custom in North America. A procession of fantastically dressed, horn-blowing youths go from house to house, collecting money or gifts of food. A related custom was "hodening" or "hoodening." A man would bear a horse's skull (or wooden horse's head) on a pole. The jaws of the horse's head were often wired and made to snap open and shut. Some of these horse skulls had candles inside them to cast an eerie light. The man bearing the skull covered himself with a stable blanket or sheet. This "hooden horse" would go from house to house accompanied by "soulers," who sang traditional

seasonal songs.⁴ The horse is a symbol of Celtic goddesses like Epona and Rhiannon. Often the soulers were children, who would sing their ancient souling
songs from door to door in return for gifts or food. In some places, special cakes
called "soul cakes," "Saumas cakes," "Soulmas cakes," "dole cakes," or "dirge
loaves" were handed out to soulers. A traditional Shropshire souler's song goes
like this:

> Soul! Soul! for a soul-cake!
> I pray you, good missis, a soul-cake!
> An apple, a pear, a plum or a cherry,
> Or any good thing to make us all merry.
> One for Peter, two for Paul
> Three for Them who made us all.
> Up with the kettle and down with the pan.
> Give us good alms, and we'll be gone.⁵
> Another, from Staffordshire, goes like this:
> Soul Day! Soul Day!
> We've been praying for the souls departed;
> So pray, good people, give us a cake,
> For we are all poor people, well known to you before,
> So give us a cake for charity's sake,
> And our blessing we'll leave at your door.⁶

These customs were ultimately adapted into the modern practice of trick-
or-treating.

The modern jack-o'-lantern has a long history. One of the colloquial names
for Halloween in Sommerset is "Punkie Night." It got this name from the
"punkies" or candle lanterns that children would make from hollowed-out
gourds such as mangold-wurzels. In other places, turnips or cabbage stalks
(called "custocks" in Scotland) were used to make lanterns. The children did
not necessarily carve faces into them. Punkies were often carved with elaborate
designs of animals or flowers. A candle was put inside and a cord run through
the top to provide a handle. The children would go from door to door begging
candles for their punkies, singing:

> It's Punkie Night tonight.
> Give us a candle, give us a light,
> If you don't, you'll get a fright.
> It's Punkie Night tonight.
> Adam and Eve, they'd never believe
> It's Punkie Night tonight.⁷

The flame in each of the punkies represented the spirits of the departed that are remembered on Samhain. All over Europe, it was customary on Samhain to leave lighted candles in the windows to guide the spirits of departed relatives back to visit their living kin. The Celts believed that the flames in their lanterns represented the spirits of their dear departed relatives, not "damned souls." Carving faces into them was probably originally an extension of this belief, not an attempt to create "demonic faces." The Celts did not believe in Satan, so Matrisciana's and Brown's statements that such lanterns left in windows were a sign that the occupants of the house were sympathetic to Satan is ludicrous.

Sometimes candles were lit for the living, as a form of divination. In North Lancashire, a ceremony of "lating the witches" takes place. People light candles and carry them over the hills between eleven o'clock in the evening and midnight. If the candle remains lit, then the person it has been lit for will be safe for the coming year, but if it goes out, misfortune is expected. Another custom is the placing of twelve candles in a ring on the floor. People jump the candles in turn, each candle representing a month of the year. If one goes out when a person jumps over it, this means that misfortune will befall that person in that month.

In Ireland and Brittany, food and drink were set out for the spirits of the departed. This was often referred to as the "dumb supper." Soul cakes may have originally been the food that was offered. Modern Wiccans often observe Samhain by serving a dumb supper at which strict silence is observed. A place is set at the table for the spirits of the ancestors.

A related custom involves the belief that all of the crops had to be harvested before Samhain. Anything left in the fields after Samhain was considered to be either blasted by the puca or to be the property of the puca (see Appendix B). Since "puca" is a term not found in ancient Celtic mythology and is probably a recent import from the Danish invaders (who called them "puki"), this custom is probably recent.

In contemporary North America, fireworks are also associated with Halloween. This was a custom of the British Guy Fawke's Day celebrations, which is celebrated on November 5 and commemorates the discovery of the plot to blow up the English Parliament Buildings. Immigrants who wished to continue the custom, despite living in a country that does not celebrate Guy Fawkes' Day, may have introduced fireworks in North American Halloween celebrations. The fireworks also fit with the fire festival theme of this holiday.

NOTES

1. Ian Corrigan, "The Samhain Rite," http://www.adf.org/rituals/celtic/samhain/samhain.html.

2. Kami Landy, with revisions by Fox Henderson and Rob Henderson, "Shining Lakes Grove Samhain 1997," http://www.adf.org/rituals/celtic/samhain/slgsamhain97.html.

3. Robert K. Barnhart, ed., *Barnhart Dictionary of Etymology* (New York: H.W. Wilson), 462.

4. Christina Hole, *British Folk Customs* (Hutchinson, 1976), 100–102.

5. Ibid., 187.

6. Ibid., 188.

7. Ibid., 162.

Chapter Eleven

Other Festivals and Misinformation

Yule Misinformation

- In *America's Best Kept Secret*, Frattarola describes December 22 as "CELEBRATION: Feast Day, TYPE: Orgies, USAGE: Oral, Anal, Vaginal, AGE: Any age (male or female, human or animal)."[1]
- In *Halloween: 'Tis the Season to be Evil*, Schnoebelen claims that "it has been said that during this time baby boys are severely tortured to blaspheme the Christ child being born."[2] The *Colorado Bureau of Investigations Questioned Documents Examiner's Occult Guide* contains this same definition.[3]
- Detective Don Rimer's "Symptoms Characterizing Occult Ritual Abuse" describes December 22 as involving "WINTER SOLSTICE Orgies."[4]
- In his book *America's Occult Holidays,* Marquis tells us that Christmas was forbidden by the early American pilgrims (which is true), but then tries to convince readers that Christmas was "an ancient occult ceremony dedicated to the birthday of Tammuz, the son of the cofounders of the occult, Nimrod and Semiramis."[5]

The Real Yule

Yule, the winter solstice (December 21), is a Lesser Sabbat in the Wiccan calendar. It is also known as Alban Arthuan. In Druid orders, the winter solstice is known to ADF as La Ceimbroadh, to the OBOD as Alban Arthan or "the light of Arthur," to the RDNA as Yule, and to the ODU as Mean Geimhridh.

The word "yule" first appeared in its modern spelling in 1475 CE. Around 1450 CE it was spelled "yoole," and in about 1200 CE it appeared in *The Ormulum* as "Yole." Previous to 899 CE, it appeared in Old English as the word *geol* or *geola*.[6] The venerable Bede recorded it about 726 CE in his history (written in Anglian Old English) as *Giuli*. The name may have originated in

Scandinavian countries, since their word for this season is similar: *jul*, or in old Icelandic, *jol*.[7] December 21 is also the Christian Feast of Saint Thomas.

The term "Christmas" cannot be traced back as far as the term "Yule." It first appeared as "Cristmessa," or "Christ's Festival," around 1100 CE. Another Old English variation was "Cristes Maesse." The expression "Christmas Eve" did not appear before 1300 CE (from "Cristenmesse Even"). "Christmastide" was first used in 1626, and although decorated trees appeared in England in the mid-1700s, the term "Christmas tree" did not appear until 1835.[8]

The winter solstice is the longest night of the year. Some cultures hold a Festival of Light to commemorate the Goddess as Mother, giving birth (once again) to the Sun God. In the Wiccan community, this custom often this takes the form of getting up before the sun rises and lighting a bonfire. The celebrants stand around the fire, "singing the sun up" in celebration of the returning light. Wiccans often appoint coveners to represent the Young Lord (or the waxing year) and the Old Lord (the waning year). They play out a ritual drama of the Young Lord's victory over the Old to mark the point from which the days will lengthen.

Druids consider Yule to be a time of rebirth and elimination of obstacles. One Druid Yule ritual calls upon the participants to "[c]ast away, O wo/man[,] whatever impedes the appearance of light."[9] In darkness, the participants throw scraps of material to the ground, each scrap signifying something that has been holding them back. A lamp is then lit from a flint and raised up on the Druid's crook in the east. The white mistletoe berries distributed in some Druid Yule ceremonies symbolize the return of the light.

Another typical Druid Yule ritual[10] honors the Earth Mother with poetry and with the participants bestowing a kiss upon the earth, either directly or with their fingertips. A gift of silver is made to the well and one of oil to the fire and tree. The boundaries between the mundane world and the otherworld are established with offerings of cornmeal to the land, water to the sea, and incense to the sky. A cup of ale is then offered to the Outsiders, cornmeal to the ancestors, herbs to the nature spirits, and oil to the gods (the Shining Ones). Individual offerings of song, poetry, story, dance, and artwork are made. Omens are read in the cauldron of Cerridwen. The waters of life are represented by a cup of water and a horn of ale. Each participant offers some liquid to the ground, makes a statement or boast, and then drinks from the cup.

Some Druid Yule rituals involve a final "sacrifice" of a willow branch to the fire.[11] Scrying is typically done to determine if the offerings have been accepted, and if the omens are bad, the offerings are repeated. Other Druid groups use holly branches as a sacrificial offering, and each participant hangs an ornament on the world tree while making a wish.[12] The waters of life may be represented by a cup of cranberry juice, which is then passed around for all to drink.[13]

Yule was another time of year that the custom of "hodening" or "hoodening" was practised. As in the Samhain hodening, a man would drape a stable blanket or sheet over himself and carry a horse's skull (sometimes a wooden horse's head) on a pole about four feet long. The jaws were often hinged and made to snap open and shut. The "horse" would go from household to household at night with a small group of attendants. His visit was said to bring fertility and good fortune to the household. One of his attendants would lead him by the reins or a rope, while another would carry a whip. Sometimes a lighter person would ride on the horse's back. A man dressed as a woman and carrying a besom (broom) also accompanied the horse. This figure, called "Mollie" or "Old Woman," was originally likely a woman, perhaps a priestess. This group would greet the householders at the front door, the hodening horse snapping his jaws and the Old Woman sweeping the entrance way to remove bad luck. The hodening party would enter the house, and the occupants would tie a red ribbon on the horse's head.

Imbolc Misinformation

- In *America's Best Kept Secret*, Frattarola defines February 2 as "CELEBRA-TION: Satanic Revels, TYPE: Sexual, USAGE: Oral, Anal, Vaginal, AGE: 7-17 (female)."[14]
- In Balsiger's *1988 Witchcraft/Satanism Ritual Calendar,* February 1 is described as "Candlemas Eve. Welcoming spring."[15]

Do you suppose that Satanists would do a ritual to welcome spring? If this seems out of place to you, you are right. This date isn't a satanic festival, though others list it as one.

The Real Imbolc

Februum, from which we derive "February," is a Latin word meaning "purification" and "atonement; thus, this month is considered a month of cleansing. Juno Februa was the Roman goddess who presided over this month.

Wiccans call February 2 Imbolc, which means "in the belly." It is also known as Imbolg, Uimelc, Oimelc, Feile Bhride, Brigid, Brigantia, or Candlemas. Many Druids also call this festival Imbolc, though the Druid order Ord Draiochta na Uisnech calls it Oimelc. It was named Oimelc (sheep's milk) because it marked the beginning of the lambing season for the Celts. This festival is a Greater Sabbat on the Wiccan calendar and marks the midpoint of the dark half of the year. At Imbolc, household fires are put out and relit, and the festival often marks the first ploughing and first planting of the year.

Imbolc is a celebration of the first signs of life returning in spring. To the Celts, this day was sacred to Brighid, a goddess whose threefold aspect rules smithcraft, poetry, inspiration, and healing. Hence one of the other names for this day is Lá Fhéile Bhríde, meaning "Brighid's Feast." Brighid is commonly honored at the Christian Feast of Saint Brighid. At Imbolc, a woman acting on Brighid's behalf blesses the fires of the smithy.

The Catholic Church in Britain incorporated this festival into its calendar as early as the fifth century. It became known as Candlemas, a Feast of Lights, or the celebration of the Presentation of Christ in the Temple. Several Popes tried to stop parades of lit candles in the streets of Rome during this period. When this failed, they simply diverted these parades into the churches so that the priests could bless the candles. It subsequently became a Church tradition that at Candlemas, the Church candles were blessed and carried around in procession. The Puritans of the seventeenth century tried to wipe out the custom, but they did not entirely succeed.

Many will recognize this date as being the contemporary "Groundhog Day." This celebration harkens back to the original festival, when people sought out signs of the approaching spring. An old Candlemas rhyme goes:

> If Candlemas Day be Fair and Bright,
> Winter will have another fight,
> If on Candlemas Day be shower and rain,
> Winter is gone and will not come again.

Another Candlemas rhyme goes:

> If the sun shines bright on Candlemas Day,
> The half of the winter's not yet away.

Candlemas is still commonly celebrated in Scandinavian countries as a festival of lights.

Wiccan Imbolc celebrations are typically dedicated to Brighid. Corn dollies or "Bride's dolls" are woven out of stalks of grain and are placed overnight in a "bed" by the hearth or entrance. The previous year's dollies are burnt and replaced with these new ones. A white wand of birch or willow may be left beside the bed. Many Wiccan covens have adopted the Church's custom of blessing candles for the coming year; candles are often dipped and blessed in a similar fashion as part of Imbolc celebrations. Pancakes are a typical festival food for Imbolc celebrations. This is also a Christian custom around Lent, which falls at a similar time of year.

Druids celebrate Imbolc or Oimelc to honor the Mother Goddess, usually in her aspect of the goddess Brighid, the patroness of poets, healers, and midwives. Some Druid Imbolc ceremonies involve eight candles rising out of a pool or other container of water at the center of the ceremonial Circle.[16] Druids often use Imbolc as a time for an *eisteddfod*, dedicated to poetry and song praising the Goddess in her many forms.

The Grove of the Great Dragon[17] marks Imbolc by making offerings of bread, grain, or flour to awen; to the God and Goddess in the form of Cernunnos and Dana; and to patron powers in the guises of Aengus Og and Brighid. An OBOD Imbolc ceremony[18] requires three images of Brighid such as a corn dolly, Brighid's cross, or statue, as well as a white triple-wick candle. A Druid strikes an anvil three times to invoke Brighid as patroness of the forge. Elemental archetypes and sacred directions are greeted in the pattern of a Celtic cross, another symbol related to Brighid. Druids representing these quarters call upon Eala the white swan, Bradan the salmon of wisdom, Nathair the sacred snake, and Torc the great boar.

Eostre Misinformation

- Tom Sanguinet claims that at "Easter, [Witches] still greatly honor (the Middle Eastern pagan Goddess) Astarte with her silly little eggs."[19]
- In *America's Best Kept Secret*, Frattarola describes March 20 as "CELEBRATION: Feast Day (Spring Equinox), TYPE: Orgies, USAGE: Oral, Anal, Vaginal, AGE: Any age (male or female, human or animal)."[20]
- Joseph "Doc" Marquis mixes his mythologies when he claims that "Easter ... is in fact the celebration of the return of Semiramis into her reincarnated form of the spring goddess."[21]

In fact, Semiramis is not associated with Eostre at all.

The Real Eostre

March 21 is the spring or vernal equinox. Wiccans call the spring equinox Eostre, Eostar/a, Ostara, Lady Day, or Alban Eilir (light of the earth). It is a Lesser Sabbat on the Wiccan calendar. Druids call this festival Eostre, Alban Eilir, Méan Earraigh, or Méan An Earraigh. In Old High German, the festival's name was Ostarun, becoming "Ostern" in Modern German. In Bede's *Ecclesiastical History,* the Christian holiday is spelled "Eastre," as it was in Old English before 899. By 1103, it had become "Estran." In Middle English (before 1387), it was spelled "Ester" or "Esterne."[22]

Eostre is a celebration of the return of life to the earth after the long winter. The festival's name was not derived, as Sanguinet claims, from the Middle Eastern goddess Astarte. It comes from the Anglo-Saxon goddess Eostre (or Ostara), who was believed to fly over the earth and leave the eggs (beginnings) of new life. Eostre's totem animal was the rabbit. Both eggs and rabbits have been incorporated into the modern Christian celebration of Easter. This date is also sacred to the Norse goddess Iduna.

The Christian festival of Easter derives from Eostre. Although Easter and Eostre do not always coincide, the system for determining the date of the Christian festival of Easter is still based on the vernal equinox, being the first Sunday after the first full moon that occurs on or after March 21.

Wiccan Eostre celebrations typically focus on themes of fertility and rebirth and often occur at daybreak. Many incorporate the ancient Greek myths of Dionysus or of Demeter and Persephone into their celebrations. For example, for the past twenty years the Aquarian Tabernacle Church (based in Washington state) has hosted a Spring Mysteries festival that recreates the Eleusian Mysteries* and Epoptaic† rituals based on these myths.[23] Wiccan Eostre ceremonies often involve blessing seeds for spring planting.

Eggs appear as significant religious symbols in many ancient cultures. Egyptians placed eggs in tombs as a symbol of rebirth, and Greeks placed eggs on the graves of loved ones to ensure reincarnation. Eastern Europeans colored and decorated eggs as offerings to bird goddesses. Single-colored eggs were known as *pysanky*, and those with elaborate designs as *krashanka*. The Saxons decorated eggs as offerings to the goddess Eostre, which is where modern Wiccans, Druids, and Christians acquired the custom. Ancient Druids also dyed eggs scarlet with furze (gorse) blossoms or madder root in honor of the sun.

Hot cross buns, familiar at modern Christian Easter celebrations, are another ancient Pagan custom. The ancient Greeks decorated buns with a solar cross as offerings to the gods, as did the Saxons. Hot cross buns are often used in the cakes and wine ceremony in Wiccan Eostre celebrations.

Druid Alban Eilir rites often include offerings of hazlenuts to the woodlands.[24] Offerings of bread and mead or beer are given to the earth for the spirits of place and the ancestors.

Beltaine Misinformation

- Lyle Rapacki, in *Satanism: The Not So New Problem*, correctly defines Beltaine, but lists it under "definitions of Satanic terms."[25] Most people pretending to be occult crime "experts" don't even get the definition right, however. For example, in *Schemes of Satan*, Michael Warnke describes Beltaine as follows:

    ... Beltane originated as a holiday to honor St Walburga (The term "Walburg" is also an old Teutonic name for the festival given in honor of the god of the underworld—Satan.) Its date coincides with the time of the year when spring planting begins, and the Celts (represented by the Druids) often

---

*   The Eleusian mysteries involved the myth of Demeter and Persephone: Persephone's journey to and from the underworld of Hades as the cause of the coming and going of spring and summer.

†   The Epoptaic rituals involve the myth of Dionysus.

used this celebration as another opportunity to offer human sacrifices.[26]

The Celtic festival of Beltaine existed thousands of years before Saint Walburga, who was named after the goddess Walgburg, not a god of the dead. Walpurgis and Beltaine are two different festivals.

- Shane Westhoelter, in his *General Information Manual With Respect to Satanism and the Occult,* describes May Eve or Beltane as "one of the most powerful witches' sabbats. The witches in attendance vow to obey their god, the 'master' disguised as an animal."[27]

One of the traditional Beltaine customs does involve "hobbyhorses" (more on this in a moment). This is similar to the custom of hodening that occurs at Samhain and Yule. This may have been where Westhoelter and others got the idea that Pagans are attending a "master disguised as an animal," though it is more likely that he was influenced by the myths created by the inquisitors.

These errors subsequently show up in police manuals.

- The *Colorado Bureau of Investigation (CBI) Questioned Documents Examiner's Occult Guide* defines Midsummer as "Festival of Beltane." The *CBI* manual also suggests that all occultists call May Eve "Walpurgisnacht."
- Actually, only Christians, a few followers of Germanic Paganism, and Satanists follow this practice.
- Lou Sloat's *Texas Ritualistic Crime Information Network Occult Crime Manual* includes "May Eve/Roodman [sic]" and "Midsummer/Beltane" separately in its list of "occult terms," as if they were two different dates.[28]
- Retired police officer and self-appointed "occult" crime 'expert' Dale Griffis handed out a list of terms "used by occultic groups" at one of his lectures in 1989, which included the same mistake that the *CBI* makes: "Midsummer: The Feast of Beltane."

Midsummer, the summer solstice, is called Litha, not "Beltane."

The Real Beltaine

Beltaine, also known as Beltane, Cetshamhain, Rudemas, or May Eve, is a Greater Sabbat of the Wiccan calendar, celebrated from April 30 to May 1. The festival is also known in Wales as Galan Mai.

Beltaine (literally "fires of Bel") was the beginning of the summer season for the Celtic peoples and was named for the solar deity known in various parts of the Celtic world as Beli, Bile, Belenos, Bel, and Belenus. In more recent times, the Catholic Church incorporated Beltaine into their calendar as the Feast of Saint John the Baptist.

Beltaine is the one of the great Celtic fire festivals, the other being Samhain. Unlike Samhain, when the fires are lit at dusk, the Beltaine fires are lit at dawn. Traditionally, horns were sounded during the lighting of the fires. It was customary in some places to blow the horn for hours. Eggs and cakes, such as Scottish bannocks, would be cooked in the fires.

Beltaine was when the Celts drove their cattle to summer pasture. It also marks the setting of the constellation of the Pleiades, an event that in some parts of the world signals the start of the fishing season.

Beltaine is an ancient celebration of fertility and life. The crowning of a young girl as May Queen, representing the Maiden Goddess, is still practiced throughout Great Britain. Originally, a May King representing the Young God, Robin, or Jack-in-the-Green was crowned as well.

Dancing around the Maypole is a Beltaine custom that continues in the British Isles to this day. Modern Wiccans have adopted the Maypole, an ancient fertility symbol, into their Beltaine celebrations. The traditional British Maypole was a young tree, which was chopped down on May Day and trimmed of all but a few branches at the top. It was then decorated and raised on the village green. In later years, many towns had permanent poles. In 1644, Cromwell's government forbade Maypoles throughout England and Wales, and many of the permanent poles were removed. When King Charles II was restored to office on May 29, 1660, this prohibition was lifted, and some of the Maypoles returned. Historian Christina Hole reports: "The shorter poles, round which the children perform a plaited ribbon dance, and which are often seen at school May Day celebrations today, do not belong to the English tradition. They come from southern Europe, and seem to have been introduced into [England] (by Ruskin) in 1888."[29]

Author (in hat) carrying the Maypole at a Wiccan Beltaine ritual

Maypole dance at a Wiccan Beltaine celebration

"Birching" is a traditional Beltaine custom. Between sunset and dawn, May birchers would go from house to house affixing branches or sprigs to their neighbors' doors. The trees or plants were either chosen for their symbolism or because their names rhymed with whatever message the birchers thought appropriate. For example, a flowering hawthorn branch was a compliment. Lime or pear branches were also compliments, as they rhymed with "prime" and "fair." Rowan was a sign of affection as its other name, "wicken," rhymed with the endearing slang term "chicken." A thorn branch indicated that the occupant was an object of scorn. Holly, briar, and plum were insults, rhyming with folly, liar, and glum. This distribution of greenery indicated how a person was regarded in his or her community, and could signal a need to mend one's ways. Unfortunately, the custom was sometimes employed for spite or revenge. Although it has died out in most places, a shadow of it still lives on with the custom of leaving hawthorn or some other complimentary plant outside the bride's door on the eve of a wedding.

May garlands are a related custom. For this reason another name for Beltaine is Garland Day. Traditionally, children used to go from door to door with their garlands, singing songs and receiving small gifts or coins in return. Often the garlands were in the form of a hoop, and in some places, games evolved where a ball was thrown through or over the hoop. Sometimes the balls took the form of floral globes, often with a May doll suspended inside. In Horncastle, Lincolnshire, young boys carried peeled willow wands covered with cowslips. Called "May gads," these wands were carried in a morning procession to the site of an old Roman temple where the Maypole stood. There, the boys would strike the wands together to scatter their blossoms in honor of the first day of summer.

At Beltaine, wells and springs were dressed, in keeping with the Celtic custom of venerating them as connections to the otherworld. Dressing involves decorating the well and surrounding area to honor it. This custom continues in many parts of Britain today, although the designs are now usually Christian.

Another Beltaine custom is the collection of dew. "May first is the magical time of greatest power for the element of water and 'wild' water (dew, flowing streams, or ocean water) is collected for the base of healing drinks and potions for the year to come."[30] Young girls would go out before dawn on May Day to collect dew and wash their faces with it. This was supposed to bring beauty and luck. Dew was also collected and kept to treat consumption, goitre, and various other ills.

Hobbyhorses also make their appearance at Beltaine, similar to the custom of hodening at Samhain and Yule. The usual form of hobbyhorse is a hoop frame, six feet in diameter, covered with cloth skirting. In front is a wooden horse's head, with jaws that snap. A man stands inside, his head hidden by a mask. The hobbyhorse travels with a group of attendants, the most important of which is often a "teaser" or "club man," who carries a padded club and wears grotesque clothing. As they process down the streets singing, the hobbyhorse will rush at young women and try to trap them under his skirts. This is thought to bring them fertility and/or a husband. The inside of the horse's skirts was formerly smeared with blacking in order to leave a mark of good fortune on the young woman, but this is not done in modern survivals of this custom. Another discontinued custom is the sprinkling of water on onlookers by the hobbyhorse when it stopped at a pool to "drink." Occasionally, the 'horse' sinks down as if dying, and songs change from happy ones to sadder ones. The teaser gently strokes him with his club. After this brief pause, the hobbyhorse leaps up, the music returns to happier tunes, and the procession continues.

Manannan Mac Lir Grove Beltaine

An example of a Druid Beltaine is the 2004 ceremony composed by Valan and held by the Moonpath Chapter of CUUPS (Covenant of Unitarian Universalist Pagans).[31] Mother Earth was honored as Hertha, the guardian of the sea was Njord, and the Sky Father was represented by Tiwaz. After the quarters were called, the Circle was cast by having each person place their left palm onto the upraised right palm of the person on their left, saying, "Hand to hand I cast this Circle." When everyone was holding hands, a Druid announced, "It is joined." The Circle was then cast with "sparks and fire," with one person from each of the quarters taking a lighted sparkler on to the next quarter to light another sparkler. The Goddess was invoked as Aine and Calleach. A May Queen was revealed from among the participants and spoke blessings to the Shining Ones. The god invoked was Aengus, the Celtic god of love. A priest representing Aengus passed a phallic rod, which circulated around the group. The May Queen received the rod last and placed it upright in a hole in the earth, saying, "Awake, O King-To-Be! Enter now the Maiden Earth and Bring joy and blessing to us all!" Omens were taken with runes. If an unfavorable omen was drawn, the participants were asked to meditate on the gods' message and consider how to respond individually. Juice was distributed as the waters of life. The participants, led by the May Queen and Aengus, then passed between two Beltaine blessing fires to bring them luck. The May Queen and the person playing the part of Aengus brought out these two fire vessels. Thanks were then given to the gods and spirits. Valan closed the rite by announcing, "Let the fire be flame. Let the well be water. Let all be as it was before. This rite is ended." The Fire-keeper then extinguished the fire with a bucketful of water to create a smoky finale.

Litha Misinformation

- In *Schemes of Satan*, Warnke lists Saint John's Eve (June 21–22) as a Druid celebration.[32]
- Lou Sloat's *Texas Ritualistic Crime Information Network Occult Crime Manual* includes Saint John's Eve in its list of "occult terms."[33]
- Balsiger's "Satanic calendar" describes June 20 as "Summer Solstice" and "June 23- Midsummer's Eve, St John's (the Baptist) Eve. Invokes the sun at the height of its strength."[34]

Balsiger doesn't seem to understand that the summer solstice and Midsummer are the same thing. Nor do Druids recognize Saint John.

- In *America's Best Kept Secret*, Frattarola describes June 21 as "CELEBRATION: Feast Day (Summer Solstice), TYPE: Orgies, USAGE: Oral, Anal, Vaginal, AGE: Any age (male or female, human or animal."[35]

- In Detective Rimer's "Symptoms Characterizing Occult Ritual Abuse," June 22 is described as occasioning "SUMMER SOLSTICE Orgies."[36]

The summer solstice does indeed honor the sun, but none of the other activities described by those writers will be familiar to Pagans. Pagan Litha celebrations do not require orgies or bestiality. Litha isn't a satanic festival.

The Real Litha

Wiccans call the summer solstice Litha, Midsummer, or Alban Heruin. Originally a Saxon solar celebration, Litha was incorporated into the Wiccan calendar as a celebration of the first fruits of the season. In some traditions, this day is celebrated as the sacred marriage of the Goddess and God. In others, it marks the victory of the Lord of the waning year over the Lord of the waxing year at the point at which the days begin to shorten. Among Druid orders, the summer solstice is called Mean Samhraidh by the ODU, Grianstod by the ADF, Alban Heruin by OBOD, and Alban Hefin (light of the shore) by other Druids.

The summer solstice on June 21 or 22 is the longest day of the year. At this time, Druids hold their most complex ceremonies, while Wiccans consider this a Lesser Sabbat. For Wiccans, it is a time of blessing the crops so that they may be ready to harvest by Lughnasad, the next Greater Sabbat.

Some Druids, starting at midnight on the eve of the summer solstice, hold vigil through the night around the solstice fire. A dawn ceremony marks the time of the sun's rising. At noon, a further ceremony is held.

A Druid summer solstice ritual written by Todd Covert for Ravens Cry Grove of the ADF serves as an example.[37] At this ritual, offerings of grain and other food were made to the hallows, and offerings of silver were made to the well, oil to the fire, and water from the well to the bilé. The bilé was anointed with fragrant oil. A Druid poured ale in the well for the ancestors and set the remainder in the cup on the altar. Flowers or fruit were placed among the hallows for the spirits of the land. Oil was poured on the fire for the Shining Ones. A large god-mask made of straw was brought forth in honor of Miach, his sister Airmid, and their father, the healer Diancecht. One of the Druids stepped forward with a sword and slashed the mask open. The participants were urged to tear the straw of the great mask apart and cast it on the fire. An effigy of the Green Man* made of herbs on a litter† was revealed when this action was completed. A Druid offered an explanation of the various herbs and their properties. The gates of the ritual site were then opened, and the people processed out with the Green Man before them. Upon reaching a suitable patch of earth,

---

*   A representation of the male energy in nature.

†   A flat supporting framework, such as a piece of canvas stretched between parallel shafts, for carrying a disabled or dead person; a stretcher.

the people were given an opportunity to offer praise offerings. The main offering consisted of having the people scatter the herbs, asking whatever they
wished in return. The seer then consulted ogham or runes to read omens. If
an omen was inauspicious, further offerings could be made and a second omen
taken. If the omen was again unfavorable, the rite would then be ended, with
due thanks made to the Kindreds. As the omen was auspicious, the rite pro-
ceeded and the participants processed back to the hallows. The waters of life
(ale) were circulated. Thanks were then given to the Kindreds, patron powers,
gods, etc. The libation cup was then emptied on the ground. Manannan Mac
Lir was called on to close the gates. A feast followed this celebration.

Lughnasad Misinformation

- In *Schemes of Satan*, Warnke claims that at Lammas, "In some of the older
  religions, the priest kings would be sacrificed in the fields as a part of the
  rituals surrounding Lammas. Lammas is also known as the festival of first
  fruits, and it was believed that the blood of the martyred priest kings would
  provide fertility for the produce of the following year."[38]

The idea of the sacrifice of the king is an old theory put forward by Margaret Murray in the 1920s and picked up by authors such as Robert Graves.
Modern archaeologists and historians have long since debunked it.

- In the *Colorado Bureau of Investigations Questioned Documents Examiner's
  Occult Guide*, the authors correctly define equinox as the "two times a year
  when the sun crosses the celestial equator and when the length of day and
  night are approximately equal." Elsewhere, however, they state, "Other
  important dates are Spring and Summer Equinox celebrations known as
  Beltane and Lammas."[39]

There is no such thing as a summer equinox; the equinoxes occur in spring
and autumn around March 21 and September 21. One can confirm their exact
dates in a given year by contacting a local observatory or by referring to an
astronomical ephemeris.

The Real Lughnasad

Wiccans often refer to Lammas as Lughnasad. This festival is one of the Celtic
fire festivals or cross-quarter days, celebrated on August 1. It is named in
honor of the Celtic Sun God Lugh. Races and games are held in his name and
that of his mother, Tailltiu. Lughnasad is a celebration of the first harvest and
often includes celebrations dedicated to mythical figures such as John Barley-
corn, who represents the life of the grain in the fields. In many areas, this was
the day that the "Lammas lands," those lands belonging to the community and
let to individuals during the summer, reverted to the community. It was a time

to gather hay and reap the wheat and barley. In some areas, a flaming wheel, known as a Catherine wheel, was sent rolling down the hillside to symbolise the descent of the year towards winter, and in Druid ceremonies a wheel is passed around the circle to symbolize the turning year.

In many churches in England, the first corn is still brought into the church on Lammas or the Sunday nearest to it for blessing, perpetuating the ancient custom of honoring the first harvest.

Typical Wiccan and Druid Lughnasad ceremonies involve offerings and partaking of bread, representing the fruits of the first harvest. At one Druid Lughnasad ceremony, written by Ceisiwr Serith of the ADF,[40] this offering of bread came as a loaf in the shape of a bull, a symbol of Crom Dubh.* The loaf was buried in the woods along with offerings of first fruits, with a Druid reciting, "Return, return, return to the unplowed field of which you are rightly lord." A diviner then sat on the mound over these offerings, covered himself with a cloth, and sought divinatory inspiration. At another Druid Lughnasad, grain was offered to Danu in the offering bowl, followed by an invocation to Brighid. Silver was offered to the well, oil to the fire, and incense and water to the bilé. A corn dolly was brought out and carried around the ring. Nine roses were woven into the corn dolly, and it was placed at the foot of the bilé, followed by an invocation to Lugh. A spear decked with greenery and blossoms was brought into the grove. It was carried once round the ring, then stretched over the fire and held there. Finally, the spear was brought out and laved nine times with water, while the following words were spoken:

> May the strength of Lugh be over us,
> May the beauty of Lugh delight us,
> May the skill of Lugh be upon us.
> Be welcome, Shining One, and behold your bride.
> Be welcome, White-Silver One, and succor the earth.
> Be welcome, Hand of Striking, and drive away the hail.
> In the Grove of the Old Ways.
> In the ring of your people.
> In the hearts of all who honor the earth.[41]

---

* Crom Dubh (crooked black) is a minor Celtic fertility God mentioned in the medieval tale "Immram Brain maic Febail (The Voyage of Bran, son of Febal)" book II, page 49 (Dublin, RIA, *Lebor na hUidre*, pp. 121a–24 [originally, f. 78]. Diplomatic edition: 10088-10112), and appears in the Scottish saying: *DiDòmhnaich Crum Dubh, plaoisgidh mi an t-ugh* (Crooked black Sunday, I'll shell the egg). Crom Dubh has come to be used to describe the first Sunday in August in Ireland. I am unaware of any practices that represent this God with loafs shaped like bulls.

Praise offerings, omens, and blessings followed. The waters of life were then hallowed and presented. The grain was hallowed with a loaf of bread brought out on the spear to represent the first loaf of harvest. Half of the loaf was broken into the offering shaft or bowl and the rest shared around the company. After the final blessing, any unused offerings, incense, and water were given to the Earth, with the words: "Mother of all, to you we return all we leave unused. Uphold us now in the world as you have in our rite."

Mabon Misinformation

- In Balsiger's "Satanic" calendar, September 20 is the occasion for a "Midnight Host. Blood ritual."[42]
- In Detective Rimer's "Symptoms Characterizing Occult Ritual Abuse," September 21 is described as involving "FALL EQUINOX Orgies."[43]
- In *Schemes of Satan*, Balsiger's associate Warnke lists "Michaelmas (September 21–22)" as a "Druid celebration."[44]

Neither Mabon, nor any other neo-Pagan festival on this date, involves any sort of blood ritual or orgies. Warnke also needs to check his Christian calendar: Michaelmas is a festival on September 29 held in the British Isles to honor the archangel Michael—and has nothing to do with Druids. In Druid orders, the autumnal equinox is known as Mean Foghamar (autumnal equinox) by the ODU, as An Fhomhair by the ADF, and as Alban Elfed (light of the water) by OBOD.

The Real Mabon

Wiccans call the autumnal equinox "Mabon," after the Celtic Deity, son of Modron (mother), who is mentioned in the story of Culhwch and Olwen. His name translates simply as "son." The festival is also known as Harvest Home or Alban Elved. Mabon is a Lesser Sabbat and the third and last harvest festival of the Wiccan calendar. It is a time of thanksgiving for the bounty of the earth that will sustain the people through the winter.

Mabon is the second of the Celtic harvest festivals. It marks the end of harvest time, just as Lughnasad marked its beginning. Both Wiccan and Druid ceremonies on this date give thanks for the fruits of the earth and for the goodness of the Mother Goddess. It is a time of canning and drying the fruits of the harvest and drying the herbs needed in the winter months.

NOTES

1. John Frattarola, "Passport Magazine Special Edition: America's Best Kept Secret," 7.
2. Bill Schnoebelen, "Saints Alive In Jesus," in *Halloween: Tis The Season To Be Evil* (1990), 3.
3. *Colorado Bureau of Investigations Questioned Documents Examiner's Occult Guide*, 114.
4. Don Rimer, "Symptoms Characterizing Occult Ritual Abuse," http://www.ogia.net/oklahoma%20gang%20investigators'%20association/occult/htm.
5. The Prophecy Club, http://www.prophecyclub.com/text2/pc-video.htm.
6. *Random House Webster's Unabridged Dictionary*, 2nd ed.
7. Robert K. Barnhart, ed., *Barnhart Dictionary of Etymology* (New York: H.W. Wilson, 1988), 1255.
8. Ibid., 170.
9. Phillip Carr-Gomm, *Elements of the Druid Tradition* (London: Element Books, 1996).
10. Rev. Robert Lee "Skip" Ellison, 2001 Yule Ritual for Muin Mound Grove of the ADF, http://www.muinmound.org/Rituals/Yule_Ritual.htm.
11. ADF, Yule Ritual, designed by the members of the Shadow Weaver Grove (now defunct) for presentation on December 16, 1989, http://groups.msn.com/thewoodedway/adruidyuleritual.msnw.
12. Valan, 2003 Yule Ritual, composed in 1999 for the Little Acorn Grove of ADF and performed by the Moonpath Chapter of CUUPS, http://moonpathcuups.org/rituals/yule03.htm.
13. Ibid.
14. Frattarola.
15. David Balsiger, *1988 Witchcraft/Satanism Ritual Calendar*, 2.
16. Phillip Carr-Gomm, *Elements of the Druid Tradition* (London: Element Books, 1996).
17. Grove of the Great Dragon, http://groveofthegreatdragon.web.officelive.com/imbolc.aspx.
18. Susa Morgan Black, http://druidry.org/obod/festivals/imbolc/imbolc_susa/ritual.html.
19. Keith Morse,"Questions and Answers on Wicca: A Christian Perspective on Witchcraft," *Personal Freedom Outreach Newsletter* 3:4 (October–December 1983), 4.
20. Frattarola.
21. The Prophecy Club, http://www.prophecyclub.com/text2/pc-video.htm.
22. Barnhart, ed., 311.
23. Aquarian Tabernacle Church, http://www.aquatabch.org/spring-mysteries-festival.
24. Oak and Feather Grove, "2004 Druid Alban Eilir Rite," held at local caves called the Fairy Holes, http://www.druidnetwork.org/rites/seasonal/groverites/eilir-oaf.html.
25. Lyle J. Rapacki, *Satanism: The Not So New Problem* (Intel, 1988), 55.
26. Michael Warnke, *Schemes of Satan* (Victory House, 1991), 131.
27. Shane Westhoelter, *General Information Manual With Respect to Satanism and the Occult* (National Information Network, 1989), 113.
28. Lou Sloat, *Texas Ritualistic Crime Information Network Occult Crime Manual*, 14.
29. Christina Hole, *British Folk Customs* (Hutchinson, 1976), 137.
30. The Center for Non-Traditional Religion, "Wicca and Paganism: A Rebirth of the Religion of the Mother Goddess," 9.
31. Valan, the Druid, Moonpath Chapter of Cups, "A Druid Bealtaine Ritual" (2004), http://moonpathcuups.org/rituals/belt04.htm.
32. Warnke.
33. Sloat.

34. David Balsiger, *1988 Witchcraft/Satanism Ritual Calendar,* 3.

35. John Frattarola, "Passport Magazine Special Edition: America's Best Kept Secret," 7.

36. Don Rimer, "Symptoms Characterizing Occult Ritual Abuse," http://www.ogia.net/oklahoma%20gang%20investigators'%20association/occult.htm.

37. Todd Covert, Raven's Cry Grove, Summer Solstice, http://www.adf.org/rituals/celtic/midsummer/rcgsummersolstice.html.

38. Warnke, 131.

39. *Colorado Bureau of Investigations Questioned Documents Examiner's Occult Guide,* 2.

40. Ceisiwr Serith, "A Celtic Lughnasad Module," http://www.adf.org/rituals/celtic/lughnassadh/cei-lughnasad.html.

41. Stone Creek Grove, ADF, Rite of Lughnasad: Feast Day of Lugh Samildanach, http://www.stonecreed.org/rituals/lughnassadh.htm.

42. Balsiger, 5.

43. Rimer.

44. Warnke.

PART TWO

NORSE/GERMANIC
PAGANISM

Heathens

Odin among the Aesir, Dvalin (sleeper) among dwarfs, Dáin (dead)
among alfs, Alvitter (all-knowing) among etins, I myself carved some
for mankind.
—The Hávamál

Ásatrú is one name for the modern-day revival of the pre-Christian religion of the Germanic tribes of northern Europe. Its roots can be found in
cultures existing from the Bronze Age to about 1300 CE. The religion is
drawn from surviving literature and current history, archaeology, and sociol-
ogy. Other names for this spiritual path include Vanatru, Odinism/Wodenism,
Irminsul, Theodism, Forn Sed, Germanic/Teutonic Paganism, Skertru, the Elder Trow, the Folkway, and the Northern Way. For the sake of simplicity, I'm
going to use the term Ásatrú unless referring to a specific path. The followers
of spirituality based on Germanic or Norse myths and customs prefer to use
the terms Heathenism, Heathenry, or Heithni rather than the term Paganism
to distinguish their path from Wicca and Druidism.

The Norse/Germanic peoples settled an area from Iceland to Russia, from
Scandinavia to the Mediterranean. They included the Angles and Saxons, Lom-
bards and Heruli, and Goths and Vikings.

Christians targeted the ancient religions of the Norse and Germanic peoples in an attempt to eradicate them. These ancient beliefs held out longest
in Iceland, which did not convert officially to Christianity until 1000 CE. The
Christian historians that followed often portrayed the Vikings and other Norse/
Germanic peoples as barbarians, but it was these Norse peoples who brought
us the concepts of trial by jury, parliaments, and Anglo-Saxon common law.
The Germanic and Norse civilizations, like the Celts, upheld the rights of
women. For example, women could own property, and they could be warriors
or clergy.

Unlike the Celts, whose traditions and stories were documented by the
early Christian clergy in the British Isles, many of the myths and stories of Ger-

manic and Norse religions were lost. None of their folklore was documented until historian and skald (poet or bard) Snorri Sturluson began collecting Norse sagas and legends two hundred years later.* Sturluson's *The Snorri* or *Prose Edda* became an important source for followers of Germanic and Norse spirituality. A collection of eddas by Snorri and others inspired by him surfaced in the 1600s: *The Elder Edda* or *Poetic Edda*. *The Poetic Edda* presents the cosmogony, the mythological lays, and the story of Sigurd and Brynhild. This text later became the "Lay of the Nibelungs." *The Younger Edda* is a prose synopsis of Ásatrú beliefs.

Some scholars believe that some of the eddas were strongly influenced by the Bible. An example is the myth of Ragnarok, the final apocalyptic battle of the gods. Many scholars believe this story imitates the book of Revelation with its end-time references. Heathens do not consider the eddas to be scripture in the same way, however, that Christianity, Judaism, and Islam have books of scripture. The eddas and sagas documenting their myths are used as a source of inspiration, but these myths are not treated as literal history in the way some Christians treat the Bible. Like other neo-Pagan spiritual paths, Ásatrú has been modified by recent discoveries and advancements in archeology and historical research.

---

*   Snorri lived 1179 to 23 September 1241.

Chapter Twelve

Ásatrú

Woden, we are awed by thy craft,
Tiw, we stay true to thee forever,
Baldur, thy brightness and boldness guide us,
Frigga, thy fruit and wisdom keep us all,
Idunna, thine apples ward our ways,
Thunar, thy thunder wards our stead,
Freia, we get freedom from thy frolic;
Frei, from thee we get a harvest of frith.
—Edred Thorsson, Midsummer blessing, *Northern Magic* (p. 49)

Like the Pagan paths growing out of Celtic myths, such as Wicca and Druidism, the Heathen spiritual paths were influenced by the romantic movement in art and literature in the 1800s. Unfortunately for Heathens, Hitler used the myths of Norse/Germanic mythology to justify his dictatorship and motivate his followers. Hitler wasn't a Heathen; he only used the mythology to support his political agenda. This usage cast a pall over Heathen spirituality for decades after World War II. Influenced by Hitler, some modern white supremacists unfortunately still use Norse or Germanic mythology to dress up their hateful practices.

In the 1970s, Sveinbjorn and Thorsteinn Gudjonsson approached the Icelandic government, known as the Althing, to demand that Ásatrú be recognized. After much debate—and a lightning bolt struck the house of the Minister of Religious Affairs (lightning is very rare in Iceland)—Ásatrú was recognized as an official religion of Iceland on par with the other state religion, Lutheranism. Meanwhile, in the United States, Steve McNallen, Maddy Hutter, and a handful of other people interested in Heathen spirituality were working to revive Ásatrú. They pieced together their modern practice by studying ancient sagas, eddas, and supporting historical documents, and the Ásatrú Free Assembly (AFA) was born.

In the early 1970s, the AFA formed the first kindreds* in the United States (which the Ásatrúar refer to as Vinland). At that time, there was also an Odinist Fellowship (OF). The AFA and OF eventually disbanded. Two kindreds survive from this time: the Arizona Kindred and the Wulfing Kindred. There are about one hundred kindreds in the United States today.[1] Under the direction of leaders such as Garman Lord, Theodish and Anglo-Saxon versions of Heathenism have also appeared since 1976.

Ásatrú tended towards patriarchy until the 1990s, when the influence of female leaders such as Freya Aswyn, Prudence Priest, and Diana Paxson revived female power in Norse Paganism. This change has created some tension within the Heathen community. Paxton, former Steerswoman of the Troth, states:

> Today the major tension is between those who consider themselves "Folkish," and believe that Germanic religion should be practiced by those who are of Germanic descent, and the "Universalists," who believe that the Germanic Gods may be worshipped by anyone who is attracted to them. Although women and gay men are more likely to be found as leaders among the latter, there are many women and gay men in the Folkish camp as well.[2]

Ásatrú, means "true to the *Æsir*" or "belief in the gods" in Old Norse. The followers of Ásatrú are known as Ásatrúar. Grammatical rules would suggest that the plural should be Ásatrúarar, but in practice Ásatrúar is used for both singular and plural forms.

Organization

The Ásatrúar organize themselves into groups, variously referred to as kindreds, hearths, garths, steadings, and hofs. Hearth comes from the Middle English (900 CE) *herth*. Hearth was derived from similar Germanic terms such as the German *herd* and the Danish *haard*. Garth is derived from the Old Norse/ Middle English (1300–1350 CE) *garthr* ("farm," "farmyard," "courtyard"). The hearth or garth is a single-family unit and the smallest unit of Ásatrú organization. *Hof* is a German word whose meanings include yard, courtyard, farm, country house, manor, palace, court, ring, or circle. "Steading" is an old term from Scotland and Northern England (1425–75) for a farm and its buildings. A hof or steading may consist of several garths or hearths. If they share a manor house or "hof," it is aligned north-south, if possible. If not, their *stalli* (altar) is aligned north-south. Some Ásatrúar refer to a group of hofs as a kindred.

---

*   Earlier in the book I said that Druids used the term Kindreds to refer to gods, spirits, and ancestors. The term kindreds, as used by Ásatrúar, refers to Ásatrú groups. Later we'll discuss some of the other terms used in Ásatrú.

Worldview

The Ásatrúar are inspired by the universe around them, which they consider to be one manifestation of the underlying Divine Essence. The other manifestation is the universe within them, passed down from the ancestors as instinct, emotion, predispositions, and memories. Modern Ásatrúar seek to live a free and productive life using tales of their ancestors and deities to inspire them. Ásatrú is polytheistic; however, the Ásatrú do not pray to their gods—that is to say, they do not surrender their will to deities or humble themselves before them. The Ásatrú see themselves as kin to the gods, not as inferior servants. The Ásatrúar commune with Divinity and honor the gods, seeking their blessing through formal rites and informal meditation. Most Heathens, like Wiccans, do not use the term "worship" to describe their religious practices. "Worship" implies subservience and separation from the Divine. While Heathens honor their ancestors and gods, they believe that their fate is in their own hands. Rather than praying for intervention, they pray for inspiration and guidance.

Ásatrú Deities

The principal deities of Ásatrú are

Odin: Father of the gods, patron of wisdom and poetry;
Thor: god of strength and might, defender of the gods and men;
Frigga: Mother of the gods, protector of family and children;
Tyr: a one-handed god renowned for sacrifice, valor, and prowess in battle;
Balder: the most beautiful of the gods, soft-spoken and bold;
Skadi: a huntress goddess of the mountains;
Heimdal: the watchman guarding the rainbow bridge to the realm of the gods;
Idun: the goddess who keeps the magick apples that renew the gods' youth;
Freya: a warrior goddess of love, fertility, and procreation;
Frey: a virile fertility god, patron of love, joy, and prosperity;
Njord: a sea god, patron of maritime pursuits.[3]

All but the last three on this list are of the Æsir. The last three are of the Vanir* (see Appendix B).

Ásatrúar believe in nature spirits called wights. They make offerings to house and land wights. Typically these offerings consist of milk, grain or porridge, honey, and mead or beer left on the altar. Yule tree ornaments are considered to be honorary offerings to the wights. Often wights are honored before and after taking trips with "land-leaving" and "land-taking" ceremonies.

---

*   The Vanir (singular *Vanr*) are gods of fertility and wisdom who reside in Vanaheimr with the Æsir.

Ásatrú Code of Ethics

The Ásatrúar subscribe to several ethical codes.* One of the simplest and oldest is called the Three Wynns. Garman Cyning of the Theodish Belief formulated the Three Wynns Code. The Three Wynns are

- Wisdom: adherence to the ancient wisdoms of our religion;
- Worthmind: the maintenance of a personal sense of honor;
- Wealthdeal: generosity with one's family and friends.

Another common code of ethics in Ásatrú/Odinist circles is the Nine Noble Virtues, which were codified by Odinic Rite founders John Yeowell (Stubba) and John Gibbs-Bailey (Hoskuld) in the early 1970s:[4]

- Courage: standing by one's principles in the face of fear
- Truth: being committed to the truth and seeing things as they are
- Honor: being ever mindful of how one's actions reflect on the community. Maintaining one's reputation and respect
- Loyalty: keeping oaths
- Hospitality: helping one another within and without the community
- Industriousness: living life to the fullest through building and creating
- Perseverance: seeing things through to completion
- Self-Discipline: taking responsibility for one's actions
- Self-Reliance: living and acting on one's strengths and assets

Another ethical code is the Six-Fold Goal:

- Right: The justice of law shaped by the lore of the Ásatrúar and administered with good judgment by those who can see the truth. Right is a call for the rule of rationality and enlightenment in the world.
- Wisdom: An ability to see and to understand (linked to memory)
- Might: Defense of harvest and frith (see below), governed by the first two goals (Right and Wisdom)
- Harvest: The reaping of things in the cycles of nature. It relates to plenty, wealth, and physical well-being. This includes all manner of economic pursuits.
- Frith: A complex concept that I will discuss in a separate section that follows.
- Love: The intrinsic desire to live. It is the pure force of life that is embodied in play and pleasure.[5]

---

* My Ásatrú friends shared most of these with me directly.

Another code is the Nine Charges of Odin, which, along with the Nine Noble Virtues, are part of the "Havamal," a first century poem. The Nine Charges are

- to maintain candor and fidelity in love and devotions to the tried friend: Though he strike me, I will do him no scathe;
- never to make a wrongsome oath: for great and grim is the reward for the breaking of plighted troth;
- to deal not hardly with the humble and lowly;
- to remember the respect that is due great age;
- to suffer no evil to go unremedied and to fight against the enemies of family, nation, race, and faith: my foes will I fight in the field nor be burnt in my house;
- to succor the friendless but to put no faith in the pledged word of a stranger people;
- if I hear the fool's word of a drunken man, I will strive not: for many a grief and the very death groweth out of such things;
- to give kind heed to dead men: straw-dead, sea-dead, or sword-dead;
- to abide by the enactments of lawful authority and to bear with courage and fortitude the decrees of the Norns.

Another code is the Twelve Ætheling Thews (or Thews). These were formulated in recent years and first appeared in the work *Beyond Good and Evil: Wyrd and Germanic Heathen Ethics*. They reflect the movement in the Ásatrú community towards family and community. The Twelve Thews are

- Boldness: bravery, courage in the face of adversity;
- Steadfastness: tenacity, the refusal to give up;
- Troth: fealty, faith, fidelity. Loyalty to one's tribe, friends, and family;
- Givefullness: generosity, the ability to give to others at the appropriate times;
- Gestening, guestliness: hospitality, or the ability to be kind with guests;
- Sooth: truth, the avoidance of lies;
- Wrake: justice, or the drive to always see the wrongs done one's tribe corrected;
- Evenhead: equality. The recognition that those of the opposite sex are equal;
- Friendship: the ability to treat those that one calls friend as family;
- Freedom: self-reliance and perseverance as well as responsibility for one's actions;

- Wisdom: adherence to the ancient wisdom of our religion and the use of it in life;
- Busyship/workhardiness: industriousness or the ability to work hard.

The most recent list of Thews appears in Eric Wodening's book *We Are Our Deeds: The Elder Heathenry, Its Ethic and Thew* (1998). Wodening's list of Thews includes the following concepts:

- *Bisignes*: industriousness
- *Efnes*: equality, equal justice for all
- *Ellen*: courage
- *Geférscipe*: community awareness, putting the good of the community above one's self
- *Giefu*: generosity
- *Giestlíthness*: hospitality
- *Metgung*: moderation or self control
- *Selfdóm*: the ability to be an individual, true to one's self
- *Sóth*: truth, honesty
- *Stedefæstnes*: steadfastness
- *Tréowth*: troth or loyalty
- *Wísdóm*: wisdom

Frith and Troth

Frith is a concept variously defined as happiness from within or joy from productivity and/or duty. While there are points of similarity among all of the above lists, frith rarely seems to appear, perhaps due to its complex nature. It is an important and universal concept that is usually considered separately. Troth and frith are both very important concepts to Heathens. Althing Canada writes, "Troth refers to loyalty, staying true, in the way that one might refer to staying true to one's spouse or one's ideals. Frith refers to peace and the interconnected web of a healthy community. Frith is boosted by such things as friendship, gift exchanging, and coming to the aid of one's community when they are in need."[6]

Ásatrúar Rachel Watkins describes frith as "protection, sanctuary, asylum, security, safety and reconciliation."[7] Ásatrú scholar Yngona Wisniewski defines frith as "maintaining security and refuge of the community."[8] Gary Penzler, an Ásatrú author from Burlington, Ontario, defines it as "the web of peace and interdependence in a happy, functioning society."[9]

Orlog and Wyrd

Like other Pagans, Heathens do not believe in the concept of original sin. Nor do Heathens proselytize. Heathens believe in a natural cause-and-effect relationship between "wyrd" and "orlog." Althing Canada defines them as follows:

Wyrd is the sum of the deeds of each Heathen's life, and that of their ancestors and anyone to whom they have sworn an oath. Orlog is the process of natural laws by which wyrd is rebalanced—those who do good deeds can expect good to come to them in turn, and ill deeds will bring ill of one kind or another, either to the individual or even to their children, if their debt is not paid in their own lifetime. In this way, the past leads to a most likely future, but through the conscientious effort of rebalancing wyrd him- or herself, a Heathen can affect his or her own orlog, choosing to voluntarily pay their own debts.[10]

Heathens consider oaths to be a sacred matter. In Ásatrú, any promise made, especially in the context of a holy ritual, is a serious commitment to the gods. The words of the spoken oath go directly into that Heathen's wyrd. If the oath is not honored, the resulting orlog may bring about disaster. Oaths sworn to a community, even if they concern small matters, are the bonds that tie a community together in frith. They foster bonds of friendship, trust, marriage, responsibility, and dependability. The Heathen believe that a community cannot exist without oaths. The consequences of broken oaths are a frequent subject of Heathen myths.

Hamingja

Hamingja is the spiritual power of the Ásatrúar. One's hamingja accumulates over time. Some Ásatrúar speak of being on this earth to learn and accumulate hamingja. When Ásatrúar die, their hamingja is left to their kin, and they go to rejoin their ancestors in a sort of collective pool. When children are born, they take some of this collective soul pool with them, accumulating hamingja until they, in turn, pass on to the ancestors.

Afterlife

Many Ásatrúar believe in an afterlife, though they do not subscribe to the dual system of heaven and hell one finds in Christianity. In Ásatrú, some who die in battle are chosen by Odin to live in his hall, Valhalla, and become members of his army of *einherjar* (single warriors) at Ragnarok. Others are taken by Freyja to live in her palace, Sessrumnir. Thralls (slaves) and those chosen by Thor go to live in his hall, Bilskirnir. There are several other halls of the gods that can also be destinations. People who do not distinguish themselves or prove themselves live on in Hel. Hel is a dark and dreary place, but not a place of torture or torment. Evildoers, such as criminals, adulterers, oathbreakers, and slayers of their brothers wind up in Nifhelheim, a place of infinite cold.

The Gothar and Althing

The *gothar* are the collective priesthood of the Ásatrú community. A priest is known as a *gothi* and a priestess as a *gythia*. Heathens do not believe that they require the gothar as a means to communicate with Divinity; they all have direct access. The gothar, however, are particularly skilled at leading rituals, though individual Heathens may lead their own. They were instrumental in the development of a form of government known as the Althing (or Thing). The Althing was a gathering at which the gothar met annually to discuss law and settle disputes. "The Thing" is defined by *The Dictionary of Northern Mythology* as "The legislative and executive assembly of free men in Germanic antiquity ... In the free state of Iceland, the Althing was the latter-day successor of the Germanic Thing and was a proper legislative and jurisdictional parliament."[11] The Thing site was protected by a marked boundary, such as a rope strung around poles. Those entering the Thing boundary were bound by tribal law to respect the proceedings and conduct themselves in a dignified manner. The three main elements of a Thing are

- the recitation of the Law, pronouncement of sentences, issuance of summons, and public announcements;
- judicial proceedings and decisions about the validity of Law, and the Law Council;
- the audience of Thing people (the Folk).[12]

Well-known ancient Thing sites include Frosta and Gula in Norway, Uppsala and Skara in Sweden, Viborg and Oresund in Denmark, and Thingvellir in Iceland.

The first Althing was held at Thingvellir in the year 1180 RE (Runic Era)* and was believed to be a continuation of the Norwegian Thing presided over by Law Speaker Thorleif the Wise. The three Icelanders who were given credit for the founding of the Althing in Iceland are Ulfljotr, Goat Hair, and Thorsteinn Ingolfsson, who was the son of the first settler of Iceland.

In the year 2230 RE, Steve McNallen held the First Annual Althing of the

---

* The Runic Era calendar used in Ásatrú was created based on the age of the oldest known runic artifact, which is dated 250 BCE. Ásatrúar fix this date as the time when Odin revealed the Runes to the Ásatrú, and count that as year 0 RE. The abbreviation RE stands for "Runic Era." The runic era calendar therefore adds two hundred and fifty years to a given date. So the year 2012 in our Western calendar would be 2262 RE.

AFA in Northern California. This first national gathering became a tradition that continues to this day. In the year 2237 RE, the Ásatrú Free Assembly was dissolved. Seven surviving kindreds of the late AFA worked together to continue the Althings and Ásatrú. In the late summer of 2237 RE, they drafted a set of bylaws and invited every known Ásatrúar in the country to an Althing to discuss and vote on them. On Midyear 18, 2238 RE, Valgard Murray and Thorsteinn Thorarinsson formally opened Althing 8 with a Tyr *blót*. This event marked the foundation of The Ásatrú Alliance. The Annual Althing of The Ásatrú Alliance of Independent Kindreds continues to this day.

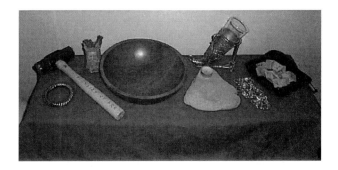

Stalli

Many Ásatrúar have altars or *stalli* in their homes. The picture above depicts a typical stalli.

The Blót

The principle religious observance of Ásatrú is the *blót*. *Blót* translates as "offering." In ancient times, this ritual involved the sacrifice of an animal, which was then prepared and eaten. The animal's blood was captured in a bowl called the *blótbolli*. The gothi presiding would asperge the assembled people and the walls of the temple with this blood using a twig called the *hlaut-teinn*. The blótbolli would then be poured out on the stone altar. A modern blót involves offering gifts to the gods in exchange for their blessings. Modern Heathens have replaced this blood ritual with an offering of drink, usually mead. Often a nonalcoholic alternative will also be provided. There are four types of blóts:[13]

- Seasonal blóts: celebrations of the cycles of the year, including Yule, Oestara, Walburga, Midsummer, Winter's Finding, and Winter Nights (more on these below).

- Deity-specific blóts: recognizing individual deites or classes of deities. Examples include the Feast of Vali, Thorrablot, Tyrsblot, Freyfaxi, and Disablot.

- Ancestral blóts: honoring the memory of ancestors and famous people. Examples include the Feast of the Einherjar and Lindisfarne Day.
- Personal blessings: marking rites of passage (births, funeral services, and weddings). They are also used to ask the gods for assistance.

A blót can be as simple as offering libations of ale to house wights and as complex as a seasonal celebration like Yule. Typically a blót involves the following steps:

- Preparation of sacred space: A hammer working or warding is often performed to sanctify the sacred space. A hammer representing Mjolnir (see glossary) is held aloft and swung, shaken, or waved in the pattern of an equal-armed cross at each of the cardinal directions as well as above and below. As the gothi or gythia turns in a circle, they announce that they are making the stead holy for kin and gods and wights, and announces that any who wish to break frith or cause harm, man or wight, should fear Mjolnir's wrath (at this point striking the ground with the hammer). If a hammer is not available, a fist may be held aloft to represent it.
- Reading: portions of the eddas, sagas, or Norse myths are recited to remind the celebrants of their past, as well as to build an understanding of Ásatrú lore.
- Rede: a statement of the purpose of the blót.
- Invocation or call: an invitation to the deities who are the subject of the blót.
- Hallowing: the beverage to be used for the libation is sanctified.
- Blessing: the asperging of the attendees, which is a symbolic blessing from the deity invoked.
- Sharing: The beverage is passed around to each participant. Each is allowed to speak a hail over the drinking horn in a procedure similar to the Sumbel Ceremony (see below). The leftover drink is poured into the blótbolli.
- Offering: the leftover beverage in the blótbolli is poured out on the ground as a libation to the deities to whom the blót is dedicated.
- Leaving or closing: the celebrants take formal leave of the deities and the ritual area is desanctified.

The Sumbel Ceremony

The sumbel (also known as a symbel or samal) is a toasting ritual consisting of three rounds. In the first round, each person hails a god or goddess, followed by the recitation of a personal story or information about this deity. Anything said over the drinking horn must be true. The person then drinks from the drinking horn or cup (or kisses the rim if they don't want to imbibe alcohol) and passes the horn to the next person in a clockwise direction. Some Heathens will not hail Loki, the trickster god, while others have no problem with this. It is considered wrong to hail the jotunar, as they are the enemies of the gods. In the second round, each person toasts ancestors and heroes. The third round consists of an oath, boast, or toast. Oaths must be serious. A boast can be of accomplishments or objectives. A toast can be to a person, the host of the sumbel, or one of the Nine Noble Virtues.

Symbols

Mjolnir

The Mjolnir or Thor's hammer is the principal symbol of Ásatrú. In Norse mythology, Thor is the son of Odin, and the god of the sky and thunder. Thursday is named after him. It was believed that lightning is the sparks created when Thor strikes his anvil with his hammer, Mjolnir. It was also believed that Thor uses Mjolnir to break up the ice in spring. Decorated replicas of this hammer were often worn as amulets, and many followers of Ásatrú wear the hammer as a symbol of their religion. Many Heathens will use a hammer as one of their ritual tools to create sacred space.

I have frequently encountered 'occult experts' who couldn't tell a Greek labrys from a Norse hammer. Some can tell them apart but think that they're both satanic. For example, Detective Don Rimer's *Ritual Crime and the Occult: The New Youth Subculture* includes "the Thor's Hammer" in its list of "Satanic symbols."

The Troth Ring

The oath ring or troth ring is another essential ritual tool in Ásatrú. It is a solid gold or silver ring used for the swearing of oaths and also as a symbol of priesthood. It is worn on the wrist of the gothi at all kindred blóts, sumbels, and functions, and it is often displayed on the stalli when not in use. Swearing of oaths on the troth ring symbolizes the unending nature of the oath. To use a troth ring or oath ring, one simply holds it and says aloud the oath being sworn. If two people were swearing oath together, as in a marriage rite, both would hold the ring, which may also be held by a gothi or gythia.

The Valknut

The symbol of the *valknut*, also known as the *valknot*, is "Hrungnir's heart" or the "knot of the slain." Hrungnir was a legendary giant of the eddas. The valknut appears on many ancient Norse stone carvings and funerary monuments. Like the pentagram used by Wiccans, the valknut can be drawn unicursally (in one stroke of the pen) and has become a popular talisman of protection. The valknut's three interlocking triangles and nine points are symbolic of rebirth, fertility, and reincarnation. The nine points also connect it with the nine worlds and nine Fates of Norse mythology. The interlocking triangles reflect the interrelatedness of earth, Hel, and the heavens. Another, modern version of the valknut, called a triceps, resembles a cutaway triangle or a triangle formed of three diamonds (three *othala* runes interwoven).

Other common symbols used by Heathens include:

- Solar wheel/Odin's cross: The solar cross is probably the oldest religious symbol in the world, appearing in Asian, American, European, and Indian religious art. Composed of an equal-armed cross within a circle, it represents the solar calendar—the movements of the sun, marked by the solstices. Sometimes the equinoxes are marked as well, giving an eight-armed wheel. (The swastika is a form of solar cross.)
- The sun cross: In its most simplified form it is known in Northern Europe as Odin's cross, after the chief God of the Norse pantheon. The Ásatrúar often use it as an emblem. The word "cross" itself comes from the Old Norse word for this symbol: *kros*.

- Celtic cross: a symbol of the Celtic Christian Church, which they borrowed from the pre-Christian Celtic Pagan emblem of the Sun God Taranis.

- *Irminsul*: a solar-phallic pillar used in religious practices by early Anglo-Saxons. Charlemagne destroyed it in 772 CE. Its exact meaning is unknown, although it may be connected with the Anglo-Saxon deity Irmin, who is possibly related to the Norse God Tyr (a theory supported by the shape of the rune letter *tyr*, which resembles the shape of the irminsul). The irminsul was likely related to the World Tree Yggdrasil, a symbol of the *axis mundi* (world axis), representing humanity and the cosmos. Modern irminsuls usually consist of an upright pole or cross, symbolizing the union of earth with the heavens, and are often surmounted or hung with a solar wheel or sun cross.

- *Aegishjálmr*: The term *ægishjálmr* translates as "helm of awe" or "helm of terror." It appears in various sagas. Originally, it probably didn't refer to a physical helmet, but rather a type of magick called *seidr*. Seidr was used to cause forgetfulness, delusion, illusion, or fear. The ægishjálmr was a type of seidr magick called *sjónhverfing*, a magical delusion or "deceiving of the sight" that affects what is seen. Seidr is well documented in the sagas, often being used to conceal a person from his or her pursuers. Sagas in which the ægishjálmr appears include the *Eyrbyggja Saga* (Chapter Twenty), the *Reykdoela Saga* (Chapter Fourteen), and the *Njáls Saga* (Chapter Twelve). A related magick was the technique called the *hulidshjálmr*, the helmet of hiding or invisibility. The method for invoking the hulidshjálmr varied, but included placing hands atop the head of the person to be concealed or throwing magical powders over them. The most famous appearance of the ægishjálmr is in *Volsungasaga* (Chapter Eighteen):

And Fáfnir said, "An ægishjálmr I bore up before all folk, after that I brooded over the heritage of my brother, and on every side did I spout out poison, so that none dared come near me, and of no weapon was I afraid, nor ever had I so many men before me, as that I deemed myself not stronger than all; for all men were greatly afraid of me." Sigurd said, "Few may have victory by means of that same ægishjálmr, for whoever comes among many shall one day find that no one man is by so far the mightiest of all."

It was believed that Fáfnir wore the ægishjálmr symbol on his forehead, between his eyes.

- The ægishjálmr was also a common magickal symbol in the Middle Ages in Iceland. It was believed that this symbol should be cut into lead and then thrust between one's eyebrows before reciting, "Ægishjalm *eg ber milli bruna mjer*" (Ægishjalm I carry between my brows). This practice was believed to assure victory in battle. Richard Wagner used the idea of the "helm of awe" in his Ring Cycle, where the ægishjálmr appears as the Tarnhelm, which makes the wearer invisible and gives him or her the ability to shape-shift.

- The Norse alphabet, the characters of which are called runes, is extremely important to Ásatrúar. The Runic alphabet is over 2,200 years old and was the first written language among the Germanic tribes. The runic alphabet is known as the *Futhark*, as this is what the first few letters of that alphabet spell. Some Ásatrúar use runes as a basis for the Ásatrú calendar, with dates reckoned according to the Runic Era (RE). One of the most popular forms is the use of runes for divination or magical writing. The *Hávamál* tells the story of how Odin sacrificed himself on the World Tree.

> I know that I hung on Yggdrasil
> For nine nights long
> Wounded by spear
> Consecrated to Odin
> Myself a sacrifice to myself
> Upon that tree
> The wisest know not the roots
> of ancient times whence it sprang.
>
> None brought me bread
> None gave me mead
> Down to the depths I searched
> I took up the Runes
> Raised them with song
> And from that tree I fell.
>
> Runes you shall know, and readable staves,
> Very powerful staves, very great staves
> Graven by the mighty one who speaks
> Carved by the highest hosts

Odin in among the Aesir,
Dvalin (sleeper) among dwarfs,
Dáin (dead) among alfs,
Alvitter (all-knowing) among etins,
I myself carved some for mankind[14]

Rites of Passage

Following the birth of a child, a naming ceremony is often held. This takes place when the baby is nine days old. The parents formally name their child and bring him or her into their community. The ceremony consists of consecrating water in the names of the gods, anointing the child using an evergreen twig as an aspergillum, and providing birth gifts. Sometimes a full blót is held to request blessings for the child.

No special ceremony is required for initiation. Many Heathens choose to swear a holy oath on an oath-ring that they will be true to the gods and goddesses of the North. If they are joining a preexisting kindred, the members may wish the new member to swear an oath of peace and respect to the kindred.

NOTES

1. Valgard Murray, "The Asatru Kindred," http://www.asatru.org/asatrukindreds.php.
2. Isaac Bonewits, *The Pagan Man: Priests, Warriors, Hunters and Drummers* (Citadel Press, 2005).
3. Edred Thorsson, *Northern Magic: Mysteries of the Norse, Germans and English* (St. Paul, MN: Llewellyn Worldwide, 1992) and Bergen Evans, *Dictionary of Mythology* (NY: Dell Publishing, 1970).
4. The Odinic Rite, "The Nine Noble Virtues and Charges of the Odinic Rite," http://www.odinic-rite.org/main/the-nine-noble-virtues-and-charges-of-the-odinic-rite/
5. Edred Thorsson, *A Book of Troth*, 1989.
6. Althing Canada, Ásatrú in Prison, http://www.asatru.ca/?page_id=2.
7. Eric R. Munson, "Some Asatru Philosophy," http://web.archive.org/web/20090322181936/http://www.destinyslobster.com/asatru/philosophy.html
8. Ibid.
9. E-mail to author from Gary Penzler, May 30, 2005.
10. Ibid.
11. Angela Hall and Rudolf Simek, *The Dictionary of Northern Mythology* (Boydell & Brewer, Inc., 1993).
12. Valgard Murray, "Althings: Past, Present and Future," citing Thorsteinn Gudjunsson, *Thingvellir*.
13. Valgard Murray, "The role of the Gothar in the Ásatrú Community," http://www.asatru.org/roleofgothar.php.
14. Unknown, trans., "Hávamál: The Words of Odin the High One, *The Elder* or *Poetic Edda* (*Sæmund's Edda*)," http://researcharea.org/books/Ásatrú_Theology.

Chapter Thirteen

The Ásatrú Calendar

The high gods gathered in council
In their hall of judgment. All the rulers:
To Night and to Nightfall their names gave,
The Morning they named and the Mid-Day,
Mid-Winter, Mid-Summer, for the assigning of years.
—"Völuspá, Song of the Sybil"[*]

The seasonal blóts of the Ásatrú calendar differ from group to group. Some dates, such as the summer solstice, are fixed. The dates of other celebrations may vary according to seasonal changes. For example, the beginning of spring varies depending on the latitude. The date of the celebration may be two months earlier in Atlanta than it is in Edmonton.

Different Ásatrúar use different systems for naming the months of the year. One system[†] for naming the months is listed below:

January	Snowmoon
February	Horning
March	Lenting
April	Ostara
May	Merrymoon
June	Midyear
July	Haymoon
August	Harvest
September	Shedding
October	Hunting
November	Fogmoon
December	Yule

---

[*] "The Völuspá" or "Prophecy of the Völva" is the first and best-known poem of the Poetic Edda. It tells the story of the creation of the world and its coming end related by a *völva* addressing Odin. It is one of the most important primary sources for the study of Norse mythology.

[†] Assembled from various Ásatrú traditions including The Asatru Alliance.

The calendars of ritual dates also vary from one Heathen organization to the next. Typically Heathen organizations don't have more than a half dozen celebrations throughout the year. The most significant are

- Yule (Júl), the most important of all the celebrations;
- Oestre/Summer Finding: a festival for the arrival of spring;
- Midsummer;
- Winter Finding or Harvest;
- a Feast for the Einherjar around November 11.

The following list contains all of the typical seasonal blóts of the Runic Era calendar as listed by modern Ásatrú organizations:[1]

- January 3: The Ásatrú Alliance lists this date as "Charming of the Plow" or *Idis-Thing*. An agricultural ritual of Northern Europe that can be traced back to ancient times. Grains and cakes are offered for the soil's fertility, and the Sky Father and Earth Mother are invoked.
- January 9: Day of Remembrance for Raud the Strong, a landowner in Norway. King Olaf Tryggvason of Norway had Raud put to death between 995 and 1000 CE for refusing to convert to Christianity due to his loyalty to Ásatrú. Olaf, who was later made a saint by the Church, confiscated Raud's lands and other wealth. Thus, Raud has become a popular figure to modern Ásatrúar.
- January full moon (or the Friday between January 19 and 25): Thorrablot or Thor's Feast. Thorrablot marked the beginning of the Old Norse month of Snorri. This festival, sacred to Thor and the ancient Icelandic winter spirit Thorri, is still observed in Iceland with parties and a Midwinter feast.
- February 2: The Ásatrú Alliance lists this date as "Barri." Other Ásatrú groups list it as "Charming of the Plough" or Idis-Thing. A fertility festival honoring the wooing of the Maiden Gerdr by Ingvi Freyr, a symbolic marriage of the Vanir god of fertility with Mother Earth.
- February 9: Day of Remembrance for Eyvind Kinnrifi. Saint Olaf had Eyvind tortured to death for his steadfast loyalty to the old gods.
- February 14: Feast of Vali. This feast originally celebrated the death of Hothr at the hands of Vali. The Feast of Vali celebrates the return of the light of the sun, triumphing over the dark days of winter. Today it is a traditional celebration of the family and involves the renewal of marriage vows. It is also a time to exchange cards and gifts with loved ones.
- March 9: Day of Remembrance for Oliver the Martyr. Oliver was an adherent of Ásatrú who persisted in organizing underground sacrifices to the gods and goddesses despite decrees by Saint Olaf the Lawbreaker forbidding such

activities. Betrayed by an informer, he was killed by Olaf's men while preparing for the spring sacrifice in the village of Maerin, Norway.

- March 21–23: High Feast of Ostara. This spring equinox festival is similar to the Wiccan festival of Eostre. Ostara marks the end of winter and the beginning of the season of rebirth. Ostara honors Frigga, Freya, and Nerthus with a blót and feast.

- March 28: Ragnar Lodbrok Day. Ragnar was a famous Viking who raided Paris on Easter Sunday in the year 1145 CE.

- April 9: Day of Remembrance for Jarl Hakon of Norway. Hakon was a ruler of Western Iceland who restored the worship of the old gods and cast out the alien religion.

- April Full Moon (or April 17–19): *Sigrblot/Sumarsdag* (Summer's Day). The first day of summer in the Old Icelandic calendar. Sigurd is the mythical hero who wooed the Valkyrie Brynhild and won the treasure of the Nibelungs. In Iceland, the festival had strong agricultural overtones, but elsewhere in the Nordic world it was a time to sacrifice to Odin for victory in summer voyages and battles. The Ásatrú Alliance celebrates Sigrbloot or the Day of Remembrance for Sigurd the Volsung on June 9.

- April 23 (Ásatrú Alliance) or 25: Yggdrasil Day. A celebration of Yggdrasil, the World Tree.

The Real Walpurgis

Saint Walburga, also known as Walpurgis, Vaubourg, or Gauburge, was named for the Goddess Waldborg. Walburga lived between 710 and 779 CE. Born in Wessex, England, she was an abbess and missionary who died in Heidenheim, Alemannia. She and her brothers Willibald of Eichstatt and Winebald of Heidenheim played an important part in Saint Boniface's ordination of the Frankish church.

Walburga was a Benedictine nun in a monastery in Wimborne, Dorsetshire when her brother Winebald brought her to his kingdom to oversee the nuns at the monastery in Heidenheim. When she died, her body was buried in Heidenheim, but was later moved to the Church of the Holy Cross at Eichstatt, arriving there on April 30, a day now known as Walpurgis. Her festival is actually the anniversary of her death, February 25.

Myths later developed claiming that Witches rendezvous in the Harz Mountains nearby on this date. Part of the reason for these myths is that after her death, Walburga's story took on some of the characteristics of her namesake, Waldborg. For example, the rock on which Saint Walburga's bones rest is said to secrete a mysterious fluid reportedly possessing miraculous healing powers.[2]

Because Beltaine, a Celtic festival, traditionally begins on April 30, some people today use the term Walpurgis to describe it. The association of Witches with Walpurgis eventually led to the belief that Walpurgis was a 'satanic' holiday. For example, Anton LaVey names Walpurgis as one of the "Satanic" festivals in his Satanic Bible.

- April 30: Walburg, Walpurgisnacht, or May Eve. This is named for the Norse fertility goddess Waldborg. As with the Celtic/Wiccan festival of May Eve/ Beltaine, it is a time of divination and a celebration of spring.
- May 1/May Day: A spring celebration featuring the Goddess Freya. Maypole dancing and bonfires are important features of this day, as they are with the Wiccan festival of Beltaine.
- May 9: Day of Remembrance for Guthroth/Gudrod of Gudbrandsal. Guthroth was a minor upland king of Iceland who opposed Olaf Tryggvason. Olaf captured and tortured Guthroth.
- May 15: Frigga Blót. A festival in honor of the All Mother Frigga.
- June 8: Lindisfarne Day. On this day in the year 1043 RE (793 CE), three Viking ships raided the Isle of Lindisfarne, officially opening what is known as the Viking Age.
- June 9: Sigrbloot or the Day of Remembrance for Sigurd the Volsung, according to The Ásatrú Alliance.
- June 19: Ásatrú Alliance Founding Day. On this date in 2238 RE, seven kindreds of the former Ásatrú Free Assembly (AFA) joined together by ratifying a set of bylaws to preserve and promote the cause of the AFA and Ásatrú in Vinland.
- June 20: Midsummer. The summer solstice. The traditional time for holding the Althing in ancient times.
- July 4: Founder's Day. Some Ásatrú kindred celebrate this day to honor the founders of modern Ásatrú: H. Rud Mills of Australia, and Sveinbjorn Beinteinsson and Thorsteinn Guthjonson of Iceland.*
- July 9: Day of Remembrance for Unn the Deep-Minded. Unn was a woman from the Laxdaela Saga who immigrated to Scotland to avoid the hostility of King Harald Finehair. She established dynasties in the Orkney and Faroe Islands by carefully marrying off her granddaughters. She later settled in Iceland.
- July 29: Stikklestad Day. Olaf the Lawbreaker (Saint Olaf) was killed at the battle of Stikklestad on this date in the year 1280 RE. Olaf acquired a reputation for killing, maiming, and exiling his fellow Norwegians who would not convert to Christianity.
- August 1: Freyfaxi or Loaf Fest. This date marked the beginning of the harvest in Iceland. It shares many characteristics of the Wiccan festival on this date, Lughnasad. At Freyfaxi, Thor is honored as the father of the fields. Celebrations include sporting events and a feast. Traditionally, the

---

* Sveinbjörn Beinteinsson (July 4, 1924–December 23, 1993), a native of Iceland, was instrumental in helping to gain recognition by the Icelandic government for Asatru. He founded the Ásatrúarfélagi (Fellowship of Æsir Faith) in 1972.

first three stalks of grain are bound and kept as an amulet to bring good fortune. The last sheaf of grain is kept for the Yule feast. The Ásatrú Alliance lists Freyfaxi as August 21.

- August 9: Day of Remembrance for Radbod. Radbod, a king of Frisia, is honored on this day for keeping Christian missionaries out of his land.

- August 21: The Ásatrú Alliance celebrates Freyfaxi on this day with a blót to Freyr and a grand feast from the gardens and the fields.

- September 9: Day of Remembrance for Herman of the Cherusci. Herman was a leader of the Cherusci tribe. He defeated three Roman Legions led by Varus in 9 CE.

- September 20–23: Winter Finding. The fall equinox. A blót is held for Odin. This is the traditional time for Fall Fest and the Second Harvest Feast. It is often celebrated as a New Year's Day. Frey and Freya, as well as Nerthus and Nord, are honored on this day.

- October 8: Day of Remembrance for Erik the Red. Eric was the founder of Greenland and father of Leif, the founder of Vinland.

- October 9: Ásatrú Alliance Day of Remembrance for Leif Erikson. See October 28, below.

- October 11–17: Winter Nights or Vetrablot. In the Old Icelandic Calendar, winter begins on the Saturday between Hunting 11 and 17. Winter Nights celebrates the bounty of the harvest and honors Freya and her protective spirits, the Disir. This was the time of year when the herds were culled and meat preserved for the coming winter.

- October 28: Day of Remembrance for Leif Erikson, the founder of Vinland, who came to the New World over five hundred years before Columbus.

- November 9: Day of Remembrance for Queen Sigrith of Sweden. Sigrith rejected Olaf the Lawbreaker's overtures of marriage and refused to abandon her gods. Her perseverance allowed the Heathens to hold sway in the Northlands for another three centuries.

- November 11: Feast of the Einherjar. The Einherjar are the chosen heroes who sit in Odin's Hall. It is a day to honor departed kin. Some Ásatrúar celebrate this day on May 30.

- November 25 or 27: Feast of Ullr or Weyland Smith's Day. A celebration of the Hunt in which the celebrants seek to gain personal luck needed for success. Weapons are dedicated on this day to Ullr, god of the bow. Many Ásatrúar recognize the great craftsman Weyland Smith on this day. Some Ásatrúar celebrate this feast on November 27. Others celebrate the Feast of Ullr on the 25, coinciding with the modern US celebration of Thanksgiving.

- December 9: Day of Remembrance for Egil Skallagrimsson. This day honors Egil, an Odinist and adventurer.
- December 20–23: Yule, the night before the winter solstice. Also known as Mother Night, the time when the New Year is born. It is a night to honor Frigga. The Ásatrú festival of Yule runs from this date for twelve nights, representing the year in miniature. The return of the sun indicates that there will be no Fimbulwinter preceding Ragnarok. It is the time of year when the ancestors of the Ásatrú are felt to be closest. The dead (*draugar*) are considered to be very active at this time of year. Odin, in his aspect of Jólnir, the god of death and transition, is said to lead the Wild Hunt over the world, seeking out evil and corruption and to escort the old year out. Frey is also honored in his aspect as the newborn Year, representing growth and promise. The Ásatrúar decorate Yule trees, representing Yggdrasil, and burn Yule logs in honor of Thor. As in Wiccan Yule log traditions, a piece of last year's log is used to light this year's. A fragment of the Yule log is preserved throughout the year to guard the house against lightning and fire.
- The twelve days of Yule culminate with Twelfth Night. In ancient times, a boar was consecrated to Frey and led out so that everyone present could lay their hands on it to swear solemn oaths. Oaths sworn on the oath boar were taken very seriously. Pork is traditionally served at the feast to honor Frey in thanks for prosperity.

NOTES

1. The Asatru Alliance, http://www.asatru.org/holidays.php; Eric R. Munson, Munson's Mead Hall, http://web.archive.org/web/20090212140931/http://destinyslobster.com/asatru/calendar.html.
2. Arthur Lyons, *Satan Wants You: The Cult of Devil Worship in America* (New York, NY: The Mysterious Press, 1988), 120–121; http://web.archive.org/web/20090212140931/http://destinyslobster.com/asatru/calendar.html.

Appendix A: Resources

Wiccan Resources

W hen I started down the Wiccan path in 1969, there weren't any organizations to support me. The Pagan community has grown and times have changed. I can't list every Pagan organization; there are far too many, and many are local and limited in scope. Here are a few organizations that are available to the Pagan who is contemplating going public:

Alternative Religions Education Network (AREN): AREN started out as the Witches' Anti-Defamation League (WADL) and later absorbed Witches Against Religious Discrimination (WARD). AREN is a nonprofit organization working to educate the public concerning "positive nature-based religions devoted to deities of either or no specific gender or attributes." This includes Wiccans, Druids, and many other neo-Pagan paths. http://www.aren.org/.

Aquarian Tabernacle Church (ATC): A Wiccan organization founded in Washington State that now has a seminary, as well as affiliates worldwide. The ATC sponsors several major gatherings. http://www.aquatabch.org/.

Ardantane: A Pagan seminary in New Mexico founded by Wiccan author Amber K and others. http://www.ardantane.org/.

Cauldron, The: A networking and information resource. http://www.ecauldron.com/index.php.

Covenant of the Goddess (COG): An international organization of cooperating autonomous Wiccan congregations and solitary practitioners. http://www.cog.org/.

Covenant of Unitarian Universalist Pagans (CUUPS): A network of Pagan-identified Unitarian Universalists who educate others about Paganism, promote interfaith dialogue, develop Pagan liturgies and theologies, and support Pagan clergy. http://www.cuups.org/.

Lady Liberty League: The antidefamation organization of Selena Fox's Circle Sanctuary (http://www.circlesanctuary.org/liberty). Circle Sanctuary publishes *Circle Network News* (http://www.circlesanctuary.org/circle) and sponsors one of the oldest major Pagan festivals, Pagan Spirit Gathering.

Military Pagan Network (MPN): A nonprofit organization dedicated to supporting Pagans in the military. http://mpnfortcampbell-ivil.tripod.com/.

Officers of Avalon: An organization representing Pagans within the emergency services (police, firefighters, paramedics). Officers of Avalon have a charity branch to raise support for disaster victims, called Avalon Cares. http://officersofavalon.com/.

Ontario Consultants on Religious Tolerance (OCRT): An excellent information resource on alternative religions. http://www.religioustolerance.org/.

Pagan Alliance of Nurses (PAN): An organization connecting and supporting Pagan nurses. http://groups.yahoo.com/group/PaganAllianceofNurses.

Pagan Federation: A British organization founded in 1971 to provide information and counter misconceptions about Paganism. http://www.paganfed.org/.

Pagan Federation International: An organization providing information and support to Pagans. http://www.paganfederation.org/.

Pagan Pride: Organizing Pagan pride events across North America to foster education and understanding. http://www.paganpride.org/.

Southern Delta Church of Wicca, ATC: An ATC affiliate based in Arkansas, very active in antidefamation work and public education. http://www.sdcw-atc.com/.

Witchcraft & Law Enforcement: What Law Enforcement Agencies Need to Know About Witchcraft: http://www.witchessabbats.com/index.php?option=com_content&view=article&id=3&Itemid=9.

The Witches' Voice (Witchvox): An educational network providing news, information services, and resources for and about Pagans, Heathens, and Wiccans (http://www.witchvox.com/). My antidefamation column, "Witch Hunts," is located on Witchvox (http://www.witchvox.com/xwitchhunts.html).

Druid Resources

An Conradh Draoithe Heireann: Website for the Organization of Irish Druids. http://www.irishdruidnetwork.org/orgs.html.

Ár nDraíocht Féin: A Druid Fellowship (ADF): An international fellowship devoted to creating a public tradition of neo-Pagan Druidry. http://www.adf. org/core.

Awen Grove: A Canadian Druid website. http://awencanada.com/.

British Druid Order, the: http://www.druidry.co.uk/.

Daven's Journal/Ord Draiochta na Uinech: Site with information on Ord Draiochta na Uisnech (Druid Order of Uisnech). http://davensjournal.com/.

De Danaan: Networking site for those in Celtic spirituality. http://www.de-danann.org/.

Druids and Celtic Paganism: Druid and Celtic mythology information site. http://www.angelfire.com/pa3/ramblingaround/index.html.

Druid Network, the: http://www.druidnetwork.org/index.html.

Henge of Keltria, the: Website for Keltrian Druidism. http://www.keltria. org/.

Mythical Ireland: An excellent website for mythology and mythical sites. http://www.mythicalireland.com/.

Order of Bards, Ovates & Druids: http://www.druidry.org/.

Reformed Druids of North America: http://www.geocities.com/mikerdna.

Heathen Resources

Ásatrú Alliance, The: Official web page of the Ásatrú Alliance. http://www.asatru.org/.

Ásatrú Folk Assembly (AFA): http://www.runestone.org/flash/home.html.

Irminsul Ættir Ásatrú: A website listing information on Ásatrú and activities in Washington State. http://www.irminsul.org/.

The Ásatrú Archive: Archive of articles and information on Ásatrú. http://www.lysator.liu.se/religion/neopagan/asatru.html.

Ásatrú Basics: Ingeborg's Unofficial Ásatrú FAQ. http://www.erichshall.com/asanew/newtotru.htm.

Ásatrú U: From the Reeves Hall of Frigga's Web. http://www.asatru-u.org/.

Appendix B: Glossary

A Glossary of Neo-Pagan Terms

Aesir: (sing. Áss): Norse/Ásatrú deities of family, society, and human endeavor. They represent craft, poetry, and bardic pursuits; thought, spirit, and order.

Alfheim: Norse/Ásatrú. The land of the elves in Asgard (q.v.).

Algron: Norse/Ásatrú. The island where Odin (q.v.) stayed for five years.

Altar: A table, stone, or other surface used in rituals on which the ritual tools are placed. In Wiccan ritual, the altar is normally situated slightly north of the center of the Circle. In John Dee's Enochian system of magick, the altar is called the "holy table" or "table of practice."

anointing: (1) To dab oil on a person or object as a ritual act of consecration. (2) Wiccaning, Paganing, or saining.

Asgard: Norse/Ásatrú. The home of the Aesir (q.v.), one of the nine worlds of Yggdrasil (q.v.).

Áss: Singular form of Aesir (q.v.).

athame: The Wiccan's traditional consecrated knife. In most traditions, each coven member will carry one, although some traditions substitute wands. The athame often has a black handle, and is often a symbol of the air element (and sometimes of fire).

awen: A Welsh term translated as "poetic inspiration" or "divine inspiration." The Welsh call a poet or soothsayer an *awenydd*.

baculum: A wand used in Wiccan rituals. See *wand*.

bard: (Gaelic): Druidism. A person who composes and recites poems or epics, often while accompanied by music. In Druid ritual, the bard is often tasked with opening the well and leading songs and chants.

Beltaine: (var. Beltane, Galan Mai, Cetshamhain, May Eve): Wicca, Druidism. A Greater Sabbat of the Wiccan calendar, celebrated April 30, marking the beginning of the summer season. Beltaine is the other great fire festival, the first being Samhain (q.v.). See *Samhain*.

bell: In Wicca, a small hand bell is often used during the casting and closing of a Circle and during rituals.

besom: A broom used in Wiccan rituals, such as handfasting.

Bilé: Ásatrú, Druid. The bilé (pronounced "bee-lah") is a tree, branch, or pole in the center of the ritual space representing the World Tree in Druid ritual. The branch or pole often has bells attached. See *World Tree*.

Bilskirnir: Norse/Ásatrú. Thor's hall in Asgard (q.v.).

Birfrost: Norse/Ásatrú. The flaming rainbow bridge between Asgard (q.v.) and Midgard (q.v.).

Blessed be: Traditional words of welcome, blessing, and farewell used by Wiccans (and Masons).

Blót: (Old Norse; trans. "blessing"): Ásatrú. A ritual celebration.

Blótbolli: (var. Blotbowli): Ásatrú. A bowl for catching ritual libations.

bolline: Wicca. A knife used for cutting herbs and engraving. Often it is crescent shaped and has a white handle. Welsh traditions sometimes call this knife a *kerfan*. Traditionally, the athame is only used to make ritual gestures, where the bolline is used as a utility knife, though some Wiccan traditions such as the 1734 tradition prescribe the use of a single knife for ritual and practical purposes. Arthur Edward Waite mentions the bolline or sickle in the *Book of True Black Magic*. The name likely comes from the *bolino*, a ritual knife mentioned in *The Key of Solomon*.

Book of Shadows: Wicca. A personal book of rituals, rites, cures, and magick. See the section on this subject within this handbook.

Breidablik: Norse/Ásatrú. The hall of Balder in Asgard (q.v.).

cauldron: A large iron pot, an ancient symbol of the Goddess Cerridwen, which is found in many ritual circles; a symbol of rebirth and regeneration.

censer: An incense burner or brazier. Represents the element of air.

chalice: Ceremonial cup or goblet, often used to represent the element of water. Used in the ceremony of cakes and wine.

Circle: Wicca. (1) The consecrated space within which a ritual is held. The Circle is a sacred space that may be created anywhere, as opposed to temples or churches in other religions, which are, of course, not portable. A Wiccan Circle is both a defense and a container, meant to keep in the energy that practitioners raise, and keep out unwanted influences. (2) A term for Pagan and Wiccan rituals.

coven: Dates to 1500–1520 CE, var. of *covent* or *cuvent*, which are found in the *Ancrene Riwle*; deriv. Old French *covenant* and *covenir*; deriv. Latin *convenire* (to agree, to be of one mind, to come together). (1) A group of people who are of one mind, who come together with a common purpose. "Coven" first appeared in reference to "a gathering of witches" in 1662 (Barnhart, 228). (2) Wicca. The word "coven" is usually used today to refer to a Wiccan group, though the popular press sometimes uses it to describe groups of Satanists, probably due to popular Christian literature. Modern Satanists actually refer to their groups as grottos or pylons. All Wiccans are initiated into the coven and become priests and priestesses, and all coveners are essentially equal. Wiccan covens are generally "closed" (i.e., for initiates only).

cowan: Someone who is not a Wiccan. May have been synonymous with "warlock" (oathbreaker) at one point, but is now generally a benign term for an outsider or noninitiate.

Craft, the: Wiccans often use this term to refer to their faith.

Crom Dubh: (crooked black): A minor Celtic fertility God mentioned in the medieval tale "Immram Brain maic Febail (The Voyage of Bran, son of Febal)" and appears in the Scottish saying: *DiDòmhnaich Crum Dubh, plaoisgidh mi an t-ugh* (Crooked black Sunday, I'll shell the egg). Crom Dubh has come to be used to describe the first Sunday in August in Ireland.

cross-quarter days: The Greater Sabbats, which fall between the solstices and equinoxes. See the section on Sabbats and Esbats within this handbook.

deosil: Clockwise or sunwise. The standard way of moving within a ritual Circle. Used for positive workings and magick involving increase and prosperity.

Einherjar: (var. Einheriar): Norse. (1) The einherjar are the chosen heroes who sit in Odin's hall.

Einherjar Feast: (var. Heroes's Day): Odinist/Ásatrú. November 11 is the Feast of the Einherjar (q.v.). It is a day to honor departed kin. Some Ásatrúar celebrate this day on May 30. The month of November is considered a month of sacrifices when obligations in honor of the departed ancestors are made.

Eljudnir: Norse/Ásatrú. The hall of the Goddess Hel (q.v.) in Niflheim (q.v.)

Eostar(a): See *Ostara*.

equinox: The time of year when the day and night are of equal length. The spring or vernal equinox is around March 21 each year, and the fall or autumnal equinox is around September 21. See the section on Sabbats and Esbats within this handbook.

Esbat: (deriv. Old French *esbatment*, "to divert oneself" or "an amusement"): A Wiccan ceremony occurring during a full moon. A monthly meeting for Wiccans. See the section on Sabbats and Esbats in this handbook.

Fensalir: Norse/Ásatrú. Frigg's hall in Asgard (q.v.).

fire maiden: Druidism. An official who lights the fire and makes an offering of incense.

Folkvang: Norse/Ásatrú. The site of Freyja's hall in Asgard (q.v.).

Fogmoon: Ásatrú. November.

frith: (Old Norse, trans. "peace"): Ásatrú. Peace, security. Ásatrúar define this as "joyful productivity," "joy in duty," or "happiness from within."

Gimli: Norse/Ásatrú. Hall of the gods after Ragnarok (q.v.).

Green Man: A sculpture, carving, or other representation of a face made of leaves, branches, and vines, representing the male regenerative energy in nature. Green men are common architectural ornaments in many old British churches.

gothar: The old Norse word *gothar* is the plural form of *gothi* (priest) or *gythia* (priestess). Gothar translates as "those who speak the godly tongue." The gothar are the priesthood of the Ásatrú religion.

gothi: See *Gothar*.

grove: Ritual space used by Druids. See also *Lundr*.

gythia: See *Gothar*.

hamingja: (var. lyke, hyde, myne, haminja): Ásatrú. Spiritual power that is accumulated over one's lifetime and passed on to one's descendants. Similar to the Eastern concept of karma.

hammer sign: Ásatrú. Making a hammer-like shape in the air over an object (such as a horn of mead) as a blessing. Alternatively, holding a Mjolnir pendant or hammer over an object. See *Mjolnir*.

hammer warding: (var. hammer working): Ásatrú. A hammer warding is usually performed to sanctify the sacred space. A hammer representing Mjolnir is held aloft and swung, shaken, or waved at each of the cardinal directions as well as above and below. If a hammer is not available, a fist may be held aloft to represent it. See *Mjolnir*.

handfasting: A Pagan or Wiccan wedding.

harvest: Ásatrú. August.

haugr: An Old Norse word for a burial mound. It is related to the archaic English word "how," which means "hill" or "hillock."

Hávamál: *Hávamál, the Sayings of Hár* is an epic poem with 165 verses that is used as one of the foundations of the Ásatrú religion.

Haymoon: Ásatrú. July.

Heimdall: (Also known as Heimdallr, Hallinskithi, Gullintanni, and Vindlér or Vindhlér.) In Norse mythology, Heimdall is a god of divination and prophecy who watches for Ragnarök from his dwelling Himinbjörg, located where the burning rainbow bridge Bifröst meets Valhalla. Heimdall is the son of the Nine Mothers and possesses the resounding horn Gjallarhorn.

Hel: (1) Norse. Hel is the daughter of Loki and the giant, Angurboda. She is the sister of Fenrir (Fenris-wolf) and Jormungand (Midgard serpent). She is the Goddess of the underworld. Her realm is Niflheim (q.v.) and her hall is called Elvidnir (misery). In her hall, her table is called "hunger" and her bed, "disease." She is described as half white and half black. (2) Ásatrú. (a) Another name for Nifhelheim, where deceased evildoers remain to suffer. (b) One of the nine worlds of Yggradrasil (q.v.).

Himinbjorg: Norse/Ásatrú. Heimdall's hall in Asgard (q.v.).

hlaut-teinn: Ásatrú. A twig used to asperge the celebrants at a blót.

Hlidskjalf: Norse/Ásatrú. Odin's high throne in Valaskjalf (q.v.)

Hnitbjorg: Norse/Ásatrú. Stronghold of the giant Suttung.

Hof: An Old Norse word whose modern German meanings include yard, courtyard, farm, country house, manor, palace, court, ring, or circle. In Ásatrú, it refers to a holy building.

hörgr: Old Norse, Ásatrú. An altar or cairn where offerings are made.

Horning: Ásatrú. February.

Hunting: Ásatrú. October.

Hvergelmir: Norse/Ásatrú. A spring in Niflheim (q.v.) under the roots of Yggdrasil (q.v.).

hyde: See *hamingja*.

Idavoll: Norse/Ásatrú. The central plain of Asgard (q.v.).

immrama (Gaelic): Druidism. Tales of sea voyages in Celtic tradition. Such journeys were made to the seas of the otherworld to find meaning or to explore realms of the mind and spirit. A typical example is the "Voyage of Mael Duin's Boat."

initiate: (1) Wicca: A new member of a coven or tradition. (2) a Wiccan holding the rank of the first degree. (2) Druidism.

Iving: Norse/Ásatrú. A river dividing Asgard (q.v.) from Jotunheim (q.v.).

Jotunheim: Norse/Ásatrú. The home of the giants (q.v.), one of the nine worlds of Yggdrasil (q.v.).

jotun: (Var. ettins, giants): Norse/Ásatrú. Giants who compete with the Æsir (q.v.). They are descended from the first being in the universe, the Jotun Ymir. The jotun represent chaos and destruction, powers of the universe that are not necessarily evil. At Ragnarok (q.v.) it is believed that the jotun will band together to defeat the Æsir (q.v.). Jotunheim is the abode of the jotun.

keeper of the well: Druidism. An official who pours the waters and makes an offering of silver.

landvaettir: Norse/Ásatrú. Land wights of the forest, earth, and streams. They are said to live in rocks and trees. See *wights*.

Lenting: Ásatrú. March.

Litha: (var. Alban Heruin): Wicca. This is the Summer Solstice (June 21), a Lesser Sabbat in the Wiccan calendar. It was originally a Saxon celebration incorporated into the Wiccan calendar as a celebration of the first fruits of the season. It is the longest day of the year. In some traditions, this day is celebrated as the Sacred Marriage of the Goddess and God. In others it is celebrated as the victory of the Lord of the waning year over the Lord of the waxing year, to mark the point from which the days will shorten.

lundr: Ásatrú: An empty grove set aside as a sacred place.

lustral bath: A bath of purification taken prior to a ritual, usually consisting of consecrated water with a little salt and/or herbs.

lyke: See *hamingja*.

Lyr: Norse/Ásatrú. Menglad's hall in Jotunheim (q.v.).

maiden: Wicca. An assistant to the high priestess in ritual.

megin: Ásatrú. A divine energy or life force that pervades everything (cf. chi).

Miach: In Irish mythology, Miach was a son of the healer god Diancecht of the Tuatha Dé Danann. He replaced the silver arm his father made for Nuada with an arm of flesh and blood; Diancecht killed him out of jealousy for being able to do what he himself could not.

Menglad: Norse. Goddess of healing. She lives in a hall called Lyr in Jotenheim.

Merrymoon: Ásatrú. The month of May.

Midgard: (1) Norse/Ásatrú. (a) Midgard is the "middle land" created by the descendants of the giant Ymir between the land of ice, frost, and eternal silence (Niflheim, q.v.) and the land of fire and the midday sun (Muspelsheim, q.v.). It is one of the nine worlds of Yggdrasil (q.v.). This land is surrounded by an ocean inhabited by a giant serpent, the serpent of Midgard, sometimes simply known as Midgard. (b) The earth we inhabit.

Midyear: Ásatrú. The month of June.

Mimir: Norse. ("The rememberer, the wise one," also known as Mim.) A god of knowledge and wisdom who was beheaded in the Æsir-Vanir War. Odin carries around Mímir's head, and it recites secret knowledge and counsel to him.

Mimir's well: Norse/Ásatrú. A well of wisdom under the roots of Yggdrasil (q.v.) in Asgard (q.v.). Guarded by the head of Mimir.

Mjolnir: (MEEOL neer) (var. Thor's Hammer): The name of the magick hammer of the god Thor. Norse peoples believed that lightning is the sparks created when Thor strikes his anvil with his hammer Mjolnir and that Thor uses Mjolnir to break up the ice in spring. Decorated replicas of this hammer were often worn as amulets, and many followers of Ásatrú wear it as a symbol of their faith.

moot: Bef. 900 Middle English *mot*[*e*] (meeting, assembly); Old English *gemöt*; deriv. Old Norse *möt*; Danish *gemoet*: (1) A meeting or assembly. (2) Odinist. A meeting or gathering.

Muspellsheim: Ásatrú. The Southern land of fire guarded by the giant Surt, mentioned in the Voluspa (q.v.). It is one of the nine worlds of Yggdrasil (q.v.).

myne: See *hamingja*.

Nastrond: Norse/Ásatrú. Site of the hall of evildoers in Hel (q.v.) where the dragon Nidhogg gnaws on corpses.

neo-Paganism: A reconstruction of pre-Christian religions to create modern Earth religions.

Niflheim: Ásatrú. The land of freezing mist and darkness mentioned in the Voluspa (q.v.). Niflheim is the home of the goddess Hel (q.v.). It is one of the nine worlds of Yggdrasil (q.v.).

Nine Noble Virtues: Ásatrú. A code of ethics in Ásatrú/Odinist circles. The Nine Noble Virtues are courage, truth, honor, loyalty, hospitality, industriousness, perseverance, self-discipline, and self-reliance.

oath ring: (var. Troth ring): Ásatrú. A solid gold or silver ring used for the swearing of oaths and also as a symbol of priesthood. It is worn on the wrist of the gothi at all kindred blóts, sumbels, and functions. It is often displayed on the altar when not in use. See *Troth ring*.

Od: (1) A Norse god. (2) Ásatrú. The gift of ecstasy and enlightenment given to humanity by the gods.

ogham: An ancient Celtic alphabet used to inscribe monuments, attributed to and named for Ogma, the Irish god of poetry and eloquence.

Okolnir: Norse/Ásatrú. A land of warmth created after Ragnarok (q.v.) that is the site of the hall of Brimnir.

Old Religion, the: An alternate term for Wicca.

Ostara: (1) Wicca. An alternate name for Eostre. See *Eostre*. (2) Norse/Ásatrú. (a) Ancient goddess of youth, fertility, and spring, known to the Saxons as Eostre (q.v.). (b) The month of April. (c) March 21–23: High Feast of Ostara. This spring equinox festival is similar to the Wiccan festival of Eostre. Ostara marks the end of winter and the beginning of the season of rebirth. Ostara honors Frigg, Freya, and Nerthus with blot and feast. (3) Odinist. The spring equinox festival, similar to that observed by the Ásatrúar.

Pagan: In recent years, followers of many earth-based religions have come to refer to their beliefs and practices as "Pagan" or "neo-Pagan" (new Pagan).

Paganing: See *anointing*, *Wiccaning*, *saining*.

pentagram: A five-pointed star. With one point uppermost, it is a symbol of Wicca. (var. pentangle). Also known as Solomon's seal, though other texts assign the name Solomon's seal to the hexagram instead. The Pentagram was regarded by the ancient Greeks as a talisman and preservative from danger, being inscribed on the threshold of a doorway. Early Christians used it as a symbol of the five wounds of Christ. Each of the five points of the pentagram represents one of the five traditional elements: spirit, air, fire, water, and earth. As the top most point represents Spirit, this symbol is said to represent the dominion of Spirit over the other four elements and the supremacy of reason over matter.

Inverted, that is, with two points uppermost, it has been used as a symbol of several different things. Within some traditions of Wicca it is a symbol of the second degree of initiation.

Satanists have also used an inverted pentagram as a symbol. They interpret the four points of the elements over the point of spirit as representing the domination of matter over reason. It also, coincidentally, resembles a goat's head when inverted, though this is probably a very recent interpretation. A symbol of LaVey's Church of Satan is an inverted pentagram on a circular field with a goat's head superimposed over it, referred to by them as the sigil of Baphomet. See *Baphomet*.

pentacle: A pentagram within a circle. Represents the element of earth. It may also be a flat, round disk with a pentacle engraved on it, worn as a pendant (usually silver) for protection, or used as a dish to represent earth or to distribute cakes in a ritual (also spelled "pantacle" in this usage).

puca: (var. pooka, puka; Anglo Saxon, trans. "mischievous spirits" or "fairy folk"; Middle English *puke*, deriv. Old Norse *puki*. Welsh *pwcca*): It appears in Shakespeare's play *A Midsummer's Night Dream* as the character Puck.

Ragnarok: (Norse. Deriv. *regin* [God] and *rok* [judgment]): Norse/Ásatrú. The destruction of the world in the final battle between the gods and the forces of evil.

Rede: Derived from the Anglo-Saxon word *raedan*, meaning "to interpret." A rule governing interpretation. (1) Wicca. A religious law or maxim. The most important guiding principle for Wiccans is the Wiccan Rede: "Do whatever you will, so long as it does not harm another." (2) Ásatrú. The part of the blót ceremony in which the purpose of the blót is stated.

Sabbat: One of the eight major seasonal Pagan and Wiccan festivals, which occur at approximately equal intervals throughout the year.

saining: (bef. 12th century): Witchcraft. An ancient Celtic blessing and protection from harm and disease, which may involve anointing with oil or water. Bobbing for apples may be the remnant of an ancient Pagan saining rite. See also *anointing*, *Paganing*, *Wiccaning*.

samal: See *sumbel*.

Samhain: The name of the ancient Celtic New Year's Eve, October 31, celebrated by Wiccans and Druids today, marking the beginning of the winter season. Samhain is the origin of the modern celebration of Halloween, All Hallow's Eve, or Hallowmas. Samhain is the first great fire festival, the other being Beltaine. See *Beltaine*.

sanctifier: Druidism. Person in charge of offerings and sacrifices in ritual.

seer: (Middle English, 1350–1400 CE): Druid. An official who performs divination and takes omens. In Druid ritual, the seer is often tasked with lighting the sacred fire.

Seid worker: Ásatrú. A Witch or wise woman who works magick.

seidr: Ásatrú. Magick.

Shedding: Ásatrú. September.

sidhe: Celtic. A supernatural race similar to fairies or elves that are said to live in the otherworld or in fairy mounds. They are first mentioned in the Book of Invasions in the Book of Leinster.

Sindri: Norse/Ásatrú. Red-gold roofed hall that will appear after Ragnarok (q.v.).

sippe: Ásatrú. Kinship, kindred, kith, and kin.

skald: Old Norse. Poet.

skyclad: Nude. Ritual nudity is common in some Wiccan traditions.

Snowmoon: Ásatrú. January.

Sokkvabekk: Norse/Ásatrú. Saga's hall in Asgard (q.v.).

solstice: The time of year when the difference in length between day and night is at its greatest. The summer solstice (longest day) occurs on approximately June 21 each year and the winter solstice (shortest day) on approximately December 21.

So mote it be: Wicca. Phrase commonly used to conclude ritual or magickal statements.

sumbel (var. symbel, samal): Ásatrú. Toasting ritual.

sunwise: Clockwise. See *deosil*.

svartalfar: Norse/Ásatrú. Dark elves or dwarves, said to be the first beings that the gods created. Their realm on Yggdrasil (q.v.) is Svartalfheim. Beings of the earth who represent industriousness and craftsmanship. Svaralfar made Mjolnir (q.v.) and Freyr's magical ship. See *Svartalfheim*.

Svartalfheim: Norse/Ásatrú. Home of the Dwarves; one of the nine worlds of Yggdrasil (q.v.).

symbel: See *sumbel*.

sword: Wicca. A ritual sword is often used in casting the Circle; each coven usually has one.

tender of the tree: Druidism. An official who dresses and censes the World Tree or bilé in ritual.

Threefold Law: Wicca. The most common Wiccan equivalent of the principle of cause and effect is the Law of Threefold Return, which was established by Raymond Buckland: "Everything you do comes back to you three times." It started as a public relations sound bite to help the public understand that Wiccans were harmless, not destructive satanic cult members. Gerald Gardner's original version was a "twofold" law. It was in a later press interview that Buckland upped the ante to make it a threefold law instead. The threefold version stuck.

Thrudheim: Norse/Ásatrú. Thor's realm in Asgard (q.v.) and the site of his hall in Bilskirnir.

thurible: An incense burner or brazier. Represents the element of air (or sometimes fire). See *censer*.

tradition: (var. trads): A denomination of Wicca. The Wiccan community is made up of many different traditions, each with its own customs and philosophies.

Troth ring: Ásatrú. A solid gold or silver ring used for the swearing of oaths and also as a symbol of priesthood. It is worn on the wrist of the gothi at all kindred blóts, sumbels, and functions. It is often displayed on the altar when not in use. See *oath ring*.

Tuatha de Danaan: Celtic. The "peoples of the Goddess Danu." A race mentioned in the *Lebor Gabála Érenn*, who arrive to settle Ireland and conquer the Fir Bolg. The Tuatha are the old gods of Ireland.

Utgard: Norse/Ásatrú. A realm in Jotunheim (q.v.) ruled by Loki (q.v.).

Valaskjalf: Norse/Ásatrú. Odin's hall in Asgard (q.v.).

Valhalla: Norse/Ásatrú. Odin's hall where the Einherjar (q.v.) await Ragnarok.

Valkyrie: Norse. Derived from the Old Norse *valkyrja* (chooser of the slain). A host of female figures first mentioned in the Poetic Edda who decide who will die in battle. The valkyries bring their chosen to Valhalla, where the deceased warriors become einherjar.

Vanaheim: Norse/Ásatrú. Home of the Vanir (q.v.), one of the nine worlds of Yggdrasil (q.v.).

Vanir: (sing. Van): Norse/Ásatrú. Deities representing the fertility of the earth and forces of nature. Norse mythology tells of the Vanir warring with the Æsir (q.v.) and eventually calling a truce. They are, therefore, sometimes classified as a part of the Æsir.

Ve': Ásatrú. An outdoor sanctuary, usually incorporating an altar or image.

Vigrid: Norse/Ásatrú. The plain in Asgard where the final battle of Ragnarok (q.v.) will occur.

Vingolf: Norse/Ásatrú. The hall of the goddesses in Asgard (q.v.).

Völuspá: "Völuspá, Song of the Sybil" is an epic poem describing Creation. One of the main texts of Ásatrú (q.v.).

wand: Wicca/Witchcraft. Often a symbol of the fire element (sometimes of air). See *baculum*.

Wicca: Witchcraft. The Old Religion. The words *Wicca*, *Wicce*, and *Wiccan* can each be used as a descriptive term for a Witch.

Wiccaning: Presenting an infant before the gods by the parents, usually assisted by a priestess and priest. This is customarily done between an infant's third and thirteenth month, though the custom varies. Also known as Paganing, anointing, or saining. Involves an oath by the parents to protect and nurture their child. See *anointing*, *Paganing*, *saining*.

widdershins: Counterclockwise. Used for banishing rituals. Symbolic of decrease and sometimes chaos.

wight: Middle English (bef. 900 CE), derived from Old English *wiht* through the German *wicht*; Old Norse *vettr* and Goth *waiht*). (1) A nature spirit or sprite. (2) Ásatrú. Spirits of nature.

Winter Finding: (var. Harvest Remembrance): (1) Ásatrú. September 20–23, the fall equinox. A blót is held for Odin. This is the traditional time for Fall Fest and the Second Harvest Feast. It is often celebrated as New Year's Day. Frey and Freya, as well as Nerthus and Nord, are honored on this day. (2) Odinist. The Fall Equinox Festival.

wyrd: Ásatrú. Fate. Refers to the Well of Wyrd that feeds the roots of Yggdrasil (q.v.). The Norns: (q.v.), a triad of goddesses that spin the fates of humankind, are also known as the Wyrds.

Ydalir: Ull's hall in Asgard (q.v.).

Yggdrasil: (var. Hodmimir's Wood): Norse. The World Tree, a key concept in Norse mythology. The nine worlds that make up Yggdrasil are Asgard, Hel, Jotunheim, Ljossalfheim, Midgard, Muspellsheim, Niflheim, Svartalheim, and Vanaheim. The World Tree is also a concept that shows up in Druidism as the bilé. See *bilé*.

Yule: Ásatrú, Wicca. December. See *solstice*.

BIBLIOGRAPHY

Alford, Clifford. *Occult Crimes Investigations.*

Anderson, Sgt. Edwin C. Jr., *Law Enforcement Guide to Occult Related Crime.* California State University Police, 1988.

Ayto, John. *Dictionary of Word Origins.* Arcade Publishing; Ltr. Prtg ed., 1990.

Balsiger, David. *1988 Witchcraft/Satanism Ritual Calendar*: 2, 3.

Barnhart, Robert K. ed. *Barnhart Dictionary of Etymology.* New York: H.W. Wilson, 1988.

Barrett, Francis. *The Magus.* New York: University Books, 1967.

Baskin, Wade. *Dictionary of Satanism.* Philosophical Library, 1972.

Bonewits, Isaac. *The Pagan Man: Priests, Warriors, Hunters and Drummers.* Citadel Press, 2005.

———. *Real Magic.* Berkeley, CA: Creative Arts Book Company, 1970.

Brown, David L. *The Dark Side of Halloween.* Logos Communication Consortium, 1998.

Carmichael, Alexander. *Carmina Gadelica.*

Carr-Gomm, Phillip. *Elements of the Druid Tradition.* London: Element Books, 1996.

CCIN Inc., *File 18 newsletter.* Vol. 3, no. 6:3.

Center for Non-Traditional Religion, The. "Wicca and Paganism: A Rebirth of the Religion of the Mother Goddess": 9.

Colorado Bureau of Investigations Questioned Documents Examiner's Occult Guide: 2, 4, 7.

Crowley, Aleister. *Magick in Theory and Practice.* New York: Castle Books, 1960.

Cuhulain, Kerr. *Full Contact Magick.* St. Paul, MN: Llewellyn Publications, 2002.

———. *Law Enforcement Guide to Wicca.* 3rd edition. Victoria, BC, Canada: Horned Owl Publishing, 1997.

———. *Magickal Self Defense.* St. Paul, MN: Llewellyn Publications, 2008.

———. *Wiccan Warrior.* St. Paul, MN: Llewellyn Publications, 2000.

Curott, Phyllis. *Book of Shadows: A Modern Woman's Journey Into the Wisdom of Witchcraft and the Magic of the Goddess.* Broadway, 1999.

———. "Exploding Wiccan Dogma." Lecture at Blessed Be and Merry Meet in DC conference in Washington, DC, October 14, 2000.

Doyle, Sir Arthur Conan. "The Speckled Band," 1892. *Sherlock Holmes: The Complete Novels and Stories.* New York: Bantam, 1986.

Dubois, William Edward Lee. *Occult Crime: Detection, Investigation, and Verification.* South Orange, NJ: USCCCN, 1990.

Ellis, Peter Beresford. *Dictionary of Celtic Mythology.* Constable, London, 1992.

Evans, Bergen. *Dictionary of Mythology.* New York: Dell Publishing, 1970.

Frattarola, John. *Passport Magazine Special Edition: America's Best Kept Secret*, insert "A Look At Modern Day Satanism": 2, 7. Calvary Chapel of West Covina, 1986.

Freedomlight Report 1, no. 3, Oct/Nov 1990: 1.

Frost, Gavin and Yvonne. *The Witch's Bible*. Los Angeles: Nash Publishing, 1972.

Green, Miranda J. *Dictionary of Celtic Myth and Legend*. Thames & Hudson, 1992.

Grun, Bernard. *The Timetables of History*. 3rd ed. London: Simon and Shuster, 1991.

Phillips, Phil and Joan Hake Robie. *Halloween and Satanism*. Starburst Publishers, 1987.

Hall Angela and Rudolf Simek. *The Dictionary of Northern Mythology*. Boydell & Brewer, Inc., 1993.

"Hávamál: The Words of Odin the High One," the Elder or Poetic Edda (Sæmund's Edda), translated by Olive Bray and edited by D. L. Ashliman. March 28, 2003.

Herold, Mary Ann. *A Basic Guide To The Occult For Law Enforcement Agencies*. Arvada, CO: Technical Research Institute, 1984.

Hole, Christina. *British Folk Customs*. Hutchinson, 1976.

Hutton, Ronald. *The Pagan Religions of the Ancient British Isles: Their Nature and Legacy*. Basil Blackwell Ltd., 1991.

Hutton, Ronald. *Triumph of the Moon: A History of Modern Pagan Witchcraft*. Oxford University Press, 1999.

Johnston, Jerry. *The Edge of Evil*. Vancouver, BC: Word Publishing, 1989.

K, Amber. *True Magick*. St. Paul, MN: Llewellyn Publications, 1990.

Kelly, Aidan. *Crafting the Art of Magic, Book 1: A History of Modern Witchcraft 1939–1964*. St. Paul, MN: Llewellyn Publications, 1991.

Kirschner & Associates, U.S. Government Publication #008-020-00745-5; *Religious Requirements of Certain Selected Groups–A Handbook for Chaplains*. Washington, DC, 1974.

LaVey, Anton. *The Satanic Bible*. New York, NY: Avon Books, 1966.

Leek, Sybil. *The Complete Art of Witchcraft*. New York: Signet, 1971.

Lyons, Arthur. *Satan Wants You: The Cult of Devil Worship in America*. New York: The Mysterious Press, 1988.

MacFarlane, A. D. J. *Witchcraft in Tudor and Stuart England*. London: Routledge and Kegan Paul Ltd., 1970.

Marrs, Texe. *Mystery Mark of the New Age*. Westchester, IL: Crossway Books, 1988.

Mathers, S. Liddell MacGregor, trans. The Greater Key of Solomon. Chicago, IL: DeLaurence Co., 1914.

McDowell, Josh Stuart McDowell and Don Stewart. *Handbook of Today's Religions: Understanding the Occult*. Here's Life Pub, 1982.

Morse, Keith. "Questions and Answers on Wicca: A Christian Perspective on Witchcraft," *Personal Freedom Outreach Newsletter* 3, no. 4 (October–December 1983): 4.

Murray, Valgard. "Althings: Past, Present and Future," citing Thorsteinn Gudjunsson, Thingvellir.

Myers, Brendan Cathbad. *The Mysteries of Druidry*. Franklin Lakes, NJ: New Page Books, 2006.

Nichols, Ross. *The Book of Druidry*. Thorsons, January 25, 1992.

O'Gaea, Ashleen and Carol Garr. *Circles Behind Bars: A Complete Handbook for the Incarcerated Witch*. Unpublished, 2000.

Parker, Russ. *Battling the Occult*. Downer's Grove, IL: Inter Varsity Press, 1990.

Pennsylvania State Police. Pennsylvania State Police Missing Persons Bulletin, Bureau of Criminal Investigation–Missing Persons Unit, 3, no. 3, "Satanism: The Law Enforcement Response."

Piggot, Stuart. *The Druids*. London/New York, NY: Thames and Hudson, 1975.

Plowman, Edward E. "The Legends of John Todd," *Christianity Today*. February 2, 1979: 19.

Random House Webster's Unabridged Dictionary. 2nd ed.

Rapacki, Lyle J. *Satanism: The Not So New Problem*. Flagstaff, AZ: Intel, 1988.

Reachout Trust. "Halloween." *Reachout Quarterly* no. 53, autumn 1998, 13.

———. "Hallowe'en Is Here Again." *Reachout Quarterly* no. 77, autumn 2007, 3.

Regardie, Israel. *The Complete Golden Dawn System of Magic*. Scottsdale, AZ: New Falcon Publications, 1990.

Russell, Jeffrey B. *A History of Witchcraft: Sorcerers, Heretics and Pagans*. London: Thames and Hudson, 1980.

San Diego County Sheriff's Association, *Gangs, Groups, Cults: An Informational Aid to Understanding*: 114.

Schnoebelen, Bill. "Saints Alive In Jesus," *Halloween: Tis The Season To Be Evil*, 1990: 3.

Sloat, Lou. *Texas Ritualistic Crime Information Network Occult Crime Manual*. n.d.

Southwest Radio Church, *The Gospel Truth*, Southwest Radio Church, 1998: 1.

Stewart, R. J. *Celtic Gods, Celtic Goddesses*. Blandford, London, 1990.

Thorsson, Edred. *Northern Magic: Mysteries of the Norse, Germans and English*. St. Paul, MN: Llewellyn Worldwide, 1992.

Valiente, Doreen. *The Rebirth of Witchcraft*. London: Robert Hale Ltd., 1989.

Walker, Barbara G. *The Woman's Encyclopedia of Myths and Secrets*. San Francisco, CA: Harper Collins, 1983.

Waring, Philippa. *A Dictionary of Omens and Superstitions*. Souvenir Press, 1997.

Warnke, Michael. *Schemes of Satan*. Victory House, 1991.

Warnke, Michael, David Balsiger, and Les Jones. *The Satan Seller*. South Plainfield, NJ: Bridge Publishing, 1972.

WATCH Network. *Be Aware!: A Handbook for the Purpose of Exposing Occultic Activity*. El Paso, TX: WATCH Network, 1986: 5.

Watkins, Calvert, ed. *The American Heritage Dictionary of Indo-European Roots*. Rev. ed. Boston: Houghton Mifflin, 1985.

Webster's New Twentieth Century Dictionary.

Webster's Unabridged Dictionary. 2nd ed. New York: Random House, 2001.

Westhoelter, Shane. *General Information Manual With Respect to Satanism and the Occult*. National Information Network, 1989.

Wood, Robin. *When, Why ... If*. Livingtree Books, 1996.

SUGGESTED READING

Adler, Margot. *Drawing Down the Moon*. Boston, MA: Beacon Press, 1986.

Anderson, William. *Green Man: The Archetype of Our Oneness With The Earth*. San Francisco, CA: Harper Collins, 1990.

Andron, Sandy. *Cultivating Cult-Evading*. Weston, MA: American Family Foundation, 1988.

Aquino, Michael. *The Crystal Tablet of Set*. San Francisco, CA: Temple of Set, 1990.

Attwater, Donald. *The Penguin Dictionary of Saints*. Penguin Classics, 1965/'66.

Barnes, L. K., ed. *The Necronomicon*. New York, NY: Avon Books, 1977.

Bass, Ellen and Davis, Laura. *The Courage to Heal*. San Francisco, CA: Harper Collins, 1988.

Belanger, Michelle. *The Psychic Energy Codex: Awakening Your Subtle Senses*. York Beach, ME: Red Wheel/Weiser, 2007.

———. *The Psychic Vampire Codex: A Manual of Magick and Energy Work*. York Beach, ME: Red Wheel/Weiser, 2004.

Biehn, Dep. Gerald and Dep. Thomas Kerfoot. "Occult Criminal Investigation Reference Material." Los Angeles, CA: Los Angeles County Sheriff's Department, n.d.

Blacksun. *Three Times Around the Circle*. Self-published, 1988.

———. *The Spell of Making*. Chicago, IL: Eschaton, 1995.

Bonewits, Isaac. "Official Report of the President to the Board of Directors on his Investigation of the John Todd/Lance Collins Affair in Dayton." Ohio: Aquarian Anti-Defamation League (February 23, 1976).

Bradbury, Ray. *The Halloween Tree*. New York, NY: Alfred A. Knopf, 1972.

Brennan, J. H. *The Occult Reich*. New York, NY: New American Library, 1974.

Brewer, E. Cobham. *Dictionary of Phrase and Fable*. 1898.

Brown, Dr. Rebecca. *He Came to Set the Captives Free*. Chino, CA: Chick Publications, 1986.

———. *Prepare for War*. Chino, CA: Chick Publications, 1987.

Brunvald, Jan Harold. *The Choking Doberman*. New York, NY: Norton Publishing, 1974.

Buckland, Raymond. *Buckland's Complete Book of Witchcraft*. St. Paul, MN: Llewellyn Publications, 1986.

———. *Practical Candle Burning*. St. Paul, MN: Llewellyn Publications, 1972.

———. *Scottish Witchcraft*. St. Paul, MN: Llewellyn Publications, 1992.

———. *The Tree: The Complete Book of Saxon Witchcraft*. New York, NY: Samuel Weiser, 1974.

———. *Witchcraft from the Inside*. St. Paul, MN: Llewellyn Publications, 1971.

Budge, E. A. Wallis. *Amulets and Superstitions*. New York, NY: Dover Publications, 1978.

Cabell, James Branch. *Jurgen*. New York, NY: Dover Publications, 1919.

Campanelli, Pauline. *Ancient Ways: Reclaiming Pagan Traditions*. St. Paul, MN: Llewellyn Publishing, 1991.

———. *Wheel of the Year: Living a Magical Life*. St. Paul, MN: Llewellyn Publishing, 1991.

———. *Circles, Groves and Sanctuaries*. St. Paul, MN: Llewellyn Publishing, 1991.

Cantwell, Gary. *Wiccan Beliefs and Practices*. St. Paul, MN: Llewellyn Publications, 2001.

Carlson, Shawn and Gerald LaRue. *Satanism in America: How the Devil Got Much More Than His Due*. El Cerrito, CA: Gaia Press, 1989.

Carmody, Agent. "Satanic Cults & Black Witchcraft: A General Overview." Glencoe, GA: Federal Law Enforcement Training Center.

Chick, Jack. *Spellbound*. Crusaders Comic Series. Vol. 10.

Cohen, Edmund. *The Mind of the Bible Believer*. Buffalo, NY: Prometheus Books, 1988.

Colorado Bureau of Investigations. *Questioned Documents Examiner's Occult Guide*.

Cooper, J. C. *An Illustrated Encyclopedia of Traditional Symbols*. London: Thames and Hudson, 1978.

Crowther, Patricia. *Lid Off the Cauldron: A Wicca Handbook*. York Beach, ME: Samuel Weiser, 1984.

Cruden, Alexander. *Cruden's Complete Concordance*. Grand Rapids, MI: Zondervan Publishing, 1968.

Cunningham, Scott. *Wicca: A Guide for the Solitary Practitioner*. St. Paul, MN: Llewellyn Publications, 1989.

D'Aviella, Count Goblet. *The Migration of Symbols*. NY: University Books, 1956.

De Givry, Grillot. *Witchcraft, Magic and Alchemy*. Frederick Publications, 1954.

Dreyfuss, Henry. *Symbol Sourcebook: An Authoritative Guide to International Graphic Symbols*. New York, NY: Van Nostran Reinhold, 1984.

Dubois, William Edward Lee. *Occult Crime Control: The Law Enforcement Manual of Investigation, Analysis and Prevention*. South Orange, NJ: USCCCN, 1990.

Dwelly, Edward. *Dwelly's Illustrated Gaelic to English Dictionary*. Edinburgh: Cairm Gaelic Publications, 1988.

Elworthy, Frederick. *The Evil Eye*. Julian Press, NY, 1958.

Emon, Sgt. Randall. "A Guide to Understanding Signs, Symbols & Terminology." Baldwin Park, CA: Christian Occult Investigators Network, 1986.

———. "The Occult and the Bible." Baldwin Park, CA: Christian Occult Investigators Network, 1986.

———. "Occult Criminal Investigation." Baldwin Park (CA) PD Training Bulletin 86, no. 2. (1986).

———. "The Occult Investigators Explosion." Baldwin Park (CA) PD, 1986.

Farrar, Janet and Stewart Farrar. *Eight Sabbats for Witches*. Custer, WA: Phoenix Publishing, Inc., 1981.

———. *The Witches' Bible, Volumes 1 and 2*, Custer, WA: Phoenix Publishing, Inc., 1984.

———. *The Witches' God*. Custer, WA: Phoenix Publishing, Inc., 1989.

———. *The Witches' Goddess*. Custer, WA: Phoenix Publishing, Inc., 1987.

Farrar, Stewart. *What Witches Do*. New York, NY: Coward, McCann & Geoghan, 1971.

Fitch, Ed. *Magical Rites from the Crystal Well*. St. Paul, MN: Llewellyn Publications, 1988.

Fraser, James G. *The Golden Bough: A Study in Magic and Religion*. MacMillan Press, 1971.

Frence, Peter. *John Dee: The World of an Elizabethan Magus*. London: Routledge & Keegan Paul, 1972.

Frost, Gavin and Yvonne Frost. *The Magic Power of Witchcraft*. West Nyak, NY: Parker Publishing, 1976.

———. *The Witch's Bible*. Los Angeles: Nash Publishing, 1972.

Gallant, Sandy. "The Difference Between the Occult and Satanism." San Francisco, CA: San Francisco PD, n.d.

———. "Handout on Occult Crime." San Francisco, CA: San Francisco PD, n.d.

———. "The Profile of a Devil Cultist." San Francisco, CA: San Francisco PD, n.d.

Gamache, Henri. *Mystery of the Long Lost 8th, 9th and 10th Books of Moses, Together With the Legend that was of Moses and 44 Keys to Universal Power*. NY: Original Publications, NY, 1983.

Gardner, Gerald. New York, NY: *High Magic's Aid*, Samuel Weiser, 1975.

———. *The Meaning of Witchcraft*. London: The Aquarian Press,1971.

———. *Witchcraft Today*. Secaucus, NJ: Citadel Press, 1974.

Gibson, Walter and Litzka Gibson. *The Complete Illustrated Book of the Psychic Sciences*. New York, NY: Doubleday, 1966.

Graves, Robert. *The White Goddess*. New York, NY: Farrar, Straus and Giroux, 1974.

Griffis, Dale. "Investigative Suggestions for Law Enforcement." Tiffin, OH: ADWG Consultants.

Guazzo, Francesco Maria and Montague Summers, eds. *Compendium Maleficarum*. New York, NY: Dover Publications, 1988.

Guiley, Rosemary Ellen. *The Encyclopedia of Witches and Witchcraft*. New York, NY: Facts on File, 1989.

G'Zell, Otter, ed. *Witchcraft, Satanism and Ritual Crime: Who's Who and What's What*. Ukiah, CA: Church of All Worlds, 1989.

Haining, Peter. *The Satanists*. New York, NY: Taplinger Publishing, 1969.

Hall, James. *Dictionary of Subjects and Symbols in Art*. NY: Harper & Row, 1974.

Hart, R. *Witchcraft*. London: Wayland Publishers, 1975.

Henrickson, Robert. *Encyclopedia of Word Origins*. New York, NY: Facts on File, 1987.

Hinnells, John R., ed. *The Penguin Dictionary of Religions*. New York, NY: Penguin, 1984.

Hole, Christina. *British Folk Customs*. London: Hutchinson & Co., 1976.

Holzer, Hans. *The Witchcraft Report*. New York, NY: Ace Books, 1973.

Hope, Murray. *Practical Celtic Magic*. Wellingborough, Northamptonshire: The Aquarian Press, 1987.

Howard, Michael. *Candle Burning: Its Occult Significance*. London: The Aquarian Press, 1975.

Hunt, Dave. *Peace, Prosperity and the Coming Holocaust*. Eugene, OR: Harvest House, 1983.

———. *Understanding the New Age Movement*. Eugene, OR: Harvest House, 1983.

Hurtag, J. J. *The Keys of Enoch*. Los Gatos, CA: The Academy for Future Science, 1977.

Hutton, Ronald. *The Pagan Religions of the Ancient British Isles*. Oxford: Basil Blackwell, 1991.

Huysmans, J. K. *Down There*. New York, NY: Dover Publications, 1958.

Jones, Larry. "Cults, Sects and Deviant Movements Seminar Notes." Boise, ID: CCIN Inc., 1986.

———. "The Emergence of Ritualistic Crime in Today's Society." Boise, ID: CCIN Inc., 1986.

Kahaner, Larry. *Cults That Kill*. NY: Warner Books, 1988.

Kelly, Aidan. *Diana's Family: A Tuscan Lineage and Aradianic Faerie Tradition*. CA: Pictish Voodoo Distributing, 1993.

———. *Hippie Commie Beatnik Witches: The California Craft 1967–1977*. CA: Pictish Voodoo Distributing, 1993.

———. *Original Gardnerian Book of Shadows Documents*. CA: Pictish Voodoo Distributing, 1993.

Kirban, Salem. *Satan's Angels Exposed*. Huntingdon Valley, PA: Salem Kirban, 1980.

Koch, Kurt. *Occult Bondage and Deliverance*. Grand Rapids, MI: Kregel Publications, 1971.

Komroff, Manuel, ed. *The Apocrypha or Non-Canonical Books of the Bible*. New York, NY: Tudor Publishing, 1949.

Koppana, K. M. *Snakefat and Knotted Threads*. Helsinki: Mandragora Dimensions, 1990.

Lamb, Geoffrey. *Magic, Witchcraft, and the Occult*. London: David and Charles, 1977.

Larson, Bob. *Larson's New Book of Cults*. Wheaton, IL: Tyndale House, 1989.

———. *Rock: Practical Help for Those Who Listen to the Words and Don't Like What They Hear*. Wheaton, IL: Tyndale House, 1982.

———. *Satanism: Larson's New Book of Cults*. Wheaton, IL: Tyndale House, 1982.

———. *Satanism: The Seduction of America's Youth*. Wheaton, IL: Tyndale House, 1989.

LaVey, Anton. *The Complete Witch*. New York, NY: Dodd Mead, 1971.

———. *The Satanic Rituals*. New York, NY: Avon Books, 1972.

Laycock, Donald C. *The Complete Enochian Dictionary: A Dictionary of the Angelic Language as Revealed to Dr. John Dee and Edward Kelley*. York Beach, ME: Samuel Weiser, Inc., 1994.

Leach, Maria and Jerone Fried. *Funk and Wagnall's Standard Dictionary of Folklore, Mythology and Legend*. New York: Funk and Wagnall, 1972.

Leek, Sybil. *Diary of a Witch*. New York, NY: New American Library, 1971.

Legge, James. *The I Ching: The Book of Changes*. New York, NY: Dover Publications, 1963.

Lehner, Ernst. *Symbols, Signs & Signets*. New York, NY: Dover, 1950.

Leland, Charles Geoffrey. *Aradia: Gospel of the Witches*. New York, NY: Samuel Weiser, 1974.

Lethbridge, T. C. *Witches: Investigating an Ancient Religion*. Citadel Press, 1968.

Levi, Eliphas. *Transcendental Magic*. New York, NY: Samuel Weiser, 1974.

Lindsay, Hal and Carlson, C. C. *The Late Great Planet Earth*. Grand Rapids, MI: Zondervan Corp., 1970.

———. *Satan is Alive and Well on Planet Earth*. Grand Rapids, MI: Zondervan Corp., 1972.

MacDonald, Margaret Read, ed. *The Folklore of World Holidays*. Detroit, MI: Gale Research, 1992.

MacLennan, Malcolm. *Gaelic Dictionary*. Edinburgh: Acair & Aberdeen University Press, 1988.

Madden, Kristin. *Pagan Homeschooling: A Guide to Adding Spirituality to Your Child's Education*. Niceville, Florida: Spilled Candy Books, 2002.

Mansfield, Hal. "Pseudo-Satanism in School Systems Today." Fort Collins, CO: Religious Movement Resource Center, 1988.

Marron, Kevin. *Witches, Pagans and Magic in the New Age*. Toronto: McLelland-Gantam, 1989.

Marrs, Wanda. *New Age Lies to Women*. Austin, TX: Living Truth Publishers, 1989.

Mathers, S. Liddell MacGregor, trans. *The Book of the Goetia, or The Lesser Key of Solomon*. Mokelumne Hill, CA: Health Research, 1976.

———. *The Book of the Sacred Magic of Abramelin the Mage*. New York, NY: Dover Publications, 1975.

Morland, David. *Demanding the Impossible: Human Nature and Politics in Nineteenth Century Social Anarchism*. London: Cassell, 1997.

McCoy, Edain. *Advanced Witchcraft*. St. Paul, MN: Llewellyn Publications, 2004.

———. *Bewitchments: Love Magick for Modern Romantics*. St. Paul, MN: Llewellyn Publications, 2000.

McDowell, Josh and Don Stewart. *Handbook of Today's Religions: Understanding the Occult*. San Bernardino, CA: Here's Life Publishers, Inc., 1982.

———. *The Occult*. San Bernardino, CA: Here's Life Publishers, Inc., 1992.

Melton, Rev. Dr. J. Gordon. "The Evidences of Satanism in Contemporary America: A Survey." Santa Barbara, CA: Institute for the Study of American Religion, 1986.

Michaelsen, Johanna. *Like Lambs To The Slaughter*. Eugene, OR: Harvest House Publishers, 1989.

———. *Your Kids and the Occult*. Eugene, OR: Harvest House Publishers, 1989.

Michelet, Jules. *Satanism and Witchcraft*. New York, NY: Citadel Press, 1939.

Mitchell, Norman E. *Hidden Practices*.

Mossman, Jennifer, ed. *Holidays and Anniversaries of the World*. 2nd edition. Detroit, MI: Gale Research, 1990.

Murray, Elaine. *Layman's Guide to New Age and Spiritual Terms*. New York, NY: Blue Dolphin Publishing, 1993.

———. *Raising Witches: Teaching The Wiccan Faith to Children*. Franklin Lakes, NJ: The Career Press, Inc. 2002.

Pazder, Dr. Lawrence and Michelle Smith. *Michelle Remembers*. New York, NY: Congdon & Lattès, Inc., 1980.

Penczak, Christopher. *The Witch's Shield: Protection Magick & Psychic Self Defense*. St. Paul, MN: Llewellyn Publications, 2004.

Pennick, Nigel. *Magical Alphabets*. York Beach, ME. Samuel Weiser, 1992.

———. *The Pagan Book of Days*. Rochester, VT: Destiny Books, 1992.

Peters, Dan and Steve. *Rock's Hidden Persuader: The Truth About Backmasking*. St. Paul, MN: Bethany House Publishers, 1980.

———. *What the Devil's Wrong With Rock Music*. St. Paul, MN: Bethany House Publishers, 1985.

Peterson, Alan Herbert. *American Focus on Satanic Crime: Volume II*. 1990.

Phillips, Phil and Joan Hake Robie. *Halloween and Satanism*. Lancaster, PA: Starburst Publishers, 1987.

————. *Turmoil in the Toybox*. Lancaster, PA. Starburst Publishers, 1986.

Pulling, Pat, ed. "BADD Advanced Ritualistic Crime Seminar Package." Richmond, VA: BADD, 1989.

————. *A Law Enforcement Primer on Fantasy Role Playing Games*. Richmond, VA: BADD, 1985.

Radford, E. and Radford, M.A. *Encyclopedia of Superstitions*. Westport, CT: Greenwood Press, 1981.

Raschke, Carl. *Painted Black*. New York, NY: Harper & Row, 1990.

Ravenwolf, Silver. *Teen Witch: Wicca for a New Generation*. St. Paul, MN: Llewellyn Publications, 2000.

————. *To Ride a Silver Broomstick: New Generation Witchcraft*. St. Paul, MN: Llewellyn Publications, 1993.

————. *To Stir a Magic Cauldron: A Witch's Guide to Casting and Conjuring*. St. Paul, MN: Llewellyn Publications, 1995.

Readers Digest Association, ed. *Folklore, Myths and Legends of Britain*. London: Reader's Digest Association, 1977.

Rinkes, Clyde, PALOMINO, Chuck and HARTLEY, Teri. *Gangs, Groups, Cults: An Informational Aid To Understanding*. San Diego County Deputy Sheriff's Association. Pleasant Hill, CA: Stuart-Bradley Productions, Inc., 1990.

Robbins, Russell Hope. *The Encyclopedia of Witchcraft and Demonology*. New York, NY: Crown Publishers, 1973.

Robinson, Herbert Spencer and Knox Wilson. *Myths and Legends of All Nations*. Savage, MD: Littlefield Adams Quality Paperbacks, 1976.

Roper, Jack. "Occult Investigation Slide Training Series Slide Script, Volume 1: Witchcraft/Magic/Satanism." Milwaukee, WI: CARIS, 1987.

Ross, Joan Carol and Michael D. Langone. *Cults: What Families Should Know*. Weston, MA: American Family Foundation, 1988.

Ryall, Rhiannon. *West Country Wicca*. Custer, WA: Phoenix Publishing, 1989.

Sanders, Alex. *The Alex Sanders Lectures*. NY: Magickal Childe Publishing, Inc., 1984.

Schnoebelen, Bill. *Wicca: Satan's Little White Lie*. Chino, CA: Chick Publications, 1990.

Schwartz, Ted and Duane Empey. *Satanism: Is Your Family Safe?* Grand Rapids, MI: Zondervan Books, 1988.

Shepard, Leslie, ed. *Encyclopedia of Occultism and Parapsychology, Vols. 1–3*. Detroit, MI. Gale Research Co., 1993.

Sholes, Jerry. *Give Me That Prime Time Religion*. New York, NY: Hawthorne Books, 1979.

Siuda, Tamara L. *The Ancient Egyptian Prayerbook*. Toronto, ON: Azrael Press, 2005.

Skelton, Robin. *The Practice of Witchcraft*. London: Robert Hale, 1988.

————. *Spellcraft*. Toronto, ON: McClelland & Stewart, 1978.

Sprenger, Johann and Heinrich Kramer. *Malleus Maleficarum*. New York, NY: Benjamin Blom, 1928.

Stackpole, Michael A. "The Pulling Report." Unpublished manuscript, 1980.

Starhawk. *Dreaming the Dark: Magic, Sex and Politics*. Boston, MA: Beacon Press, 1982.

———. *The Spiral Dance: A Rebirth of the Ancient Religion of the Great Goddess*. San Francisco, CA: Harper Row, 1979.

———. *Truth or Dare*. Boston, MA: Beacon Press, 1987.

Summers, Montague. *The History of Witchcraft and Demonology*. London: Routledge & Kegan Paul, 1965.

Suster, Gerald. *The Legacy of the Beast*. York Beach, ME: Samuel Weiser, 1989.

Sutton, Hilton. *Familiar Spirits, Witchcraft & Satanism*. Harrison House Inc., 1989.

Symonds, John, ed. *The Confessions of Aleister Crowley*. London: Arkana, 1979.

Temple of Set. "General Information and Admissions Policies, Year XXI." San Francisco: Temple of Set.

Terry, Maury. *The Ultimate Evil*. New York, NY: Doubleday & Co., 1987.

Turner, Robert. *Elizabethan Magic: The Art and the Magus*. Shaftesbury, Dorset: Element Books, 1989.

Two Disciples. *The Rainbow Bridge*. Danville, CA: Rainbow Bridge Productions, 1981.

Tyson, Donald, ed. *Three Books of Occult Philosophy: Henry Cornelius Agrippa of Nettesheim*. St. Paul, MN: Llewellyn Publications, 1993.

Underwood, Peter. *Dictionary of the Supernatural*. London: Harrap, 1978.

Valiente, Doreen. *An ABC of Witchcraft, Past & Present*. Custer, WA: Phoenix Publishing, 1973.

———. *Natural Magic*. Custer, WA: Phoenix Publishing, 1986.

———. *Witchcraft for Tomorrow*. Custer, WA: Phoenix Publishing, 1978.

Waite, Arthur Edward. *The Book of Black Magic and Ceremonial Magic*. New York, NY: Causeway Books, 1973.

Walker, Barbara. *The Woman's Dictionary of Symbols and Sacred Objects*. San Francisco, CA: Harper Collins, 1988.

Waring, Philippa. *A Dictionary of Omens and Superstitions*. New York, NY: Ballantine Books, 1978.

Watkins, Calvert, ed. *The American Heritage Dictionary of Indo-European Roots*. Rev. ed. Boston: Houghton Mifflin, 1985.

Watson, William. *A Concise Dictionary of Cults and Religions*. Chicago, IL: Moody Press, 1991.

Wedeck, H. E. and Wade Baskin. *Dictionary of Spiritualism*. London: Peter Owen, 1971.

Wedge, Tom. "Seminar Package on Occult Crime." Bellefontaine, OH: Self-published, 1982.

Weinstein, Marion. *Earth Magic: A Dianic Book of Shadows*. Custer, WA: Phoenix Publishing, 1980.

Wilcox, Laird, ed. *Guide to the American Occult: Directory and Bibliography 1988*. Orange, NJ: Priority One Consultants, 1988.

Wilson, Colin. *The Occult: A History*. New York, NY: Random House, 1971.

Wood, Robin. *When, Why...If*. Livingtree Books, 1996.

Woodrow, Ralph Edward. *Babylon Mystery Religion*. Riverside, CA: Ralph Woodrow Evangelistic Association, 1966.

Wright, Harry. *Witness to Witchcraft*. New York, NY: Funk & Wagnall, 1957.

Zane, Thomas. *Occult Influenced Crimes.* Daytona Beach, FL: Daytona Beach Community College, 1988.

Zilliox, Larry and Larry Kahaner. *How to Investigate Destructive Cults and Underground Groups: An Investigator's Manual.* Alexandria, VA: Kane Associates International, 1990.

Video

A Cutting Edge/Jeremiah Film. *Pagan Invasion Series Volume 1: Halloween: Trick or Treat.* Jeremiah Films, 1990.

Children of the Circle. *March on Fort God: Paganism Emerges in the Bible Belt.* Arkansas: Whitlock Independent Cinemagraphic Coverage of America, 2003.

Jubilee Christian Center. *From Pagan to Pentecost.* San Jose, CA: Jubilee Christian Center Productions, 1991.

Periodicals

Wheeling News-Register. "P & G Vows To Sue Those Spreading Satan Rumors." April 25, 1990.

The Battle Cry. Chick Publications, May/June 1990.

Bivens, Terry. "Bedeviled by a Wild Rumor, They Fight Back." *Philadelphia Inquirer,* August 1, 1982.

Brooke, Tal and Russ Wise. "Goddess Worship." *SCP Newsletter* 23, no. 2 (Winter 1998/'99).

Cabal, Alan. "The Doom that Came to Chelsea." *New York Press,* June 3, 2003.

Cultivate Ministries newsletter, July 1990.

Exodus newsletter 1, no. 6 (April 1987): 1.

File 18 1, no. 10 (December 1986); 2, no. 87-1; 2, no. 87-5; 3, no. 6; no. 88-4; 5, no. 90-5. Boise, ID: CCIN Inc.

Freedomlight Report 1, no. 3 (Oct/Nov 1990).

Hornblower, Margot. "Rumor Bedevils Proctor & Gamble." *The Washington Post,* April 18, 1985.

MacDonald, Jim. "Tracking the Devil." *New Hampshire Star,* July 16, 1990.

Morrison, Clarke. "Faith Uproar Unfolds At Erwin Middle School." *The Asheville Citizen-Times,* May 17, 2001. http://www.citizen-times.com/news/07071837.shtml.

Morse, Keith. "Questions and Answers on Wicca: A Christian Perspective on Witchcraft," *Personal Freedom Outreach* Newsletter 3, no. 4 (October–December 1983): 4.

Peterson, Peter. "Flag, Torch, and Fist: The Symbols of Anarchism," *Freedom* 48, no. 11: 8.

Plowman, Edward E. "The Legends of John Todd." *Christianity Today,* February 2, 1979.

Reese, Pat. "Signs of Satan." Special Report. *The Fayetteville Observer,* August 1, 1988.

Salmant, Sandra. "P & G Drops Logo; Cites Satan Rumours." *The New York Times,* Business Day section, April 25, 1985.

Southwest Radio Church. *The Gospel Truth.* July 1988.

Stevens, Phillips Jr. "The Dangerous Folklore of Satanism." *Free Inquiry Magazine,* 1989.

———. "Satanism: Where are the Folklorists?" *New York Folklore* 15, nos. 1–2 (1989).

"The Nobel Search for Devil-worshippers and Other Godless Commies." *San Diego Reader* (May 6, 1986): 22.

Victor, Jeffrey S. Victor. "A Rumour-Panic About a Dangerous Satanic Cult in Western New York." *New York Folklore* 15, nos. 1–2 (1989).

Websites

Guiley, Rosemary. *The Encyclopedia of Witches and Witchcraft.* New York: Facts On File, 1989; and Leslie A. Shepard, ed. *Encyclopedia of Occultism and Parapsychology,* 3rd ed. Detroit: Gale Research, Inc., 1991. http://www.themystica.com/mystica/articles/h/hand_of_glory.html.

House Shadow Drake. http://www.shadowdrake.com/folklore/hand.html.

Hunter, George. "Teasing Sparks $10 Million Lawsuit." *The Detroit News.* http://detnews.com/2001/schools/0107/04/a08-243315.htm.

Madrak, Stanley. "Amulets, Spells, Charms and Taboos." http://www.moodymanual.demonbuster.com/part2-w1.html.

———. "Exposing Caribbean Witchcraft." http://www.moodymanual.demonbuster.com/caribbe1.html.

———. "Forbidden Practices of the Occult." http://www.moodymanual.demonbuster.com/forbidd4.html.

———. "Occult ABC - Exposing Occult Practices and Ideologies." http://www.moodymanual.demonbuster.com/part2-w4.html.

Reachout Trust. Testimony of Niki. http://web.archive.org/web/20030228124213/http://www.reachouttrust.org/regulars/articles/testimony/niki.htm.

Religious Tolerance. http://www.religioustolerance.org.

Roper, Jack M. Bio. http://members.aol.com/jackmroper/jacksbio.htm.